Operation Rumination Synopsis

Statistics suggest that 7.3 percent of all living Americans are currently serving in the military or have served at some point in their adult lives, and that half of all veterans are now over the age of 60. Author Rick Vuyst delves into his own personal thoughts *as one of the 92.7 percent who never served* in the military. To understand better he spends an entire year with veterans listening to their stories. In the process he wrestles with the fact he never served and reflects on the freedom he enjoys with a price paid for by others.

Approaching the age of 60, he chooses a 2-mile stretch of beach where he can run, reflect, train and ruminate. The goal was to voluntarily engage in a personal "boot camp" of sorts to meet the physical fitness requirements of a 17 to 21-year-old entering the Army (run, push-ups, sit-ups). He corresponds with young men currently in boot camp that summer and visits with veterans of World War II, Korea, Vietnam, Iraq and Afghanistan wars. He ruminates on what he learns as he trains, often culminating in sit-ups and push-ups next to a lighthouse on Pere Marquette beach in Muskegon, Michigan. He turns back the clock by capturing stories and changing physically, mentally and emotionally.

Veterans are all around us in our daily lives, but, unless we hear their story, in many cases those stories and lessons are lost. They pass by us just as a ship passes a lighthouse, except in this case they pass by us on the street, in the store, at church or at work in our daily lives. The veterans he visits inspire him, humble him, educate him, challenge him. They in turn share with Rick thoughts they had stored away from experiences in the past. Many times he is told over the course of the year by veterans, that he was "stirring up thoughts and memories long forgotten." Rick himself uses the physical training to help clear his own "brain fog" running to and from the lighthouse. The veterans he met with helped him experience the gamut of emotions, as together, they experience sorrow, joy, regret, laughter, tears, frustrations, accomplishment and more during the course of their conversations. Their stories are told in Rick's words in *Operation Rumination*.

In the book's denouement, Rick unties his thoughts and shares them with you: the common threads he found among the veterans, lessons learned, the results of his Army physical training test and how he got there, and settles his life-long regrets for having never served. He ultimately better understands the meaning of "selfless service" after a year of rumination and why it is a valuable characteristic to demonstrate to one another.

ISBN 978-1-61808-177-3

Printed in the United States of America

White Feather Press

Reaffirming Faith in God, Family, and Country!

Operation Rumination

Turning back the clock

Rick Vuyst

Foreword

I spent two years in Vietnam as an infantryman; I am a combat vet. It is very common for we combat vets to say—because it's true—that you will never understand being in combat by learning about it from others. Many wives and families and friends have tried to understand what their loved one experienced—frequently to no avail.

Well, Rick Vuyst may have heard that truism, but it did not slow him down from his goal of understanding and honoring those of us who did serve our nation in combat.

Rick is a nearly 60-year-old man in pretty good physical condition and is a great businessman. Rick hosts a weekly radio show (where his "stage name" is Phil Dirt) on the same station from which I record my weekly military talk-radio show, *Frontlines of Freedom*. Rick has been on the air for 25 years—I am just pushing 12 years. So, I have known Rick casually for over a decade, but it was only recently, as this book began taking form, that we became real friends.

Did Rick merely do some research to write this book? No. First, he determined the physical training requirements for an 18-year-old to get a maximum score on the Army's physical fitness test—a 2-mile run, sit-ups, and push-ups. He's working on getting into that level of shape—and this while wearing an army physical training shirt. He is experiencing as much as he can of the military culture.

He interviewed at length veterans from WWII to our current conflicts. He talked with them and listened to each serious, sad, or funny story. To the extent that anyone can do so, Rick reached into the minds, hearts, and feelings of these veterans—and he recorded them with both accuracy and compassion. It's worth noting that all the vets showed three characteristics: All have a sense of humor. All manifested selfless service and pride in their service. And all continually through their lives have set goals.

Several of the vets he interviewed are my friends—good friends. Yet, I learned more about each of them than I had known before—this both surprised and blessed me. Rick helped me get to know some of my good friends even better.

I believe that this is the most unique book I have ever read. Rick never served in our military in any way—yet, he has always been a patriot and a good citizen, and he is a guy who sets goals and then gets the job done. Rick's facts are only as good as the

memories of the vets he talked with—but he touched the hearts of those men and women and shares what he learned and experienced with accuracy, dignity, and grace.

If you care about the deep feelings of our combat veterans, I am certain that you will greatly enjoy reading *Operation Rumination*.

**Denny Gillem
Lieutenant Colonel, US Army (Retired)
Host, Frontlines of Freedom**

Table of Contents

Dedication

To those selfless servants that quietly and under the radar serve others each and every day.

This book is dedicated to all those who have made the ultimate sacrifice in the service of their country and fellow man. We honor the dedication of those who now serve. And for those veterans who now live among us in our daily lives we honor their service.

To those who practice the discipline of continual goals and to the storytellers who improve our lives and instinctively know that understanding is a two-way street.

The Lighthouse

For those in peril and distress
between the light and darkness
Giving blind sight
illuminating the night
It is a pillar of faithfulness.

*We may pass in darkness but are connected by
this symbol. A lighthouse is both lonely and
welcoming at the same time. We are drawn to them
as the dramatic edge between land and water. A
presence that stands between light and darkness. It
symbolizes stability in an ever-changing world. A
reminder there is a light on waiting for us.*

"Anyhow I have learned one thing now. You only really get to know people when you've had a jolly good row with them. Then and then only can you judge their true characters."

— Anne Frank

Chapter One

Operation Rumination Commence

I HAVE MOMENTS WHEN MY IMAGINATION rises like mercury on a hot summer day. On my personal journey, I think the heat from the road rises and mixes with cooler air. It creates visual waves on the horizon, something of a personal mirage of imagination. Since I was a boy, I imagined placing myself in historic moments … telling and retelling stories from times past. Since the days of my adolescence, I've closed my eyes and tried to imagine how I would react to a weighty moment in time. When you take history and seat yourself in the middle of it, the ensuing rumination is mentally adventurous, if not at least entertaining.

I place myself in a room of wooden chairs and tables, the movements on the wood floor interrupt the sounds of voices. The heat is excessive and oppressive. Despite the conditions, the meeting participants in the room soldier on. It all began in May of 1787 and now, September 17, 1787 they meet in a closed meeting room after a long, hot Philadelphia summer. I'm not quite sure if the summer was as oppressive in relation to others as they lead me to believe. By agreement, the meeting is closed to the public and so were the doors and windows in the spirit of confidentiality. The framers in the Pennsylvania State House are hammering out a constitution. Maybe I think, it is less summer heat and more so fashion over function. It's hard to smell good as a gentleman when clad in a coat and vest of wool attire. The lack of a breeze made the sweaty, stale air pungent. The advent and invention of air conditioning was well over a century away, and electricity would have to come first for that matter. Ben Franklin, one of the framers in the room had famously dabbled with the concept of electricity himself. At this moment I surmise it's quite possible the heat and oppressive environment has sped up the arduous undertaking of finding consensus within the group. I watch as, after enduring the heat of summer, the group signs the blueprint for freedom and democracy. The US Constitution. Adjournment sine die, no further meeting dates are scheduled. It's time to move on and see what the future holds.

Ben Franklin made the closing argument in a speech he wrote. James Wilson read it, however, because Franklin was too weak to present it. Wilson said, "I doubt too whether any other Convention we can obtain, may be able to make a better Constitution. For when you assemble a number of men to have the advantage of their joint wisdom, you inevitably assemble with those men, all their prejudices, their passions, their errors of opinion, their local interests, and their selfish views. From such an assembly can a perfect production be expected?" Good question.

Fast forward to a visit at the Capitol, and, while viewing the oil on canvas scene of that meeting, I can't help but imagine what it would be like to have been there. In the famous painting 'Scene at the signing of the Constitution of the United States' by Howard Chandler Christy, there is Ben Franklin, front and center. Washington is imposing and prominent, standing on a platform and Franklin is seated. Franklin is 81 years old and in poor health. It would be a mere two years and 7 months later that he would die. It is with that background, my imagination envisions an overheated and fatigued man at the conclusion of the final meeting, being somewhat annoyed when a lady asked him what the gathering had produced.

"What have we got a republic or a monarchy?' she asked.

Franklin replied, "A republic, madam, if you can keep it."

Today with images and information at our fingertips twenty-four seven, we can graphically see how freedoms and liberty are threatened worldwide. The grand experiment of democracy has endured. But it's messy. Progress is usually messy. The world has watched our pursuit of unalienable rights. They come with a price.

A respected friend of mine reminds me that we should be teaching students less about their rights and more about their obligations.

Through the centuries many have observed, maybe none more famously in tome as Alexis de Tocqueville. Accorded the status of a classic in the United States, the Frenchman's visit to check out the American experiment and subsequent writing of *Democracy in America,* suggested an organized society could, as Franklin had instructed the woman, "keep a republic." The expanding bourgeoisie in a free democratic society would have to agree to join forces to defend it.

The French diplomat phrased it this way, "Furthermore, when citizens are all almost equal, it becomes difficult for them to defend their independence against the aggressions of power. As none of them is strong enough to fight *alone* with advantage, the only guarantee of liberty is for everyone to combine forces."

It is those joined, or, as Tocqueville put it, "combined forces" of liberty that have preserved our rights through all these years … many years beyond his observation. For me that poses a problem. Regret.

I never served.

Statistics suggest that only 7.3 percent of all living Americans have served in the military at some point in their lives. That means today 92.7% of us walking around with unalienable rights have not "combined forces" to defend. Sure, I guess to a degree we have because we pay taxes, but those are famously expected like death. Now, an older man, I regret not having served in a branch of the military to, as Doctor Franklin suggested, "keep the republic." Who are those 7.3% who have fought for freedom? And what stories could they tell?

A Story to Tell

I NOTICED HER OUT OF THE CORNER OF MY EYE. I COULD tell there was something interesting about her. Seated in the front row to the left as I gave a speech, she seemed particularly intent on my words as I spoke of my parents surviving the 'Hunger Winter' in Holland during the winter of 1944-1945. Nazi-occupied Holland experienced a famine in the bitter cold winter of 1944-1945 with estimates that, by the time the Netherlands was liberated in May of 1945, well over 20,000 people had died of starvation. Transportation was difficult in a war-torn region, and the Nazis punished the Netherlands by blocking food supplies. I recall stories told by my Dad, who would have been 15 years old at the time, stories of eating tulip bulbs made into a soup or rations of sugar beets mixed with sauerkraut to stay alive.

After my speech, as people gathered around, she pushed her way through the group. An elderly lady and all of at the most 5 feet tall, she navigated her walker to the front of the line. I could tell she had a resolve and purpose.

"I have a gift for you," she said.

She had already turned and pushed back through the cluster of people before I could engage her in conversation. I put the book in my bag, only later that night to pull it out as I prepared for the next day. I realized the lady was Diet (pronounced Deet) Eman and the book was her story titled *Things We Couldn't Say*. Now, 98 years old, she had endured the Great Depression as a youngster and endured World War II in Nazi-occupied Holland. She is an example of courage, faith, and had survived extreme danger and unbearable loss. Together, with her fiancé and other citizens of World War II Holland, they formed an underground resistance movement to save the lives of Jews in danger of being part of Hitler's "final solution." Before the end of the war, Diet, her fiancé and others in their group, were arrested and sent to concentration camps. Many, including Diet's fiancé, lost their lives. Diet survived and lived an amazing life both during the war and long after the end of World War II. Now, 73 years after the end of the war, on a May day, this 98-year-old remarkable woman handed me a book through the crowd and walked away. I didn't realize the scope of how remarkable and how courageous her life was until she was gone.

If I hadn't connected with her and then researched, I would not know her story. It was a "sonder" moment. Sonder is a great word for emotions that currently lack words. The profound feeling of realizing that everyone, including strangers passed in the street or in a setting, have a life as complex as one's own, which they are living despite one's personal lack of awareness of it.

Yet once again my imagination rises, and I seat myself in the center of it all. I can tell a story, but can I live it? It is true that stories preserved and well told can slow the hands of time by enlightening those on their own personal journeys. The next 7 months would be interesting. I would inject myself into the lives of others to learn their stories. I would physically train and use the time for reflection. I would engage in salubrious activity despite external influences to the contrary. It won't be easy. I will have to "bootstrap" my way through it. In my younger working days, the descriptive phrase was used on me often. The analogy is the straps attached to the boots to help yourself pull them on are imagined, as though you're lifting yourself off the ground by pulling on the bootstraps.

Difficult work. I got the point.

I confirm my imagination with an affirmative resolution. My mind would ruminate on hesternal events and stories to see what I could learn. I have no idea where this will lead. Operation Rumination was born.

OPERATION RUMINATION

30 May 2018
Mission commence 1930 hours 0030 Zulu
176 meters above sea level Latitude 43° 13′
25.7952″ N Longitude 86° 20′ 10.8564″ W
Pere Marquette Beach Muskegon Michigan USA
Downrange 1.73795 nautical/ 2 statute miles
to target. ETA 16 Mike.
82 degrees F 27C Dew point 70 F (21 C)

Definition of Ruminate

ruminate[roo-muh-neyt]
ruminated; ruminating: to go over in the mind
repeatedly and often casually or slowly. To chew
repeatedly for an extended period to engage in
contemplation.

ALBERTO ARRIVED ON A WARM, MAY DAY, DARK, MYSTERI-
ous and imposing. It's not as though he had arrived unannounced
or without invitation. The National Hurricane Center announced
on May 25 that Alberto would be the first named storm of the
Atlantic hurricane season. Sultry ocean waters like the Gulf of
Mexico to tropical systems are the equivalent of sugar to candy
or a drug to an addict. It sustains and completes them. It's very
natural, similar to bread rising, where the yeast is an organism
that lies dormant until it comes into contact with warm water.
Once reactivated, yeast begins feeding on the sugars in flour, and
releases the carbon dioxide that makes bread rise. Anyone who
has frolicked in "sultry" ocean waters knows the intoxicating effect of warm waters. As the tropical systems move over land,
however, reality settles in, excitement wanes and the sultry supply is gone, causing systems to dramatically weaken.

Alberto was an overachiever … it continued on to be what
would become a historic track into the Great Lakes, reaching

Lake Michigan as a tropical depression on Wednesday, May 30th, all the while looking as impressive as it did over the gulf. Its arrival on May 30 in the Great Lakes was distinctive in that the 30th of May was the "traditional" Memorial Day. From 1868 to 1970 Memorial Day was on May 30, regardless of what day of the week it fell on to honor the sacrifice of fallen heroes who died in the service of our country, protecting the freedoms we enjoy today. After 1970 the date of Memorial Day was moved to the last Monday in May to provide a long, extended holiday weekend for campers, grillers and those ready to kick off the unofficial start of summer. This time the more traditional Memorial Day May 30 parades, remembrances and events were cancelled or moved indoors due to Alberto's persistence as far north as Michigan in 2018.

Alberto wasn't about to change my plans on May 30, because I was a man on a mission. A few days previous, on the long week-

Alberto Arriving on Pere Marquette Beach

end Memorial Day holiday, knowing I would take this mission, I was attuned to the complaining about how "hot it was" or how "fast the weekend goes" or how "before you know it we have to go back to work" type of complaints I was hearing. I was personally told by some cantankerous acquaintances that I didn't care about veterans causes or needs. That stung.

I decided I would focus on real life **heroes not just on Memorial Day** but for the balance of the year in a concerted and disciplined intentional approach to learn something about both myself and others. Instead of a scheduled moment of silence on Memorial Day weekend, I would physically train and ruminate for the next 7 months. Turn back the clock on my regret. Operation Rumination commenced. Could I turn back the clock? I surmised that possibly I could conceptually, certainly in my imagination.

- I would capture stories before they were lost. Lessons learned.
- I would engage in physical training and try to return to the physical ability of a younger age.
- I would collect pictures. They are snapshots of moments in time preserved regardless of the clock's relentless advance.
- I would write about my findings.

In 1977, the year I graduated from high school, morale for things military was low in our country. Jimmy Carter had pardoned the draft dodgers, and during 1979 and 1980 the Iran hostage crisis dragged on. The mandatory draft had ended a few years before, and volunteer rates were low for a short time after the Vietnam War. That all changed with the 1980 election of Ronald Reagan and the 1986 release of the movie *Top Gun*. From 1977 to 1980, however, I was young, single, draft free and naive. I went right to work, got married in 1980, having children at a young age, jumping feet first into adulthood unprepared for what lie ahead. Years later, on a beach in Michigan just prior to the age of 60, I would reflect. This included my personal lack of service and reflection of the sacrifices made by others to secure the freedoms I had enjoyed for years.

I decided to try to turn back the clock and meet the criteria of an age group, 17 to 21-year-old, for physical fitness standards to enter the Army as a reflection on lost opportunity to serve as others have over the years. As I trained to meet the criteria, I used the post run return walk as time of reflection and rumination of the undeserved blessings and gifts I enjoyed. I chose Army because 3.1 percent of all living Americans have served in the Army, 1.7 percent in the Navy, 1.4 percent in the Air Force and 0.8 percent in the Marines, while the remaining 0.5 percent served in either non-defense or reserve roles. I also chose Army because the PT testing physical requirements fell right between the Marines and other branches of the military like Navy. As an example, the timed-tested run is 3 miles for Marines, 2 miles for Army and 1.5 miles for Navy or Air Force. I was also thankful none of the physical requirements was a swim test. I like the water, love the beach, enjoy water sports like skiing, but I'm not a good swimmer. I'm not naturally buoyant. Oh, I'm optimistic and cheerful, it's the floating for long periods of time or the rise to the top of water part where I struggle … more like sink.

APFT
ARMY PHYSICAL FITNESS TEST

I WALK INTO AN ARMY/NAVY SURPLUS STORE. THE EMployee behind the counter glances up as the doorbell rings upon my entry. His attention returns to a small TV and the game show in progress. I'm the only customer in the store. I look over racks and racks of camouflage, boots and equipment. I know what I'm looking for. A rack of PFUs, the acronym printed on the tag in the collar of the shirts. PFU meaning physical fitness uniform or training uniform is a military uniform used during exercise, calisthenics, drills, and, in some cases, casual periods of time off during initial entry training in the US Army. They are not flashy or fashionable, simply basic grey with bold, block, black letters of "Army" emblazoned across the front.

I rifle through the rack looking for my size. They smelled sweaty and some were seriously stained. Some, more than stained, had a pungent aroma that turned my stomach. I find two in my size and bring them to the counter. I pay 4.99 plus tax for each of them and promptly take them home to run them through the washer and dryer. It's time for PT ... physical testing. Older veterans threatened me I had to do it in combat boots. Younger veterans assured me my running shoes would do just fine. A grey PFU with black shorts and running shoes would be my exercise "uniform" for the next 7 months.

I was coached by an active-duty soldier, required to do the test every 6 months, that it would be best to train in this order ... push-ups first. Sit-ups next. Then the run. That is how I would be tested. They warned me the sit-ups could impact the legs for the 2-mile run. I'm ready ... I think.

Out of a maximum score of 300 (100% for each of three criteria) I would need at least a minimum of 180 or better to eke by and pass the requirements for a 17 to 21-year-old Army recruit. In this case a 59-year-old wearing a grey PFU. I would train to score at least a 60% in each event (push-ups, sit-ups, run) to pass my APFT and pass my PT requirement as a 17 to 21-year-old.

So, let's break down the requirements.

First the push-ups. A 100% score for a 17 to 21-year-old is 71 push-ups in two minutes. Ninety percent is 64 push-ups. Eighty percent is 57. Forty-nine push-ups in two minutes is good for a 70% score. Forty-two in two minutes is 60% for the minimum passing grade.

Next come the sit-ups. The Army is considering throwing out the sit-ups, because sit-ups can be hard on the spine and potentially damaging. They are looking to replace them with "planks." For now, sit-ups is and has been the requirement, so I'm all in. The standards for a 17 to 21-year-old would be 78 sit-ups in two minutes for a 100% score. Are you kidding me? That's more than one full sit-up every two seconds. Seventy-two gets you a 90%. Sixty-six sit-ups will score you 80% and 59 a 70% score. Fifty-three sit-ups in two minutes gets you a passing 60% grade for the minimum requirement. I'm shooting for a 60% score, because the recruits, who went through basic this summer, told me in our correspondence that the sit-ups were the toughest part and a drag on their total score. I would say my goal at this point is 53 sit-ups in two minutes and to avoid throwing up in the process.

Finally, will be the run in my PT test. It is a 2-mile sprint with grading for a 17 to 21-year-old as follows. Thirteen minutes (which is absolutely ridiculous) would score 100%. For a 90% score I would finish the run in 13:42. If I were to run it in 14:27, I would have an 80% score. 15:12 gets me in at 70% and 15:54 scores me at the 60% minimum requirement for a 17 to 21-year-old.

When it's all said and done, I need a score of 180 or better, and have to do at least a 60% score in each proficiency. Hopefully my rectus abdominis will cooperate, my hip flexors will still have some youth in them, my arms will push up my score, and my legs carry me to a passing grade. I would train on the 2-mile Muskegon beach and at the Y the rest of the year.

Even if I don't pass, I figure it will be worth it. I remind myself that doing something is better than doing nothing, and doing more is better than doing something. The day after my 59th birthday we'll see how I did as I wear my PFU for the final time. If anything, the time invested in reflection and rumination will make me a better man.

There is such a thing as positive rumination and negative rumination. Rumination can be problem solving gone wrong. Rumination, or replaying things in your mind over and over, is another word for worry. Worry is not healthy. People with ruminative thought patterns can experience depression or anxiety as a result. I've had plenty of occasions of *unhealthy rumination* in my life; this time it was going to be healthy; this time would be different. I have always had difficulty living in the moment. My mind either races forward to the future or dwells in the past. I'm not a good "relaxer."

The beach I would run on for my 2-mile runs is a favorite place for me to take pictures of sunsets on Lake Michigan. I love a good picture. You can't contain or hold a moving moment, but you can with a picture. A picture is simply a moment frozen in time. It can be said a photo goes beyond being frozen in time and actually turns back the clock when we view it. Either way, I see the beneficial element of rumination and reflection in photos as "chosen-frozen" memories and recollections. There is benefit in stopping the clock. Pictures can give us a time-out from the running clock.

My plan was to also collect stories. To listen. A story, before

Channel and lighthouses at "Rumination Beach"
Pere Marquette Muskegon Michigan

it is lost, is captured and feels to me in a small way a successful slowing of the hands of time. Those moments are captured … to be revisited, to be shared. So, I planned for who knows what would happen, and who would cross my path in the next seven months. A plan is much better than hoping. I would work the plan to try to meet my goals, bearing in mind it was General Dwight Eisenhower quoted as having said, "Plans are worthless, but planning is everything." I surmise he was trying to say that the knowledge gained while planning is crucial to the actions you take in the moment, and the investment in planning will help nudge you to the start.

THE PLAN

- Healthy Rumination for 7 months - June through December
- Collect stories and learn from veterans of World War II, Korean War, Vietnam War, Iraq War, Afghanistan War. (Those in the 7.3% sector of the population.)
- Find common threads and wisdom from the veterans who had experienced something I had not.
- Train on the beach rumination site. Core work (with age men become soft in the middle.) Less long distance and more sprint distance (Interval training). Find the lactate threshold. Lots of push-ups, meet the standard of 71 push-ups in 2 minutes.
- Document all of the above via storytelling.

Granted, it was an unusual resolution and plan that had popped into my head. I told very few people, because they probably would think I wasn't normal. Then again I reminded myself,

"Don't hang out with Norm … he's a troublemaker."

Anything in life, whether good or bad, right or wrong, do it long enough, hear it long enough, it becomes the norm. When I was young there was always a dirty "communal" Tupperware plastic cup on the sink for hydration purposes. This was before the small disposable paper cups we have today. The kind your dentist hands you when they say rinse and spit. They've abandoned that too as today it's usually vacuumed out of your mouth.

I, out of personal necessity, would take the communal plastic cup and rinse it, quickly filling and then dumping the water out three times before filling it. Now I do it all the time. Today, when I fill a plastic, Styrofoam or paper cup with water, I find myself rinsing it the same way. I even count. It is the norm. I understand those old plastic Tupperware cups are collector's items now. People sell them and convert them to some French country shabby chic decor. I've abandoned that method of hydration, but the vessel I now use gets the same treatment. However ridiculous, it became the norm.

I recognized that when it comes to your health and how you feel, it is easy to accept the norm. With your health if you don't pay attention to what you put in your body or how you care for your body, soon feeling the way you do becomes normal. I wanted to push it, not accept the norm, test my position.

Maybe it's all about "GIGO" or garbage in garbage out. William D. Mellin was an Army mathematician working on early computers in the 50s and 60s and is credited with coining the phrase, "If the problem has been sloppily programmed, the answer will be just as incorrect." Unlike the digital recycle bins we now have, I picture him with trash cans full of punch cards and piles of corrupted tape. Sometimes the norm is garbage that needs to be discarded.

It's about a positive attitude, surrounding yourself with others attuned to positivity. Negativity has to be confronted. If not, a negative environment or person will slowly become the norm until negativity is normal. Diet is the same way. What you put in your body affects how you feel and function. What becomes the new normal is accepted, without the realization anymore what feeling good feels like.

It's about accepting the reality of entropy. A physical law of nature that, left untouched, everything will steadily deteriorate. Or as W.B. Yeats said in the poem *The Second Coming*, "Things fall apart; the centre cannot hold." You engage in the battle and that includes encouraging others around you.

There were a number of moments of encouragement. In impromptu locker-room meetings at the YMCA, I enjoyed my conversations with a former Army MP and drill sergeant. He was curious and interested in my Army PFU I would wear when working out at the Y. Johnny is an impressive man, almost 60 years old and built like a muscular, very fit young man. I would watch him place hand weights or dumbbells standing them on end on the floor. He would then place two weight end plates from barbells on end, one in each hand balancing them on the upright hand weights. With his feet on a stability exercise ball, while balanced and suspended above the floor, I would watch him do push-ups.

I asked him what motivated him to stay in such great shape? Johnny told me it wasn't necessarily motivation as it was a way of life. When younger and in the military, it was exercise every day. He never stopped, it was a way of life, daily exercise, and still is, a habit. A healthy norm. Together we've laughed, because, over time in the course of conversation, we learned we are the same age.

"How old are you?" Johnny said.

"I'll be 60 next year," I said.

Johnny smiled. "Me too."

"Graduated from high school in 1977?" Johnny asked.

"Yep, 1977."

"What month is your birthday in Johnny?" I asked.

"December, 1959."

We laugh. "My birthday is November 27 Johnny, I'm just a couple weeks older than you."

Johnny is one of those guys that can move from laughter and a smile to a serious conversation rapidly. A thinker. And a healthy norm takes more than exercise and I know it. I asked him what is the secret? Give me something, something that gives me the edge to stay in great physical shape like him. I saw Johnny's face become serious and intense. He set down his clothes on the bench and approached, looking me in the eyes.

"Don't eat after 4PM," said Johnny. "Your digestive system needs a chance to rest. Toxins will build in your body. If you give your digestive system a chance to rest from digesting, the organs can purge toxins during periods of sleep and rest. I eat well during the day, but I go to bed hungry."

If you look at Johnny, it's hard to argue with success. There are a lot of guys half his age that would like to have his physique. I told him I would test his theory.

"30 days," said Johnny, "30 days."

I thanked him for the advice and turned back to my locker to get my clothes. It caused me to think I should discipline myself to chew my food better too, like my doctor had advised me. Well chewed food gives the digestive system an additional break. Maybe I should give my digestive system a break. Try it even though "intermittent fasting" is no fun for me. Regardless, a smile, banter, or a thumbs up from my friend Johnny would frequently encourage me in the process.

There were moments of discouragement. Moments I asked myself what I was doing. One blustery brisk morning I ran the beach to the breakwater and out to the end. I did my push-ups first then rolled on my back on the concrete next to the lighthouse to do my sit-ups. I took off my favorite pair of running sunglasses and set them next to me on the concrete. I had no sooner done a few sit-ups when a gust of wind caught hold of those favorite glasses and slid them across the remaining breakwater surface. My impulse was to jump up and grab them, but it was too late. It took seconds but seemed like slow motion as I watched those glasses slide and skidder off the end of the breakwater into the cold lake. I lay back on the cold concrete looking up into the sky. Those running sunglasses and I had been through years and a lot together. They were comfortable. I always wore them when running, even on cloudy days. It was the norm. Another cold, chilly gust and spray from the water blew across me. I questioned my sanity out there alone. I continued my sit-ups and chuckled thinking, *I'm sure a fish will be caught next summer in Lake Michigan wearing my glasses.*

My mind would race as I would run the beach. I was ruminating. You also play head games as you run, for example, juxtaposing the words quandary and quagmire against each other.

You're alone with your thoughts.

I also picked up trash while ruminating on my return trip. Why do some people leave trash on the beach thinking someone else will pick it up? What causes them to be that way while others I would see volunteering their time to clean the beaches? The juxtaposition of selfishness and selfless service pursued my thoughts all summer long. You see both all around you. I would engage veterans, selfless servants, to understand those who would risk their very lives in service for others.

A group of 20 volunteers went out on a July summer morning to spend 2 hours picking up trash left by beach goers on the stretch of beach I was training on. On a 1.1 mile stretch of that beach 45.5 lbs of trash was picked up.

- 1,883 cigarettes and cigarette filters
- 257 food wrappers
- 5 plastic take-out containers
- 4 foam take-out containers
- 297 bottle caps
- 205 straws
- 30 forks, knives and spoons
- 6 plastic beverage bottles
- 7 glass beverage bottles
- 7 beverage cans
- 6 plastic grocery bags
- 17 other plastic bags
- 7 paper bags
- 7 paper cups and plates
- 15 plastic cups and plates
- 6 foam cups and plates
- 7 sandals or shoes
- 6 bandages
- 7 pieces of clothing
- 11 beach toys
- 2 fishing buoys
- 3 fishing nets and pieces
- 3 ropes
- 19 six-pack holders
- 18 other plastic and foam packages
- 1 other plastic bottle

- 7 strapping bands
- 4 tobacco packages and wrappers
- 2 condoms
- 1 diaper
- 6 tampons or tampon applicators
- 28 balloons
- 150 cigar tips
- 5 cigarette lighters
- 32 construction materials
- 37 fireworks
- 26 pieces of discarded food
- 3 dental floss picks
- 159 foam pieces
- 42 glass pieces
- 1,472 plastic pieces

It is a question that bothered me all summer. Not, "why was there trash on the beach?" Rather, "why are some inclined to be *selfish* and others *selfless*?" Why are some inclined to selfless service and others are not? Were they raised that way? Is it ingrained in them? Is it taught? I got a different answer from everyone I asked. I thought about the veterans I got to know over the course of the year and reflected on the historic words,

> *"Ask not what your country can do for you —*
> *ask what you can do for your country."*
>
> **– John F. Kennedy**

Selflessness is easy to overlook as a key to happiness. It, even at the surface, seems to be contrary to happiness. Isn't the pursuit of happiness and unalienable rights by its very nature selfish? Not necessarily. But I surmised in my thoughts that ***selfish happiness is short lived. Selfless service lasts a lifetime.*** It also transcends the span of your life. Because the effects of selfless service on the people around you encourage them to live their lives differently; it has a compounding positive affect. Like the ripples caused by a stone dropped in water. Selfless service is self-perpetuating in many ways. Is it a fulfillment of purpose? Our lives can be lived for any number of purposes. A purpose greater than one's self is a phrase I would hear often throughout the year. I would seek answers during Operation Rumination.

"The great lesson of biography is to show what man can be and do at his best. A noble life put fairly on record acts like an inspiration to others."

-Samuel Smiles

Despite discrimination and slight
Virgil valiantly did what was right
Even when grounded
With courage unbounded
He never gave up the fight.

Chapter Two

What Couldn't be Done He Did it

I HAD READ HIS BOOK **BLUE SKIES** AND *Thunder*, so I was looking forward to the opportunity to have coffee with Virgil Westdale. I place my recording device on the table and turn it on. Born in January of 1918, now 100 years and 7 months young, with a lifetime of experiences that exceed those of most people, I ask Virgil Westdale *the* question.

"Please tell me, Virgil, your secret," I said. "How have you stayed so positive despite the setbacks and obstacles you've had to surpass in your life?"

Virgil calls the good times "blue skies" and the struggles "thunder." He is one of very few Army Combat Veterans who actually witnessed the first Veterans Day (WWI Armistice) at the 11th hour of the 11th day of the 11th month of 1918. Virgil was 11 months old on that day! With a shrug of his shoulders he pauses and looks down as he collects his thoughts. I press him for an answer. He lifts his head and smiles. He sets his coffee on the table and begins to recite a poem from memory...

"Somebody said that it couldn't be done,
But he with a chuckle replied
That "maybe it couldn't," but he would be one
Who wouldn't say so till he'd tried.
So he buckled right in with the trace of a grin
On his face. If he worried he hid it.
He started to sing as he tackled the thing
That couldn't be done, and he did it."

"I learned that poem in the 7th grade" he says.

I sit there mesmerized while he recites the poem, understanding he had accomplished, served and done more in his 100 plus years of life than I could ever hope to. I first met Virgil at a National Judo invitational held in Grand Rapids, Michigan where he was honored.

"Maybe I should have shared that at the Judo conference" he says with a smile.

The poem was written by Edgar Guest whose family settled in Detroit, Michigan in 1891. In 1895 Guest was hired as a copy boy for the Detroit Free Press, where he would work for almost sixty-five years. Some 88 years after memorizing the poem of Edgar Guest, Virgil Westdale sits across from me over a cup of coffee, reciting the poem with a twinkle in his eyes, all from memory. I sit across from him, thinking his mind is like a computer with personality … lots of it. I know from reading his book that Virgil was an expert at using the slide rule. He was amazingly accurate and skilled during a time when electronic calculators and computers did not yet exist.

This did not stop him from doing complicated things … "it could be done and he did it."

At one point in his service during World War II Virgil Westdale was transferred from the infantry to the artillery, because of his piloting experience and ability to use flight instrumentation. It was a time when they called the slide rule a "computer." He was in the Fire Direction Center of the Headquarters Battery of the

522nd Artillery of the 442nd Regimental Combat Team. Virgil and the Fire Direction Team operated "computers" which were specially designed slide rules that computed latitude and longitude angles and settings for firing on the enemy. Forward observers selected the targets and called in coordinates, which were then mapped out on a large map. It was Virgil's job, using a slide rule, to calculate the direction and elevation of the targets on which the 105mm howitzers would fire. Commanding officers relied on him, because he could operate a slide rule under pressure. One mistake, one miscalculation could be a deadly one, resulting in firing on their own infantry being supported by the artillery unit. Often those calculations and decisions needed to be made quickly and under pressure. Once the calculation was made, the radio man commanded "fire for effect" to the gun crews. The howitzers would be adjusted to the specifications Virgil had provided. He knew the calculations had to be absolutely correct. Over the course of the war, the 522nd Artillery never once dropped artillery on its own men. *They knew what had to be done and they did it!*

"What is the secret to being creative, to being inventive?" I asked Virgil.

"I love new thoughts and learning," he said. He looked down to collect a thought and then looked up at me with a youthful twinkle in his eye. "I'm kind of a sucker for it," he said.

Virgil was not coddled by his father. "I had a great Mother," said Virgil, "who filled the void." At an early age he developed an appetite for learning. He shared with me a story how as kids they would help their dad with planting, caring for and harvesting the watermelon crop. When eleven, one summer day, his curiosity got the best of him. Using his pocket knife, he and his sister began cutting deep triangular plugs out of the melons to see if they were juicy and red. They cut into a number of watermelons but never found one ripe enough to eat. Each time they were careful to put the plug back into the melon and rotate the melon, so the wounded area was against the cool earth and out of sight. When harvest time, came a few weeks later, his dad was furious when spoiled melon after spoiled melon was discovered. What began as an innocent error made by a child, turned into an irate father, causing Virgil to stay out of his line of fire for a long time. It wasn't until years later that his relationship with his father improved, but he never was close or felt valued by his father. I asked Virgil why that story sticks out in his memory and why he shared it with me.

"I think the best way to live life is positive," said Virgil. "I'm not a holy roller," he said "but I was very much influenced at a young age by my Mennonite friend, Vernon Kaufman."

In the fall of 1940 Virgil Westdale was enrolled and studying at Western Michigan College, now Western Michigan University. By the fall of 1941 he had added a flight course to his college workload, and by February of 1942 was the proud owner of a private pilot's license, passing with "flying" colors issued by the Civil Aeronautics Administration. Like many young men in the early 1940's, college would now have to wait. He volunteered to serve his country joining the WTS or War Training Service, hoping to fly for the Air Corps. He would train as a pilot, including acrobatics training, in a Waco UPF-7 open tandem cockpit biplane.

Over time, he progressed to perform acrobatics in the sky with his flight instructors considering him at the top of his class. "That's where you can run into trouble," said Virgil, describing a time he did a power-on stall, pulling the nose of the plane up slowly until the airplane would not climb anymore, even though the engine RPM was greatly increased, causing the plane to stall and drop as the nose fell. Losing control of the plane, the elevator flaps ripped the control stick out of his hand. Wrestling with the stick, his airspeed had risen past the red warning line, and he was heading at a high rate of speed for the valley below. He managed to fight the UPF-7 out of its headlong plummet and never forgot it.

"The most vulnerable pilots are the ones who have logged around only 80 hours of flying time," said Virgil. "You're vulnerable and you don't know it. You think you know everything and you don't." It was a lesson learned, and he resolved to never fly again without his full attention. "Lessons you never forget," said Virgil.

"Yesterday, December 7, 1941—a date which will
live in infamy—the United States of America was
suddenly and deliberately attacked by naval and
air forces of the Empire of Japan."
-Franklin Delano Roosevelt.

With a father of Japanese descent, Virgil Nishimura had reason for concern. The events following the bombing of Pearl Harbor included Executive order 9066, signed by Franklin Delano Roosevelt on February 19, 1942, the same month Virgil had received his pilot's license, causing thousands of Japanese Americans to be upended. Japanese Americans were sent with few belongings from their homes to ramshackle shanties in concentration camps right here in America.

By May of 1942, Virgil's pilot license was taken from him by a CAA inspector with no explanation offered. By October of that year, Virgil had made arrangements with a lawyer to appear before a judge to change his name, because "Nishimura" was, as he told the judge, difficult to spell and pronounce. From that day forward American born and American citizen Virgil Nishimura would be Virgil Westdale.

Because no pilot's license is needed to join the Army Air Corp, and with a new name, Virgil enlisted on October 30, 1942. Passing the physical and taking the oath by November of 1942 he had his pilot's license back. He had his eye on the P-51 Mustang and wanted to fly one of them someday. Virgil trained to fly via instrumentation versus contact flying in the spring of 1943, and became an expert pilot. He passed his instrument and commercial flight exams and became eligible to go into active duty with the Air Corps or had the option to instruct new pilots. He chose teaching young pilots, and the summer of 1943 was the time of his life teaching them to fly. He was supporting the war effort and using his talents in the process.

Again, without warning or explanation in a stunning development in August of 1943 via a letter from the War Department, he would be demoted from Air Corps flight instructor to Army private. Virgil felt he was being punished for being "half-Japanese" and was devastated by the developments. By late August he was to report to Fort Custer as an Army private. To add insult to injury, just weeks before he was training pilots in instrumentation flight, now he was sent to pull KP duty scrubbing grease off hot kitchen stove hoods.

In short order his next assignment was to Camp Shelby in Hattiesburg, Mississippi, where the 442nd Regimental Combat Team was training. It was basic training and unit training with the infantry for 7 months. One month before being shipped out, he was reassigned to the 522nd Field Artillery Battalion of the 442nd RCT and assigned to the Fire Direction Center of the Headquarters Battery. Hand-picked to do mental math quickly, Virgil was ideal with his pilot and instrumentation skills. Using a slide rule, he could quickly and accurately calculate, supporting the men on the front lines with artillery calculations and skills developed during his pilot training. Virgil said there was a lot of pressure in the process. Commanding officers wanted the calculations quickly, but you certainly did not want to make a mistake, as lives were at risk from artillery fire that could go awry. By May 2, 1944 Virgil and the 442nd Regimental Combat Team shipped out of Newport News, Virginia headed for Italy. The risk of German U-Boats was an ever-present danger in the crossing of the seas of the Atlantic Ocean.

Virgil Westdale served during World War II with the 100th battalion 442nd Regimental Combat team 522nd Artillery Battalion, distinguishing itself by helping push the Germans out of Italy, freeing the "lost battalion" in France in one of the most ferocious battles of World War II, and rescuing the prisoners of the Dachau Concentration Camp. After the war, President Harry Truman made remarks to the 442nd Regimental combat team on the grounds of the White House and said "You fought not only the enemy, but you fought prejudice and you have won. Keep up that fight, and we will continue to win, to make this great Republic stand for just what the Constitution says it stands for: the welfare of all the people all the time."

Virgil Westdale, November 1944

At a time when the United States openly doubted the loyalty of young Japanese Americans enlisted from both Hawaii and the continental United States, the men of Virgil's group would go on to become one of the most highly decorated units in American history. For its size and duration of service, the 442nd Regimental Combat Team was the most decorated of any unit in American military history. The Japanese American soldiers of World War II demonstrated true courage, sacrifice and loyalty in the face of discrimination. The 100th battalion 442nd regimental combat team was honored with a Congressional Gold Medal on November 2, 2011 at the US capitol in Washington DC for their perseverance, patriotism, courage and sacrifice during World War II.

Virgil was dubbed "the tall one," because, unlike the 5 1/2 foot tall Japanese Americans or Hawaiian Japanese Americans he served with, Virgil stood out at 6 feet tall.

"I'm not 6 feet tall anymore" said Virgil, balancing the coffee in both hands as his shoulders bounced up and down in a hearty chuckle at his own expense.

As I chatted with Virgil over coffee, I was struck by how he could recall difficult memories of the past with a serious look on his face. And how he could transition from head down in reflection to a twinkle in his eye and a grin followed by a chuckle. He lived the poem he had recited to me.

"So, he buckled right in with the trace of a grin, on his face. If he worried he hid it. He started to sing as he tackled the thing that couldn't be done, and he did it."

He related a story of how, traveling through Germany, he spent a night in an abandoned warehouse in November. Cold. No heat. Concrete floor. Nothing to eat. When they did have something to eat it was usually "K-rations" in a brown, cardboard box.

"The breakfast rations were the best," said Virgil with a smile.

The breakfast K-ration box usually consisted of:

- Canned meat product (ham and eggs)
- Biscuits
- Compressed cereal bar
- Powdered coffee
- Fruit bar
- Chewing gum
- Sugar tablets
- Four cigarettes
- Water-purification tablets
- Can opener
- Wooden spoon

The dinner and supper rations included a candy bar and cheese.

"The candy bar was the worst," said Virgil. "It was like wax. We would try to melt them, but they wouldn't melt," he said, laughing with a glimmer in his eye. In the same breath he said those who were hungry didn't mind as he recalls and describes the images of the people liberated from Dachau at the end of the war. They had made it to the concentration camp at Dachau so fast, the supplies couldn't keep up.

"I ran around knocking on doors of homes to give clothing and food and that's a way I could help," said Virgil.

I was struck by how he could move from painful thoughts to finding humor. Sitting across from him I thought of the Duke

Ellington quote, "Gray skies are just clouds passing through" or as Virgil would say "blue skies and thunder."

RAIN AND SNOW

OUR CONVERSATION TURNED TO WHEN THE 442ND WAS called in to rescue the 141st Regiment 1st Battalion, which had advanced too far into enemy territory and was cut off by the Nazis closing in around them. There were many casualties in the effort to save the 141st, which became known as "the lost battalion." It was the 522nd artillery battalion's job to pound away and soften the German position entrenched on forested high ground. The artillery would have to be accurate and effective if the 141st was to be saved. It was during that assault a specific event seemed to stand out in Virgil's mind. He was standing with his artillery unit under camouflage netting, and described a low fly-by pass of a German Messerschmitt, roaring past him at close range. I can see in his eyes the recollection is clear, even today and still poignant in his mind. Once a pilot always a pilot. He talked of the German pilot being so low he could clearly see him sitting in the cockpit roaring by at what he estimated to be 200 mph and low to the ground. The weather was inclement, and Virgil watched as the pilot pulled the nose up to clear the trees full throttle and up into the heavens and the clouds. Just like that he was gone. In the course of our conversation Virgil repeated for emphasis saying, "It was raining and snowing at the same time."

Infamous storms are memorable and named by weather agencies. We personally remember storms as markers for certain events in our lives. We remember where we were at a given moment and what the weather was like. It made me realize that the weather during key moments in our lives becomes embedded in our memory. "Storms" are something we carry with us throughout our lives and ground us for future stresses. "It was raining and snowing at the same time." We retire some weather events in our minds as a marker for something that makes us what we are today.

THE STING OF DISCRIMINATION

VIRGIL DID NOT LEAVE EUROPE AFTER THE WAR WITH HIS unit, due to a first sergeant who had slighted him and left him off the list. To this day he does not know why. His unit left in September of 1945 after the Third Reich had completely fallen, and all areas of Germany were securely in Allied hands. He was left to fend for himself and had no other recourse than to join up with GIs from another unit. It wasn't until late November he would board with other GIs on trucks headed back to France. This would make it possible for him to make it home for Christmas 1945.

One night on their travel for France through Germany, bumping around in the back of a truck, near a small town, his unit stopped to stay overnight in a cold, damp building with concrete floors. Virgil and his friend, Rhinehart, instead opted to knock on doors of German homes to try to get something to eat and a warm, comfortable place to sleep. At one home, after knocking, he explained in German to the homeowner their intentions. The homeowner said he didn't have room but took them to another house a short distance away. "These people are Nazis," said the man, rapping on the door and disappearing into the darkness, leaving Virgil and his friend to face them alone. Cold, hungry and tired they stood their ground. The door opened slightly, and he put his combat boot in the door crack. He needed a place to eat and sleep. **"He did what he had to do."** After some discussion by those in the room, the door opened slowly. "Kommen Sie bitte." (Come in please.) There were 12 Germans at the table for a big dinner party. He and his friend took a seat at the table with his "back to the wall." Virgil called the next moments of sitting in silence, the longest moments of his life. "30 seconds." He will never forget the lady who took compassion on them. She got up and fetched two plates out of the cupboard and set the plates in front of them. "Bless her heart," said Virgil, "you never know what a person is capable of."

He will never forget a person seated at the table. "I think he was SS," Virgil said. During the course of the meal the individual

Virgil Westdale, December 1944

never smiled, never talked, just stared. Not a word. Virgil kept his luger handy, including in his bed that night. The next morning the hostess woke them with a knock on the door. She had prepared a breakfast of eggs and toast and even handed them sack lunches as they left.

On a cold truck ride through Germany to France, a homemade German cheese and sausage sandwich made their journey more tolerable. Besides, Virgil was finally heading home. He never did make it home in time for Christmas. It was January 5, 1946 when his ship of GIs arrived in New York harbor. They stood proudly at attention as they passed the Statue of Liberty. Virgil saluted her, understanding she represented what they had fought for … the statue represents freedom.

OPERATION RUMINATION

IT SEEMS WITH VIRGIL THAT AGE OR ANY OTHER REALITY like ethnicity is not an obstacle or consideration in impeding progress.

"I'm going to turn 60 next year," I say. Virgil takes a sip from his coffee and grins. "You have a long way to go," he says.

I laugh as I ask Virgil, now over 100 years old, what is the secret to staying young and healthy? He smiles and his sense of humor shines through as he says, "When I'm served cake, I always scrape off the frosting." I'm not sure whether or not to believe him and whether or not that's *the* secret. He proceeds to say that, "Your diet and exercise are important. I didn't each much sugar," he says waving off the sugar and adding only cream to his coffee. Virgil told me he would dance every Sunday. I ran into a friend of Virgil while in Florida. Out of the blue his name came up in our conversation. His friend told me Virgil *is* an amazing dancer even now over the age of 100.

He also notes, managing stress and always learning, are keys to staying young. "I like to learn new things," says Virgil. I nod my head in acknowledgement, recognizing the friend who introduced me to Virgil had told me he received 25 US patents and earned an international award for his work with photocopier components. Then upon "retiring," he went to work for the TSA, returning to the world of aviation and national security. He has an appetite for learning and always … continual goals.

As we get up to walk back to my car, I ask Virgil if, looking back, he is glad he served his country. "It was my duty, I'm an American," he says.

After I drop him off at home, I ruminate on how when the War Department discovered he was part Japanese, with a caucasian mother and Japanese father, he was demoted from instrument flight instructor to Army private with no explanation. His background is investigated by the FBI, Navy intelligence and War Relocation Authorities. I'm sure the only thing they ever found was that Virgil Westdale served his country with duty, honor, skill and bravery. And a very big reason why he did just that is because

...

"Somebody said that it couldn't be done,
But he with a chuckle replied
That "maybe it couldn't," but he would be one
Who wouldn't say so till he'd tried.
So he buckled right in with the trace of a grin
On his face. If he worried he hid it.
He started to sing as he tackled the thing
That couldn't be done, and he did it."

Virgil Westdale (left) and author Rick Vuyst

The course that he would chart
His work he would take to heart
With multiple roles
And continual goals
He would finish what he'd start.

Sid Lenger
US Navy
Seaman 1st Class USNR
LST 651
April 1944 to November 16, 1945

Chapter Three

Continual Goals

ONE-HUNDRED YEARS OLD AND still busy. Still working. Still creating. Outdoors at Sid Lenger's home, I walk along row after row of concrete walls, tiered along a steep embankment with Sid's daughter Lavonne. Walls made of discarded concrete slabs from a municipal sidewalk project, walls built by hand piece by piece when in his sixties. A stratum of both ingenuity and hard work, they provide layers of garden beds now maintained by his daughter.

Walking into the house there are his multiple paintings everywhere … one covers an entire wall. The cabinets in the kitchen area are all built by him. Lavonne leads me to the basement and there is Sid Lenger. Mixing and editing video and layering sound and music on his Mackie sound mixer board for a travelogue on Michigan. Models of Japanese Kamikaze planes hang from the ceiling, and mementos and pictures and medals hang on the wall. There is a framed certificate of honorable discharge from the United States Navy, dated November of 1945. A statue of a

20mm gunner is on the desk with 20mm shells.

Sid Lenger is reviewing his latest travel video and editing, rearranging, making sure it is done right. After World War II, he established Lenger Travel, and expanded the business by taking photos and movies of every place he went, countries in every corner of the globe. I look at a world map on the wall with pins pushed into every country he's visited.

Sid's back is to us as Lavonne and I watch over his shoulder. He is editing a Michigan travelogue and an image pops up on the screen that seems to define the example he has set in his life.

> *All that you do*
> *Do with all your might*
> *Things done by halves*
> *Are not done right.*

"Finish what you start," says Lavonne. Born the day after the attack on Pearl Harbor in 1941, today she works the garden of the huge, terraced backyard in stone, assembled by Sid years ago. She has now picked up where Sid left off and manages the area with the same vigor and energy Sid exhibited. I watch her as she shows me the layout and work to be done. She manages a full calendar for her Dad, and cares for him and the house with precision and competence. I look at the activity calendar she maintains for her and Sid. Every day, every box, is full of scribbles and appointments. They are planning a trip to Frankenmuth for video of a gazebo like the one in *The Sound of Music*. I thought to myself with a smile, *Lavonne, even at the age of 76, the apple doesn't fall far from the tree.*

In high school, Sid Lenger won a contest in 1936 for his drawing ability, and credits his ability to paint and draw as God-given gifts. After graduating in 1937 from Lee High School, he helped his father at Lenger's Market, which specialized in meats. At the time, posters hung in stores and public places everywhere with an image of Uncle Sam pointing at you and captioned "I want you." Everyone had to register, so, at the age of 18, Sid

Lenger registered for the draft.

Sid married his wife Beulah in February of 1941. He had a high draft number, so it wasn't until April of 1944 that he received his letter to head to Detroit for a pre-induction physical examination. He passed that exam, and, with a wife and two children at home, he was instructed to get his affairs in order. The day before Memorial Day 1944, he left for 6 weeks of basic training at the Great Lakes Naval Academy in Chicago. After that it was more training near Norfolk, Virginia at Camp Bradford.

The question in Sid's mind was: how his wife Beulah and his two children could live on $48 a month income with a house payment of $25 a month? Training to leave to fight for his country in the Pacific theatre, Sid already had the responsibility of a daughter and a son.

Sid served in the Navy on the LST 651 which saw extensive action in the Asian Pacific theatre during World War II. The ship was launched in 1944 at the Chicago Bridge & Iron Co. in Seneca, IL. He refers to the LST, named as such for Landing Ship Tank, as "Large Slow Target" with a grin on his face.

An LST is a landing ship "tank" used during World War II to carry tanks, vehicles, cargo, and land troops directly onto the shore with no docks or piers. It is an oceangoing landing craft that could beach and withdraw over and over again carrying large amounts of men, tanks and other equipment. The LST ships were designed without a keel, so that they could roll up onto the beach. But without a keel, they weren't as stable as other ships. "We got used to it," Lenger said. "It slides a little bit. I remember in Panama getting sea sick. Sickest guy in the world, I thought I was going to die," said Sid.

One of the few surviving LST ships of the time, the LST 393, is located today near my home in Muskegon, Michigan, and I think of Sid every time I drive by it docked in the harbor. Sid himself has been a longtime volunteer for the LST 393 Museum. He was involved in the restoration process of the LST 393 in Muskegon, Michigan and gave tours for a period of time on the ship. I've sat in the parking lot looking at the ship, peacefully docked in Muskegon Lake, imagining what it would be like to be onboard with Japanese kamikaze airplanes attacking from all directions while out on the ocean. I've walked the deck of the ship, trying to imagine the crew, the aroma, the intensity, heat of the South Pacific and sounds of the LST in action.

He recalls for me what the Japanese air assault looked like before his ship would land 500 Marines on the beach.

"All we could see were flares and tracer bullets that lit up the night," Lenger said. The Japanese aircraft ultimately failed to stop the US attack, and Lenger's ship successfully landed Marines on the islands they approached.

Sid had the presence of mind to take an 8mm movie camera with him on the ship, but of course is quick to point out he couldn't use it when at general quarters. The ship had two twin 40mm guns, four single 40mm gun mounts and 12 of the 20mm guns. It was powered by two General Motors 900-horsepower diesel engines. The ship had a length of 328 feet and beam of 50 feet. Sid served as quartermaster in the wheelhouse and on the ship's navigational charts. Sid had to log weather conditions and travel distance every 15 minutes in the ship's log. I look up and view a great photograph of him, hanging on the wall, as a quartermaster and helmsman in the wheelhouse, smiling as he stands at the steering ship annunciator. During general quarters he manned a 20mm gun on the ship's deck. He recalls the ship, notorious for being durable in battle, arriving back to port so damaged from attacks they felt they would have to scrap it. In a battle of attrition fought on land, on sea, and in the air, the allies wore the Japanese down, inflicting irreplaceable losses on Japanese military assets in the Solomon Islands campaign.

He particularly recalls the Battle of Okinawa in the Pacific, especially a 14-day stretch, where "they never got down to the sack," taking turns for quick naps leaning on the gun. "About 1,500 people were killed the first two days and that's the battle we were in. We were in that whole mess for 14 days and no sleep," says Sid. Okinawa was one of the bloodiest battles of the Pacific war. "We were in the first wave at Okinawa," Sid tells

Sid Lenger in the ship's wheelhouse

me with tears in his eyes. "Okinawa was the longest battle of the war."

The LST was a key component in the battle, with the invasion beginning on April 1, 1945. The intensity of Kamikaze attacks was historic and numerous during this time, with the Japanese pulling out all the stops and fighting to the death. I think of what a kamikaze attack would have been like to experience as I look up at the model Japanese Mitsubishi Zeros, hanging from the ceiling of a basement room where Sid edits his movies and paints his pictures. Okinawa proved a key battle to provide a fleet anchorage, troop staging areas, and airfields in proximity to Japan in preparation for the planned eventual invasion of the Japanese mainland. It showed the tenacity at which the Japanese would fight. I'm convinced that tenacity to fight to the death, and the volume of kamikazes in that battle, as well as casualties at Okinawa, played a factor in Truman's decision to later use the atomic bomb and avoid such an amphibious assault on the mainland of Japan.

The Captain would say, "Starboard side, commence firing," as they would wait until attacks were within one mile of the ship. "When they're coming down at 300mph you don't have much time at that point," Sid said. He relied on his loader and friend David "Goldie" Goldsboro to load the magazines or "box" as he pointed and held the trigger down. Lenger credits David with "being a hero" on the ship, quickly, efficiently and without fail, loading the magazines he estimates as weighing as much as 70 pounds. "We were one. I couldn't do nothing without him, he couldn't do nothing without me," says Sid.

Sid recalls a plane approaching their ship at a high rate of speed. "He just kept coming, skipping over the water. I could see our shells were hitting him. I shot him and just prior to hitting the ship, pulled up and over the ship's starboard side so close we could see the whites of the pilot's eyes. He ascended a short distance and then plummeted into the ocean."

"Once you kill someone you never forget it," he says, pausing to talk and overcome with emotion.

I ATTENDED AN EVENT ON WEDNESDAY, JULY 11, 2018 for the reunion of Sid Lenger and David "Goldie" Goldsboro. The LST 651 that Sid and Goldie served on moved troops during the last major battle of World War II, the Battle of Okinawa. Lenger and Goldsboro's battle station was on a 20mm anti-aircraft gun called Sky 9 on the starboard side of the ship. Sid was the gunman, or as the Navy calls it "the pointer," and Goldsboro was the loader.

Of the 139 who served on the LST 651, Lenger and Goldsboro are two of the remaining four who are still living. The two were in the Pacific near Japan when the United States dropped the atom bomb on Hiroshima and Nagasaki, with Imperial Japan surrendering on August 15, 1945. According to the US Department of Veterans Affairs statistics, less than 500,000 of the 16 million Americans who served in World War II will survive 2018. I viewed a graph of statistics from the US Department of Veterans Affairs that by 2025 less than 100,000 of the 16 million that served will be surviving. The Department estimates that the US loses about 362 WWII veterans per day. It is a reminder that every day memories of World War II, "the sights, sounds, terrors and triumphs" pass away with this generation of American heroes.

OPERATION RUMINATION

I ask Sid what the secret to longevity is. He has shared with me that both his faith as well as hard work are important keys to a full and long life. However, in one of my visits with Sid, he made a special point to remind me that as he put it, "times have changed. Today we always have to get paid," says Sid, "and make more instead of being content with what we have and making do."

I smile and listen, thinking I'm sure I'm not the only one who has heard this story. Sid continues, "I was making $12 a week when I got married. We had $25 for our honeymoon to Mammoth caves in Kentucky." They stayed in teepees on the site for $1 a day, which included breakfast. When they returned from their honeymoon, he still had $10 left of the $25.

Many who I have met from Sid's generation, including my dad, were good with managing money, not spending what they didn't have, and finding contentment in what they had. Not quick to spend, they would save and invest in their families and the future.

I press further, however, knowing our greatest generation's penchant for frugal financial practice, working hard, saving, giving to others, serving.

Sid tries to explain to me that when you work hard, keep going, keep busy, there is always something to do. At this point Lavonne interjects into our conversation two words. **"Continual goals,"** says Lavonne.

It resonates with me and strikes a chord. All the veterans over

David "Goldie" Goldsboro (left)
Sid Lenger (right)

the age of 80 I had talked to in this year had that exact same characteristic. **Continual goals** ... even today at the age of 100. One of them put it this way, "You rest you rust." Lavonne puts it this way, "You don't retire."

I have met some people this past year who do not have continual goals, and are of a younger age. They seem to me to ... just exist. Because of my focused rumination this past year, I clearly see their countenance, demeanor and health is different from those who have continual goals.

Sid Lenger is an example to me as one who combines service to others along with continual personal goals. When you add a sense of service to the characteristic of having continual goals ... you have a winning combination that makes a difference.

> *All that you do*
> *Do with all your might*
> *Things done by halves*
> *Are not done right.*

An expert story crafter
Told a half century thereafter,
Things he could not repeat so
He had to go incognito
And today tells with abundant laughter.

Chapter Four

We Did Not Exist

THE PACING OF THE DELIVERY OF A joke can have a strong impact on its comedic effect, and Al Johnson has it down cold. I watch as Al Johnson, now 95 years young with microphone in hand, holds the attention of a crowd listening to his story. A story that for years, because of its secretive nature, could not be told. Now, years later and "declassified," he is free to share, and holds the audience in the palm of his hand.

Born July 5, 1923, and with his wife born in 1921 seated in the crowd, he is asked how long they have been married. "71 years," says Al, to a robust round of applause. As the applause dies down, and waiting for effect, he pauses until the room goes quiet, then says, "I was 5 and she was 6 at the time."

He listens as an audience member asks if it was difficult not to say anything for 50 years about the secret strategic mission he had engaged in during World War II. With a wry grin on his face he says, "Not really. I had a lovely wife, she told me don't talk, don't write, just shut up." The crowd bursts into laughter and I look to the back of the room where his wife is seated. She's laughing as hard as everyone else at the impeccable delivery of his punch line.

The inevitable follow up question comes from the audience and Al is ready.

"What was more difficult, being over there during World War II or being obedient to your wife?"

Al immediately answers lifting the microphone close to his mouth and with a dry look on his face, "Yes," he answers. More laughter.

Al Johnson served in the OSS during World War II, a precursor to Special Forces Green Beret and the CIA. At the time, it was an organization "that didn't officially exist." Only now can the stories be told.

Al was drafted into the Army and was going to be a medic. "I hated it," he said. After being drafted, he went to Fort Custer in Battle Creek, Michigan. He was then sent on a bus to Abilene, Texas for 6 weeks of a hot and dry environment for basic training. After that it was on to Fort Sam Houston in San Antonio, Texas and the Army hospital there. He looked for opportunities to volunteer for something more exciting.

"I didn't want to have to go to a hospital and be a bedpan jockey," he said.

After Fort Sam Houston, Al was sent to a "holding camp" in Denver, Colorado to wait to be assigned to a hospital. It was there he saw a notice on the bulletin board about a need for volunteers for hazardous duty. That posting came with the caveat of phrases like "short life expectancy" and a "temperament to be behind enemy lines." Al volunteered and signed up.

It was the OSS or Office of Strategic Services, a precursor to the Special Forces Green Beret and the CIA. It would provide the US and allies with grass roots intelligence from the field. Al was in the French group, and would work with the French underground called the "Maquis" of FFI or French Forces of the Interior, a French resistance movement during the German occupation of 1940-1945. His OSS group would spearhead the southern invasion of France weeks before Operation Anvil, the Allied landing in southern France. They were there 6 weeks before the Allies arrived and created chaos, providing intelligence until the American's had overtaken them; then they had to get out.

The Joint Chiefs of Staff authorized the creation of OGs or Operational Groups that would consist of specially selected, trained and physically hardened US Army soldiers capable of waging war behind enemy lines. These were the forerunners of today's Special Forces operational units.

He repeated they would be an organization that "didn't exist."

After volunteering and being vetted by the FBI, they went to Washington DC and were sworn in as spies. One training location was the rolling hills of the Congressional Country Club 12 miles outside Washington DC. It was four-hundred acres leased to the US government to serve as a training ground for the OSS, the forerunner to the CIA and American Special Forces. They couldn't train in a standard Army camp because "they didn't officially exist," so they trained in the national parks which were closed during World War II.

They learned to survive off the land at Camp David. "We were given a canteen of water and sent out to live off the fat of the land," said Al. They learned well. Al said the local farmers would be missing a few chickens from time to time. He pauses for effect and then deadpans, "For years I couldn't look a chicken in the eye."

They did additional basic training in Algiers. It was strenuous physical training: running, calisthenics, rope climbing, weapons training, hand-to-hand combat training. Their minds and their bodies were being finely tuned for survival behind enemy lines. "The first plane ride I ever had, I jumped out of the plane," Al said. They practiced "drops" from a C-47 and eventually were awarded their wings and their diplomas. Their next stop was in occupied France, deep into enemy territory.

They also practiced jumping out of hot air balloons when taking British commando training. This gave them the nearest example of slipping out of the bottom of a B-24 Liberator. Al described the basket under the balloon as an 8-feet square with a hole in the middle. The ball turret under the B-24 Liberator had been removed before takeoff, leaving a large hole in the bottom of the plane about 60 inches in diameter. A sheet of plywood was put over the hole, so no one would accidently step into the hole and fall out.

The B-24 bombers they were in were not decorated; they were non-descript, black in color and secretive like their mission. They would fly the black planes at about 500-feet of altitude to avoid radar detection. It dawns on me that meant they would be slipping out of the turret hole at 500 feet and on the ground in a big hurry.

"Wow I can't believe you would jump at 500 feet Al," I said.

"You need 350 feet for the chute to open," says Al. "Then it's just 150 feet to the ground. The munitions would go out first, then the troopers. This was done so the munitions wouldn't land on us on the ground."

Al pauses and you can see he is cooking up a thought. "The English said they had better parachutes than the Americans. The Americans had their main chute on their back and reserve chute on the front in case the main chute didn't open," he says. Then a wry grin appears on his face as he says, "The English would say if their main chute doesn't work you can bring it back and we'll replace it."

Al's jump and entry into France behind enemy lines took place in darkness at 1:20AM on the night of August 14, 1944. They were to first capture a hydroelectric plant, then harass the Germans, and also collect information to radio back to London headquarters. Their drop zone was at Eguzon, France, 400 miles behind German lines. They would capture and hold a hydro-electric plant there. After that it would be ambushes to slow down German troop movements and activities, as well as sending messages back to London of German troop movements in the area. They had the use of up to 1,200 FFI (French Forces Interior) at any time. Any ambush they planned was well reinforced with fighters. In a conversation at Al's kitchen table, he explained to me it was psychological warfare as well as physical warfare. "The German's never knew when and where we were going to hit them next," he said.

They were effective in creating chaos for the Germans. They would proceed to effectively spearhead the southern invasion of France weeks before Operation Anvil, the allied landing in southern France. Al is asked by a person in the audience if he learned to speak any French while in France. "Just enough to get my face slapped," he says.

Al tells me they didn't have to live off the fat of the land in France like he had learned at Camp David. He pauses and grins at me. "The French underground or "Maquis" and the French fed us well. Wine, bread and cheese," he says.

He opens and exhibits the silk map that the military used during World War II, laying it on the table. The United States and

LE BLANC, FRANCE SEPT. 1944

Al Johnson (back row second from left)

Britain produced these silk and cloth maps for Allied soldiers to use as escape maps. If shot down over enemy-occupied territory in Europe, they would help airmen and soldiers to evade capture. In the case of Al Johnson and his OSS compatriots, they used them *having voluntarily jumped* into enemy-occupied territory. Made of silk or cloth, unlike paper, they could handle moisture and would not make noise when opened. A number of World War II veterans brought these maps of France or Germany back with them after the war.

After their mission in France, Al Johnson and the OSS returned by ship back to the US. It was December 1944 and they were given a 30-day leave to visit with family for Christmas before their next assignment. Sworn to secrecy, in the OSS, and unable to tell them what he had done; it was awkward for both him and his family. He cut his leave short and returned early.

After their December leave in 1944 their adventure was only beginning. Many miles lie ahead in the journey for their OG. After additional training, they redeployed to the China-Burma-India theatre, where they trained Chinese guerrillas for combat against the Japanese. It was a train ride to Denver, then Los Angeles and Camp Pendleton, then San Diego. Al boarded a ship to participate in the war effort, this time in the Pacific theatre. They sailed to Australia and then India, arriving in Bombay harbor. They had spent 30 days out on the water in travel. Next a 5-day train trip to Calcutta. Their mission began there to train and equip Chinese Commando units that could work behind Japanese enemy lines. From there they crossed the "Hump" (the Himalayan Mountain range) that separated China from India. Here the trip was many days on the hot, twisting, curving Burma road chiseled out of the Himalayan mountains.

In France they had been assigned to work with an existing underground network behind enemy lines. In China they were to recruit, train and then operate an underground espionage group behind enemy lines. One of their tasks was to disrupt the flow and cut Japanese supply lines. The enemy was responsible for the removal of large quantities of rice to Japan to support the war

Al Johnson home on leave December 1944

effort. It was their mission to put a stop to it. The Chinese were starving to death. Al Johnson, parachuted into the rice paddies of central China, or as he called it, the "Hengyang-Paoching-Changhou rice triangle." It was their job to disrupt the supply of rice back to Japan. During their stay, their temporary home would be a Buddhist temple. The environment, from heat to mosquitoes to malaria, was dangerous and challenging.

In addition, trying to train Chinese in the OSS methods was difficult on many fronts. Al cites a physical example. "The parachute harness was a problem because the Chinese were much

Al Johnson Calcutta India 1945
(back row second from left)

smaller," said Al. The straps were made to fit Americans. "We would cinch up the harness as far as possible to keep them from falling out."

Speaking to the group, suddenly Al pauses and goes blank. He stands with microphone in hand and taps his forehead with his free hand.

"Just a minute … the connections aren't working," he says.

"Do you need to reboot?" an audience member yells out.

"What is that?" says Al. "Is that Chinese?"

They engaged the Japanese in guerilla fighting in tough conditions, resulting in a number of wounded and casualties. During skirmishes it was usually 16 OSS providing the frontal assault with allied guerillas on their left flank and Chinese Nationals covering their right flank. It was dangerous guerilla warfare to assist the Chinese in rooting out the Japanese.

Then on August 6, 1945 they heard the message coming through on the radio, an atomic bomb had been dropped on Japan. "What's an atomic bomb?" said Al. They were told they were to stay on and extend an additional 30 days. "The Japs on the interior were not ready to give up," said Al.

They weren't happy about their extended stay but did their duty. Finally, it was time to go home. Eventually it was a flight to Calcutta and a boat trip to Seattle that would return Al Johnson to the United States after months behind enemy lines. A train ride to Camp Meade in Maryland to be processed and discharged ended Al's "secret mission." He was home.

Al Johnson and the men of the OSS had penetrated enemy lines, lived off the land, and caused large scale damage to an enemy, impairing both the Germans and the Japanese in the cause to keep them from being able to function effectively. Their mission was extraordinary under difficult and dangerous circumstances. All this, from a group of men and an organization that "didn't exist."

It would be 50 years before he could talk about it. Their existence and their mission remained classified until 1995. I can't imagine what it would be like to have participated in these heroics and be unable to tell others about my experience. Al Johnson, like many World War II veterans, returned to the United States and began their lives raising families in neighborhoods like yours and mine. If you met him in the grocery store or at church, you would never know what he did as a young man in the service of his country.

In 2009 Al Johnson received the Knight of the Legion of Honor medal from the French government. Created by Napoleon, the Legion of Honor is the highest honor that France can bestow upon those who have achieved remarkable deeds for France.

Al Johnson received the Congressional Gold medal in 2018.

Of the 1,100 that served in the OSS, only 100 are living, and only 20 of them showed up to receive their Congressional Gold medal. Al Johnson was one of them. We look at his medal together, an impressive, sizeable gold medal dated 3-21-2018. Al flips the page in a notebook for me, and I read a letter addressed to "Ellsworth" Johnson.

The Congress of the United States

requests your presence at a

Congressional Gold Medal ceremony

in honor of

Office of Strategic Services

on Wednesday the 21st of March

Two thousand eighteen

At three o'clock in the afternoon

Emancipation Hall

United States Capitol Visitor Center

Washington, District of Columbia

The invitation goes on to ask for the favor of his reply and to RSVP to the Speaker. All guests must reply and have a ceremony ticket for entry. I laugh at the irony of the final statement, "this invitation is non-transferable." I think to myself, no doubt, Al Johnson is one of a kind and the service of the OSS in World War II was an amazing one-of-a-kind feat by a select few.

I look at the medals in front of Al. I think they are beautiful, but could never compensate for the sacrifices made by him and others. In my rumination I think, *it's not about compensation*; they are a symbolic recognition, so the stories are heard and the sacrifices made are remembered. We learn from the past and can never repay heroes like Al Johnson for what they have done.

They answered the call of duty.

"You were taught to be content with what you have," says Al. "I was a Depression-era kid." Again, with perfect timing he adds, "we always moved when the rent was due."

Al wraps up his presentation and an audience member hollers out, "Stand-up comedy will be your next career!" Al looks over and deadpans, "I just hope to get home after this."

Al Johnson November 2018

OPERATION RUMINATION

AL JOHNSON AND THE MEMBERS OF THE WORLD WAR II OSS are true American heroes. They risked their lives in the war effort without acknowledgement until years later. Fifty years later. Life can be serious business, especially when put in a position of life and death like Al Johnson was behind enemy lines.

I ruminate on the fact that many of the veterans I have met have a great sense of humor. That was certainly the case with Al Johnson, his monologue fed off the audience with casual skill and delivery. He was particularly adept at deadpan delivery, dry humor or dry wit with the deliberate display of a lack of emotion. He has had years of practice. Laughter truly is the best medicine, and people who have a good sense of humor use it to their advantage. We hear of studies that tell us a light-hearted attitude may help you live longer and that a sense of humor increases longevity in the retirement years. It can improve your life mentally as well as physically. A proclivity for well-timed jocularity makes life brighter and increases perspective.

Humor is a coveted trait … we gravitate towards it. Those with a great sense of humor tend to not take themselves so seriously. All of these benefits not only benefit the individual, but benefit those who surround them. *I ruminate on how we can serve others with a sense of humor.* How whimsy and wit can occasionally see us through together. You never know who might need a smile at just the right time, and you're the one to deliver. A smile, a laugh, is inexpensive, but the benefits can be priceless.

I believe a little timely self-deprecating humor is a sign of intelligence, humility and demonstrates greater levels of happiness and self-assurance. I went to a gathering where Al Johnson was to speak to a group of Civil Air Patrol cadets. The host during the introduction said he had spotted Al and his wife in the grocery store, after 71 years of marriage still holding hands. Al grabs the host's arm and interrupts saying, "Oh that's not about love, we do that so we don't fall over." Spontaneous laughter.

Perfect timing. Ice is broken. He hasn't even started, and he has the audience in the palm of his hand.

I walk away from Al's home after a visit with him and smile as I get in my car. I love how his face lights up when he thinks of something funny to say. You know it's coming because he pauses until you're ready.

"I sold beauty supplies all my life," says Al, "I had to have a sense of humor."

As I back out of the driveway I think, *he served others in heroic, brave ways as well as in simple ways throughout his life.* From jumping out of an airplane behind enemy lines, to providing a laugh or a simple smile, Al Johnson has served his community well. He is a true American hero.

Disaster they would circumvent
Their country they would represent
With bravery as an attribute
They jumped in with a parachute
And freed those bound in internment.

Frank Krhovsky
US Army
World War II
511ᵗʰ Parachute Infantry Regiment
Paratrooper 11ᵗʰ Airborne
1945

Chapter Five

With Flying Colors

RING THE DOORBELL ON A BEAUTIFUL fall day. The leaves are colorful and falling from the beech and maple trees along the drive. Adele opens the door and welcomes me, leading me to Frank Krhovsky seated in a chair in the living room. As I set up for our interview, I sense the history, the stories, the lessons to be learned from Frank and Adele and a lifetime of experiences. I thank Adele for her hospitality and thank Dr. Frank Krhovsky for his service.

It all began with basic training for Frank Krhovsky at Camp Walters in Texas, with, as he calls it, "the basic stuff" of calisthenics, routine and exams followed by a transfer to Camp Livingston in Louisiana for radio school. With more basic training on tap Franks said, "Me and my buddies we got sick of it. Let's join the paratroopers," they decided. Being a paratrooper sounded exciting. First there was the physical exam to clear and Frank had one problem. You cannot go into a job that requires you to go to Airborne school or into aviation-related assignments if you can't pass red/green color vision testing. Protanomaly, which is a reduced sensitivity to red light, deuteranomaly which is a reduced sensitivity to green light, is the most common form of color blindness. People with deuteranomaly and protanomaly are collectively known as red-green color blind. I laugh with Frank and his wife Adele, and assume that when they give you the 6-minute warning by turning on the red paratrooper jump lights in the cargo compartments they want you to be able to differentiate between green and red before you jump out the door. Frank wasn't going to take no for an answer; he was going to be a paratrooper with his buddies. He slid off to the side of the room, and, lifting dirt and dust off the floor, smudged it out in the margin. He turned in his paperwork, and, because that part couldn't be read, he was waived through. Being a paratrooper simply sounded too exciting, and he wasn't letting his buddies leave without him.

It was off to Fort Benning, Georgia and parachute school. Frank recalls calling his cousin, also named Frank, who was at the main base at Fort Benning to inform him of his intentions.

"Are you out of your mind?" asked cousin Frank.

The first week was nothing but calisthenics, and if you got out of step with the group it was off to the side and 25 push-ups. By the second week they were jumping out of 35-foot towers with a harness. "You would drop 20 feet before the line goes taut, and you would slide into a sand pit. Some of the guys were frightened so he jumped for them.

By the fourth week of training they were packing their own shoots and were jumping everyday out of an airplane. Five jumps out of planes each week. Frank estimated those early training jumps were at around 1,100 to 1,200 feet altitude.

"The first jump is easy, because you don't know what to expect," said Frank. "Sure, you have a little anxiety, but you do what you have to do," he said.

Demolition school followed, then to the west coast and on to New Guinea for further training, running and calisthenics. Just like that, a 19-year-old young man from Ionia, Michigan was in the South Pacific and in the middle of World War II.

"What did that feel like?" I ask Frank.

"Warm," he says. "If I was going to fight in World War II, I wanted to be in the South Pacific, because I dislike cold weather. I didn't want to go to Europe." We laugh and I concur. I too am a warm-weather person.

World War II for Krhovsky was in the Philippines. The Japanese occupation of the Philippines occurred between 1942 and 1945, when Imperial Japan occupied the Commonwealth of the Philippines during World War II. The Japanese invasion of the Philippines began only hours after the attack on Pearl Harbor in December of 1941.

Frank's first jump in active duty for his regiment was about 60 miles outside of Manila. The entire regiment jumped, including glider pilots gliding in. From there they dispersed. It became a race along the Tagaytay Ridge on foot from Tagaytay to Manila. That's 68.1 kilometers or over 42 miles in two days with full gear to try to get there ahead of the Japs to prevent them from blowing the bridges.

Frank Krhovsky

Approaching the airbase at Nichols field south of Manila, he was walking along with his friend "Dutch." At one point they noticed the ground rustling to their left. Dutch noticed there was someone in a fox hole, so Frank took out grenade and threw it in. The grenade came back. "The Jap threw it back out, so I yelled hit the deck!" Frank said. "When a grenade goes off the shrapnel goes upward so we hit the ground. I took another grenade, pulled the pin and this time waited to the count of three. They blow at the count of five," said Frank. "I threw it in, and we killed the Jap."

Now situated in the Japanese-occupied Philippines, history was about to impact the life of young Frank Krhovsky. General Douglas MacArthur, the US commander in the Philippines, contacted the commander of the 11th Airborne General Joe "Jumpin Joe" Swing. Interestingly, it was General Swing, who years later in the mid 1950s, as the director of the INS under President Eisenhower, would implement "Operation Wetback," utilizing special tactics to deal with illegal border crossings into the United States by Mexican nationals.

Now, however, as Allied forces retook territory the Japanese had invaded at the beginning of the war in the Pacific, the fate of prisoners of war (POWs) was of major concern to the Allied high command. This was particularly true in the Philippines, where thousands of American and European civilians were being held prisoner. General Douglas MacArthur ordered his subordinates, including General Swing, to make every effort to liberate camps in their areas of operation as quickly as possible. Daring raids were planned and organized to free prisoners and internees ahead of the attacking American forces.

At Los Baños, some 40 miles southeast of Manila, was an internment camp for more than 2,000 civilians who had had the misfortune of falling into Japanese hands at the beginning of the war. The internees, who were at the camp in the late winter of 1945, were of many nationalities. The majority were American, and of every age, including infants. For more than three years, the internees at Los Baños, along with POWs in other camps, had waited patiently for the day when their liberators would arrive.

"It was an escapee of the concentration camps that had tipped off the Allies of the Japanese intentions," said Frank.

Prisoners were being starved to death. They were allowed only 1 cup of a rice per day which, after winnowing, yielded only half a cup of edible rice.

"It was rumored that ditches had already been dug, and gasoline was at the ready for mass killings," added Adele. "The Allies believed that Japanese captors would slaughter them all before they could be rescued."

Because Los Baños was located in the 11th Airborne Division's area of operations, Frank Krhovsky and other paratroopers from his division would be those liberators. It would come in the form of an assault from the skies.

The 511th Parachute Infantry Regiment met at Bilibid prison, which had been abandoned by the Japanese to prepare for the assault. With time of the essence, they spent a couple days collecting information. Frank was among 130 who volunteered and were trucked to Nichols field for what would be a daring and dangerous mission. He was one of 130 volunteers who were administered last rites and told they expected half would die in the raid.

They slept that night under the wings of the eight DC-7s that would fly them in to the concentration camp at Los Banos. By 6AM they were in the planes, while the rest of the regiment traveled to south of the camp via amtrac. Amtracs were amphibious tractors, also known as LVT (Landing Vehicle Tracked,) and would travel at a right angle or the enemy would hear the motors of "amphibs."

At Nichols Field outside Manila, the paratroopers boarded the eight DC-7s, and the pilots started their engines. After takeoff, each of the jump planes circled the field until all were airborne and had joined the formation. At 0640 the planes headed southeast over Laguna de Bay toward Los Baños. Laguna de Bay lake is the largest inland body of water in the Philippines, just south of Manila. Fifteen minutes later, the pilots signaled a six-minute warning by turning on the red paratrooper jump lights in the cargo compartments of their airplanes. I asked Frank what was going through his mind. "We don't talk to each other in the plane. Only deep thoughts of going out of that plane," he said. At 0700 Frank and the other paratroopers stepped to the door and jumped out. The Los Baños raid was in progress.

The 11th Airborne volunteers jump over Los Banos

They jumped at 7AM. "We did that because the Japs would be doing morning calisthenics, so they would not be armed at the time," said Frank. The key on the initial attack would be to take out the six machine gun watch towers. As the men in the amtracs reached the beach in support of the raid at Los Bonas, the 15 men in each plane would do a dangerous jump at 400 feet. "You jump out dropping 100 feet before your shoot opens," said Frank. "We had to go in low for the element of surprise." When they hit the ground, it was a full-on run through the fence into the encampment. They were carrying "Tommy guns" also known as Thompson submachine guns. GIs like the Tommy gun for its dependability and knock-down fire power. It was perfect for close-quarter fighting and could be fired from the hip.

"We landed about 200 feet from the perimeter and went into the camp at a dead run," said Frank. "We killed close to 300 Japanese in 30 minutes. Of the 200 rounds I carried I had about 60 left when it was over. We didn't lose one man in the raid."

The Paratroopers found a starving horde of internees, and they had to move quickly to bring the prisoners down to the beach. A Japanese regiment was only 10 miles away. Some of the prisoners hesitated, wanting to take along their belongings. "There was no time for that," said Frank. They were able to get all the prisoners out, many who were civilians rounded up at the start of the war. They were loaded in the amtracs for their ride to freedom. Frank recalls striking up a conversation with a young man on the ride back. He was a young man named David DeVries, ironically for Frank, from of all places Grand Rapids, Michigan. Only 15 years old his Mom and Dad were missionaries in the Philippines when he was captured. He asked Frank why they did it?

"We were going to get you out or die trying," said Frank.

Back in Grand Rapids, David's rescue and the daring rescue of detainees was reported in the Grand Rapids Herald. The young man said he was rescued by someone named "Kazooski" from West Michigan and does anyone know who he is? The errant pronunciation and spelling of the name made it easy for John Krhovsky in Ionia. He knew right away it was his son, Frank.

A Silver Star

During his time with the 511th in the Philippines, as Allies fought to push the Japanese out of the occupied Philippines, Frank Krhovsky demonstrated that volunteer spirit in an act of valor. It earned him the Silver Star. On my visit to their home, Adele showed me both the Silver Star and a Purple Heart, hanging in a frame along with memorabilia like a metal ripcord handle that he had brought back from one of his chutes. The Silver Star medal is awarded to members of the United States Armed Forces for gallantry in action against an enemy of the United States.

He recalls how he earned that Silver Star. One of the unit's Army scouts was stuck on a hill, trapped in his position by two enemy machine-gun nests.

"The scout that we had, his name was Tennessee, and he was pinned down by gunfire," says Frank.

Frank volunteered to go up there, and his commanding officers agreed, that if only one man went up "instead of a bunch of men," it would save lives. They put their confidence in Krhovsky.

I asked why he volunteered? He shrugged his shoulders and then Frank said, "My thoughts were getting up there. I was focused on knocking out those nests and getting Tennessee out of there."

Krhovsky crawled on his stomach and back up the hill under machine-gun fire from the two nests. He had to lay low and stay close to the ground. "Depressions and grass saved my life," he said. It was a slow and arduous one-hour ascent 50 yards up that hill.

"You know when you're doing all of this, you're never afraid for some reason or another. There's no fear. I got up there, got within a short distance of those machine gunners, and I threw a grenade. And lo and behold, I killed both men in the pit," said Krhovsky. He moved on to the next machine-gun nest. Pitching the grenades from his back on the ground, four machine gunners in two nests were neutralized.

"Back safe and sound." Tennessee said. "You can court martial me if you want but I will never scout again."

The war ended in August and before returning home in January of 1946, he teamed up with a Japanese meteorologist who ironically became his friend. From August to December they worked together to teach Algebra to a number of GIs who did not have an education.

Frank came home and completed his undergraduate work in three years instead of four at Aquinas College. He then applied to enter medical school and earned his Master's degree in anatomy at the University of Michigan. The young heroic paratrooper from Ionia came home after the war, went to school, became a doctor and raised a family in East Grand Rapids.

I asked Frank what kept him healthy. Now 93 years old, what could he say to me a man about to enter his 60s about longevity. "Stay active" was his response. Adele agreed. In all the time she has known Frank, he has always been active, including their hunting trips together around the world. Together they have hunted everywhere across the world except New Zealand and Australia. "Whether hunting, skiing or yard work, I have always seen Frank active," said Adele.

I ask Frank what drove him, what was the motivation to accomplish so much in his life. More than seven decades later, he sees his time in the 11th Airborne as an opportunity to give of himself during World War II, part of a great generation that came together to sacrifice what they could to make the world a better place. We conclude and agree together that Frank has the same characteristic, the same thread I have found in the other long-living veterans … continual goals.

OPERATION RUMINATION

Now 93 years old, Frank says to me, "I had to do something." I think, "boy did he do something in his life." Life is a gift.

I learn that Frank Krhovsky and his fellow paratroopers had freed Frank Buckles, a World War I veteran, in that daring raid on Los Banos. Frank Woodruff Buckles' life spanned the Twentieth Century. Frank Buckles was born on February 1, 1901. At the age of 16, he witnessed the European theatre of World War I, serving in the United States Army as an ambulance driver. In 1940, he had accepted an assignment to expedite the movement of cargo for the American President Lines in Manila. In World War II, he became a prisoner of war in the Philippines and was imprisoned for 39 months. His stay in the Philippines was impacted by the Japanese occupation during World War II, resulting in him spending over three years in Japanese prison camps at Santo Tomas and Los Banos. He was rescued by Frank Krhovsky and the 11th Airborne Division in their daring raid on Los Banos. After his return, Frank Buckles settled down in West Virginia where he lived until his death on February 27, 2011, at the age of

110! I ruminate on the thought. This man lived to the age of 110 years as an American, contributing to society. Living to an old age of 110, because of the heroics and bravery of a 19-year-old young man from Ionia, Michigan named Frank Krhovsky, who heroically had crossed his path. I ruminate on this thought. What do we … no, what do I do, with the time that is given us on this earth and what is our impact? We may never know.

Frank Krhovsky's Dad was an excellent gymnast who tried to get into the Olympics. Unfortunately, his dream never materialized. Ruminating on the thought, I think Frank inherited part of his "continual goals" motivation from his Dad. Adele shows me a photograph of Frank with his Dad. I look at it and think, yes that's it … the apple doesn't fall far from the tree. Continual goals. Despite obstacles, including something as common and simple as color blindness, truly Frank Krhovsky and his generation set the example in their accomplishments, and passed … **with flying colors.**

Frank Krhovsky and his dad

The plants in the garden she would raise
She has tended them all of her days,
To the heavens above
It's a labor of love
While in faith she works and prays.

Chapter Six

Work and Pray

L IKE AN ENDLESS ARMY OF PARA-
troopers released from an airplane, seeds and fruits
travel the winds of the world, catching a breeze when
the time is right. They colonize a distant fertile valley or plain.
Many plant families have adopted this remarkable method of
dispersal. As children we called the samara seeds of a maple tree
"helicopters." Nature's ingenious method of wind dispersal for
seeds that resemble airborne helicopters or parachutes. The dan-
delion is another great example of seed translocated by the wind
when the time is right. A swift breeze at the opportune time can
move the seed to a location far, far away.

The winds of war were blowing worldwide in the early 1940s.
Those winds would soon carry thousands of American nurses
thousands of miles from home. They would plant the seeds of
healing and comfort for allied troops engaged in a massive war
effort. The need for nurses in the South Pacific during World War
II would instantly translocate young people from small-town
America halfway around the world. Army nurses were stationed
in the Hawaiian Islands, Australia, New Zealand, the Fiji Islands,

New Caledonia, and the New Hebrides, also known as Vanuatu Island. The nurses would arrive in areas under Allied control. In the South Pacific, nurses were stationed in areas that were outside a direct Japanese ground threat, yet near enough to the front lines to aid servicemen in need. Nurses usually found themselves assigned to hospitals far from combat areas, where they cared for soldiers who had been evacuated from the front lines. Marian Cyberski found herself in Australia to care for soldiers engaged in the Pacific theatre.

Marian Cyberski

Born May 31st, 1919, Marian, now approaching the age of 100, lives in the small home in Lansing, Michigan, where she has lived since 1949 raising her seven children. Today she patrols the house, instructing electricians that were there the day I visited to do a repair and answering the phone as the pharmacy calls with prescription information. We walk out to the garden where she shows me bins and buckets of compost she has cultivated. The garden is beautiful and manicured, a combination of ornamental plants and edible plants. She shovels the processed "black gold" in 5-gallon pails for use in her yard and she gives some of it away. She plucks some leaves of kale and picks some cherry tomatoes and hands them to me. Marian says she has been battling congestive heart failure for the past 15 years, but you wouldn't know it the way she still runs that household and garden like a fine-tuned military regiment.

"The doctors tell me all the valves are leaking," she says, "but the good Lord has been kind to me, and I am exceedingly grateful." Marian sits at the kitchen table with her prayer books close at hand and rosary beads at the ready.

Early in 1942, Marian and three other girls from the Order of St. Francis school of Nursing, who worked together in a hospital in Duluth, Minnesota, decided to go to the theatre one afternoon. They went to see the movie *To the shores of Tripoli* a movie about the life at the Marine Training Base in San Diego on the eve of the Japanese attack on Pearl Harbor, starring John Payne who enlists in the US Marine Corps and falls in love with a Navy nurse, Lieutenant Mary Carter, played by actress Maureen O' Hara.

"We really liked those good-looking Marines" said Marian. "I decided I'm going to join and take care of the boys."

It was Marian's mom, Elizabeth or "Lizzy," who raised nine children on a farm in Lidgerwood, North Dakota and instilled in them a hard-working ethic. Lidgerwood is a small town in Richland county North Dakota. The population was at 652 people as of the 2010 census. We have all been to big cities where industry, art, business, science, and government are the "harvest" of civilization. The grass roots of civilization are found in small towns like Lidgerwood. Things like faith, neighborhoods, hard work, generosity and family are the foundations there. The culture of our country is passed on from family to family in these small towns. Marian inherited her strong faith and hard work ethic from her Mom in small-town Lidgerwood.

Marian's mother "Lizzy" was the oldest child in her family

and never got a full education. There were many responsibilities with a large family which precluded a formal education for Lizzy. She never forgot it. Her Mom was going to see to it Marian got an education. For her high school education, Marian was sent by her mother to an all-girls school in Little Falls, Minnesota called the Order of St. Francis. The primary reason was that the mother of the Franciscan Order, Sister Mary Immaculate, was her mom's sister. Marian says she cried all the way from Lidgerwood to Little Falls, Minnesota, about a two-and-a-half-hour drive. There she would work to pay for her education by scrubbing corridors, washing dishes, cleaning toilets and working in the hospital.

I asked Marian how her Mom lived to be almost 105 years old, healthy enough to live in her own home until she died.

"She didn't smoke or drink did she?" I said to Marian

Marian looked at me with a wry look and a roll of her eyes and while shaking her head responded, "My Mom was a good Catholic. She said her rosary every day."

"She was a good Catholic and worked on a farm her whole life." said Marian. "Feeding chickens and doing laundry by boiling water on the stove and then running the clothes through an old-fashioned wringer, taking care not to get her hair and fingers caught in the wringer. It was always work and pray."

Her Aunt, Sister Mary Immaculate, thought for sure she had a prospect as a nun in Marian Cyberski. She would have to take a vow.

A "VOW OF POVERTY ... WORK AND PRAY."

MARIAN SAID, "I'M A GOOD CATHOLIC, BUT I DIDN'T want to be a nun. I disappointed my Aunt."

It was after high school, early in 1942, that Marian and three other girls from the Order of St. Francis School of Nursing went to the movies. Their lives would never be the same. Military service and a world war would send these young ladies to locations around the globe.

In addition to the good-looking Marines in the movies, she

was particularly smitten by a young man who would play his guitar and sing the *Red River Valley.*

> *From this valley they say you are going,*
> *I shall miss your bright eyes and sweet smile,*
> *For alas you take with the sunshine*
> *That has brightened my pathway awhile.*
> <u>*Chorus:*</u>
> *Come and sit by my side if you love me,*
> *Do not hasten to bid me adieu.*
> *But remember the Red River Valley*
> *And the girl who has loved you so true.*

Eighty-two Army nurses were stationed in Hawaii, serving at three Army medical facilities that infamous morning of December 7, 1941, a day that will live in infamy. By the time World War II was over, more than 59,000 American nurses had served in the Army Nurse Corps during the war. Marian Cyberski was one of those nurses.

When the US entered World War II, following the bombing of Pearl Harbor on December 7, 1941, it is estimated there were fewer than 7,000 nurses on active duty. By 1945, more than 59,000 Army nurses were assigned to hospital ships and trains, flying ambulances and field hospitals at home and overseas. Military service took women like Marian Cyberski, from small towns across America familiar with the small-town life of Lidgerfield or Little Falls and transported them around the world. Marian would be shipped out to Brisbane, Australia to serve in World War II.

Australia's paranoia with a possible Japanese invasion peaked after the fall of Singapore in February of 1942. For Australia, that dramatic victory of the Japanese over the British signified the breaching of the so-called "Malay Barrier," a distance between Japan's military expansion and the Australian home front.

The Australian government and military planners were deeply worried about the prospect of a Japanese invasion, and plans were devised to defend Australia in the event of large areas of the mainland being occupied by the Japanese. Australia openly admitted its concerns to its citizens and implemented a massive civil defense program. There were public announcements about the Japanese threat with posters, pamphlets and radio recordings. The fear was real.

Due to the tropical conditions of the South Pacific, however, malaria, not an invasion of Australia was the big problem for American soldiers. An insidious disease, it was considered by many the "other foe" in the battle-torn South Pacific. Typically, not fatal to the infected soldier, it would take soldiers out of action for a prolonged period as though they had been wounded in battle. Malaria is a tenacious disease that can have long-lasting effects on the infected person. With violent chills, fever, and weakness, a bedridden soldier needed the care of the nurses who came to their aid in hospitals across the South Pacific. Unfortunately, the damp, hot, swampy environments encountered on many Pacific islands were ideal breeding grounds for the mosquitoes that transmit the disease. Marian was one of the thousands of nurses who came to their aid in the Pacific theatre during World War II. They volunteered to serve and served well. In the case of Marian Cyberski, the inspiration found in the cinema of a small Midwest town would send her on a journey and change her life forever. The winds of war would carry her far away and then back home again, to plant seeds, to serve, to work and pray.

OPERATION RUMINATION

MARIAN WENT ON THE 'TALONS OUT' MICHIGAN HONOR flight of World War II veterans to Washington DC in April of 2015. It was there she had the opportunity to meet Bob and Elizabeth Dole at the World War II memorial. A great experience.

Today she soldiers on, maintaining her home and tending to her garden day by day. She epitomizes the veterans I have met this year with ***continual goals*** and does it as taught by her mother years ago ... she works and she prays. I reflect on the hard work ethic I have seen demonstrated by her generation. They "dig in" and do what needs to be done, just like they did during World War II. Her prayer books and her rosary beads are laid out on the dining room table. She tends to her garden and prays, always active even as she approaches the age of 100. Her faith and continual goals keep her young and moving forward as each day her mantra remains ... work and pray.

Marian Cyberski (lower left) with Bob and Elizabeth Dole at the World War II Memorial Washington DC

He expertly cared for munitions
From his perch at lofty positions
At high altitude
With great aptitude
Al always completed his missions.

Al Schumacher

US Army Air Corps

Staff Sergeant WWII

44th Bombing group U.K. (Eight missions)

577th squadron 392nd Bombing group RAF air
base Wendling England (22 bombing missions)

Chapter Seven

Everyday is a Good Day...Some are

Just Better than others

GET OUT OF MY CAR AND STEP UP ON
the front porch about to knock on the front door of a well-
kept home with a large yard. The door opens before I can
knock. He was waiting for me. Al Schumacher was, that morning, what I surmise he had been all his life … organized and
ready to get to work … disciplined and focused yet friendly.
Books, maps, shell casings, pictures, and notebooks lay spread
out on the kitchen table. In a phone conversation, Al had agreed
to meet with me, and one week later there he was, prepared for
the "mission" and ready to get to work upon my arrival. During
the course of our conversation, he told me that flying in bomber
planes was not like it's depicted in the movies. You don't just
run to a plane and take off. An early breakfast, which is your last
meal of the day until your return, and then hours and hours of

79

preparation go into a mission run. He seemed to have particular respect for the ground crew chief who was in charge of the plane when on the ground. They walk around with a clipboard asking the crew upon their return, "What's wrong with the plane?" He was going to see it was fixed. Years later Al Schumacher himself would emphasize to his three sons,

"See if you can fix it. Take it apart but remember you have to put it back together.

If you can fix it but can't put it back together it is still broken," he says.

Right from the start I knew Al Schumacher was one of those "Greatest Generation" guys they talk about. I knew this would be special. Al Schumacher flew in eight bombing missions over World War II Germany with the 44th bombing group out of Norwich UK, before being reassigned to the 392nd Bombing group after it had almost been wiped out. He would fly 22 missions over Germany with the 577th squadron of the 392nd bombing group, operating out of the RAF air base in Wendling, England. Thirty times he left and returned on bombing raids over Hitler's Nazi Germany.

Al Schumacher was drafted in 1943 as a teenager, living in Blue Island, Illinois, an industrial suburb of Chicago. It was the Great Depression and work was hard to come by. His Dad worked a variety of jobs to try to make ends meet, and, as I talk to Al, I can't help but think a hard work ethic was instilled in him at a young age. I asked him about his health at 93 years of age, and he credits it to his faith and to "working all his life." He worked for a farmer in grade school at the age of 10, pulling and planting onions for 10 cents/hour during the great depression.

A work ethic coupled with what was yet to come in his young life, I sensed the foundation placed prior to the age of 21 "steeled" his personal characteristics for life. Still in high school when Pearl Harbor was bombed, he graduated in 1942, knowing as the world was at war, at some point his name would be called. It didn't take long and soon he was off to Chicago to be inducted. It was July of 1943, and Al, as an 18-year-old was quick to volunteer when they were asked for volunteers to the Army Air Corp. He was sent for three months of basic training to the Miami Beach training center to become a pilot. "They ran us pretty good," said Al, "it was hot and it rained." It turned out to be a weeding-out process. The Army Air Corps needed ground and air crews as well as pilots, and, in the process, Al and most of his training class "washed out" as he put it. At that time it was determined they had enough pilots, so he and others were sent to "armorer and gunner" school in Buckley, Colorado.

"It was a lot cooler there," said Al smiling.

It was there he would be taught how to operate a 50-caliber machine gun as an armorer and gunner on a B-24 Liberator bomber. As part of their training, he recalls being put in a cage on the back of a pickup truck, and, while standing at 35 mph, told to shoot catapulted clay pigeons with a 12-gauge shotgun as practice.

"They were moving targets," says Al "and you never knew where they were going to pop up. We didn't hit many of them," he says laughing, "but it was good practice."

Up in the air on a B-24 you would have to be ready. Hitting moving targets while you yourself are standing in an airplane traveling at better than 200 mph I'm sure is a trick. Performance maximum speed of a B-24 was approximately 300 mph at 25,000 feet, with a service ceiling of around 32,000 feet.

The last thing you would want to do is hit your own wing either forward or aft while firing a 50-caliber machine gun in the waist of the plane.

His job was armored gunner, and he was to check the bombs as well as be a waist gunner on a 50-caliber machine gun positioned in the "waist" behind the wings, firing from an open "window." The 50-caliber Browning machine gun was used extensively during WWII, and was the gun Al used from his position in the B-24. Years later while out pheasant hunting Al had the opportunity to fire on the birds but instead set down his rifle. His desire to fire a gun had diminished to the point he was OK with putting down the firearm. His memory raced back to the time he had fired his 50-caliber gun on the B-24 and one shell didn't exit the barrel. The second shell caused the gun to explode. Saved from burns, because he was standing, leaning back and wearing an oxygen mask, leather helmet and goggles, the sensation came rushing back years later in a field. He recalled the deadly power of firearms when on one flight the pilot instructed all gunners to open up their guns at once. Aloft in the heavens in a B-24 the pilot wanted to experience the effect of recoil while in-flight of all eight guns onboard unleashing their deadly arsenal.

"Don't do that again" said the pilot. "I was afraid we were going to shake the plane apart," he said.

The pilot insisted they wear oxygen at 10,000 feet, because he didn't need anyone getting light headed or passing out. Before takeoff it was Al's job to check the safety pins and safety wire in every fuse on the bombs. Once aloft, when they reached 10,000 ft altitude, it was his job to pull the safety pins on the bombs before needing oxygen. He would put the pins in his pocket. This was done with the bomb bay doors open. He would work out in the open and could see the ground from his position on a catwalk no more than 8 inches wide. He couldn't wear a parachute, because he wouldn't be able to squeeze between the bomb racks. Once his job was done, the pilot would take the plane up to anywhere between 18,000 to 25,000 feet.

The risk of serving on a B-24 was there even before crossing enemy lines on a bombing run. *You had to get off the ground.* Consider having roughly 3,000 gallons of fuel in the wings, which is around 10 tons of liquid combustible, combined with around 4 to 5 tons of bombs on board. Taking off with roughly 3,000 gallons of 100-octane fuel loaded, makes the plane itself an incendiary bomb if something went wrong. The fuel would be in the wings, half on each side. The wing on a B-24 is visible and exposed inside the cabin, which looks like a spartan steel hull. Al says with two banks of nine cylinders, the four 18-cylinder engines, rated at 1200 hp, were assigned the responsibility to power the plane with a weight of 32,605 lbs empty, and a maximum takeoff weight of 64,000 pounds.

When you reach proper ground speed and airspeed, you have to decide to raise the wheels at some point. Al recalls a takeoff where the pilot and crew felt they weren't going to make it beyond the end of the runway. You're committed at ground and air speed, but the weight of the plane is fighting back. He remembers the plane laboring, wheels up and committed to take off, thinking if we crash you have all this fuel and all these bombs on board. It would be quite an explosion. I read some B-24 plane specs that had the fuel capacity rating as high as 3,614 gallons! He recalls just barely getting airborne and the sensation of the runway seeming to come up to him until slowly, painstakingly slowly, the ground drops away and they get enough height, buzzing the tops of English homes as they fight to get altitude.

"I'm sure that made us Yankees not very popular with the England residents in those towns" says Al with a grin on his face.

I page through a neatly organized notebook Al has on the kitchen table of page after page of missions flown by the B-24 bombing group. Targeted runs on Berlin, Essenburg, Hesepe, Essen, Schwabisch Hall, and other targets over Germany like

Al Schumacher (top row far right)

the railyards around Hitler's Berchtesgaden retreat. I look at one dated 18 March 1945 to the Third Reich capital of Berlin, targeting the Rheinmetal Borsig Armament Works, an ordinance depot. I focus on the lists of names on that mission and there he is:

18 March 1945
Air Corps flight #901
577 Sqdn
RW (right wing)
Schumacher A.H. S/Sgt.

As I page through the notebook, Al's mind drifts back to a "secret mission" for which they could be court-martialed for divulging. Generally, they were assigned specific sites, and, if unable to find their target on a mission, they were instructed to focus on oil refineries or marshalling yards for factories. This bombing raid was over a wooded area from 20,000 feet, for which they could only surmise was a stockpile of military hardware stashed by the Nazi's, along with human lives ... it shows in Al's eyes that it bothers him to this day. "Only the navigator knows exactly where we were," he says. We loaded and unleashed plane after plane of high explosive bombs, incendiary bombs or jelly gas phosphorus bombs, that melt as they burn, along with fragmentation bombs into that wooded area, with a volume of planes and bombs that would cause you to believe every square inch of the area was decimated. Years later it would become evident they were providing ground support to troops fighting in the Battle of the Bulge, the German offensive in the Ardennes, December 1944. His squadron had bombed an area where the Germans had massed tanks for an attack. Later, ground forces reported the area "having more iron than wood" in the wooded area they had bombed.

SMOOTH AS SILK

A "COLD STEEL" METAL PLANE WITH OPEN WINDOWS AND open bomb bays at 20,000 feet altitude must have made the battle with the elements rough at times. Wearing oxygen masks due to the thin air, they would sometimes inadvertently "unhook" the oxygen tubing due to movement. On several occasions, they literally saved each other's lives by reattaching another crew member's tubing. They wore clothing layers and electronically heated flight suits notorious for not working. "You never knew if they were going to work," Al said, "so we would wear heavy clothing and try to keep warm by stomping our feet and waving our arms." They knew when they got back to their quonset hut on the base, a little coal stove waited to warm them. The problem was the coal would have to be rationed. They were allotted a bushel of coal a week. From time to time they would take matters into their own hands and "requisition" some coal from the area villages, he says with a mischievous smile on his face.

They also would wear white silk gloves.

"Have you ever had your tongue stuck to a frozen flagpole?" Al grins as he asks me.

The combination of cold steel, moisture and temperatures aloft below zero made it necessary to protect skin contact with cold, moist metal.

"We took a lot of ribbing for wearing white silk gloves," said Al, but it was the only way you could hold on up there."

On one occasion the silk gloves helped Al communicate and assure a fellow crew member. While in flight, the fellow waist gunner had signaled him for help. Al checked the oxygen line and it was intact, so he held out both hands in a questioning manner. The crew member pointed to the sleeve of his jacket. Al could see the jacket was gashed open and reached in to remove a chunk of metal. He then reached back into the gash in the jacket and ran his hand along the arm and shoulder area of the waist gunner hit by the shrapnel. He held up his hand to reveal his white silk glove....no blood. He did it again to assure the worried waist gunner. Again, no blood on the silk white glove. His relieved fellow crew member wiped his brow signaling understanding in a "whew" expression of thanks to Al.

"Most people don't realize all we had up there was a first aid kit," says Al. "If someone is injured or hit it would be hours before they would get to a hospital."

The crew would also wear silk scarves to block the noise of the plane and improve communication in the mike. Silk was an important fabric as part of their ensemble. It could also save their lives if shot down over enemy territory. Al unpackages silk maps from a worn, old green pouch. One of the few things he brought back with him from WWII, he treasures them. Once offered $150 each for the silk maps he said they're not for sale. Silk maps were used, because they could be folded and carried and would make no noise when folded or unfolded. Unlike paper they would stand up to moisture. Crew members on flights would carry these maps with them. If shot down, they would have to find their way out of Germany using the maps. They knew part of their obligation was to tie up the Germans and waste their time looking for them if shot down behind enemy lines.

On January 16, 1945 it was his faith that helped him deal with fear. "Okay God, we did what we could do now it's up to you." Losing an engine hit by flak deep over Germany, they were closer to the Russian front lines than their own. The B-24 Liberator

Silk Maps carried by Al Schumacher WW II

had a range of 2300 miles with 5000 pounds of bombs and a maximum range empty of 3500 miles. Not trusting the Russians, they made the decision to head back to their lines rerouting the available fuel to three operating engines. You burned more fuel on three laboring engines than you did if you had four engines running efficiently. Keeping the engines cool was tough, as each engine would use 50 gallons of oil! They had to slow the plane to conserve fuel and were losing altitude, so much so that before exiting Germany, they were low enough, just a few hundred feet, that the Germans shot at the plane with rifles. The laboring engines were red-lining for hours. The plane would take a position of surrender with wheels and flaps down, and, they in turn, threw everything out to reduce weight, including the guns, to make it back on fuel. They had to detour around major cities to avoid being shot at and used radar blocking chaff in what must have felt like an eternal trip over enemy territory. "Yes we were afraid" Al said, "but God put forth his hand. We had no choice, we had to do it." The B-24 managed to get across the border and just into France, where they crash landed the plane in Nancy, France. Armed only with their sidearms, they had to work their way across France, hitchhiking rides and between rides. Walking, they eventually made it to Paris, boarding a plane and flying back to the RAF Wendling air base. It was business as usual with no welcoming party as they were scheduled to fly another mission the very next day.

"It's like they say, when you fall off a horse the best thing to do is to get right back on," says Al.

Planes shot down over Germany were corralled by the Nazis and reassembled for both research and use. Al explains to me that as the war wore on they understood that from time to time an Allied war plane would be flown by the Germans who would position the plane in formation as a "friendly ally" only to wreak havoc on the mission. The P-51 Mustang, with a Rolls-Royce Merlin is a British liquid cooled V-12 piston aero engine, allowing it to exceed 15,000 feet in altitude and compete with the German Messerschmitt planes patrolling the skies over World

War II Europe. Aware of this conundrum and positioned as a waist gunner, protecting the flank of an American B-24 bomber, Al one day had a split-second decision to make. A P-51 was bearing down on his B-24 bearing arms.

B-24 Liberator crash landing in Nancy, France

Al pressed the mike. "P-51 bearing arms. Warning shot."

No sooner had the words left Al's mouth he was on the trigger firing a burst in the direction of the P-51. He didn't feel right firing on a P-51 Mustang, but felt it was the right thing to do if the plane didn't bank away. The plane did bank at the last second "almost hitting the propellers of the B-24 in the process," says Al. When back on the ground Al's name was called, summoned by two MPs to report to headquarters and his commanding officer.

"Did you shoot at a P-51 today staff sergeant?"

"Yes I did sir"

"We're not playing games here this is life and death" said the commanding officer.

Al was cleared of the incident and surmises the pilot, who said he just wanted a clean look at a B-24, was in big trouble for the incident.

"You think you know what you would do in a stressful situation," says Al, "but you really don't know until it's over" he says. "Would you fire at an intruder into your home? You don't know what you'll do until put in that situation to make a split-second decision."

Al talks of the Messerschmitts and attack planes that would lie in wait, hidden by the sun above, and waiting for attack on vulnerable targets. They were instructed to be on guard and "constantly move their guns up and down and side by side" to make sure enemy combatants knew you were awake and alert in the event they dared to attack your position in flight.

He fondly recalls a B-24 pilot named Bill who impressed on the crew that it doesn't matter the bars you have on your shoulder or the stripes on the sleeve of your arm once you're up there.

It's kind of like life. "Trust in God every day. And enjoy it. Make someone laugh and do little kind things. Open doors for others," says Al.

When Al left England at the end of World War II it was ironically on a flight of a B-24 back to the United States. From his base in Wendling, England it was a flight to Scotland, then to Iceland, to Greenland, on to Newfoundland and finally touch down at an airfield in Westover field in Massachusetts USA. There were no welcoming crowds, bands or fanfare. Al tells me he never really felt welcomed home until his participation in a "Talons Out Honor Flight" to Washington DC in May of 2015. He went on the Honor Flight with his grandson, and it was an "experience of a lifetime."

After their return from World War II to Massachusetts it was on to Sioux Falls, South Dakota for honorable discharge on October 27, 1945. His long journey was complete with a Greyhound bus ride to Chicago and on to Saugatuck, Michigan to start his post-war life.

Years later Al is at the Kalamazoo Air Zoo watching an old restored B-24 fired to life. The pilot of this flight recognizes Al knows that when the engines start it is "Spit and Sputter" twice until finally with a cloud of smoke the engines one by one fire to life. The pilot senses Al's intimate relationship with the plane and offers to him to climb on board for the flight from Kalamazoo to Flint Michigan.

"How you get home is up to you," says the pilot.

Al's son says "You're getting on that plane."

The pilot insists on Al "buckling in" for the flight, which is completely contrary to his experience of standing the entire flight when a waist gunner on a B-24 in World War II.

"I wouldn't take a million dollars to do it again" says Al, "but I wouldn't take a million dollars not to have the experience again."

When he returned from the war, he was setting pins in a bowling alley for work, but heard that General Motors was hiring. He drove from Saugatuck to 36th and Buchanan in Wyoming, Michigan to apply. He was hired, but couldn't start that day, because his wife Esther was in the car waiting. He returned the next day to work and worked there for 32 years retiring in 1980. After 4 years they asked him to move to Grand Rapids to become a supervisor.

Al, JUST LIKE OTHER AGING VETERANS, TALKS OF HARD work and continuous goals. He talks of his friend who lives in Sisters, Oregon, a much respected and loved navigator named Russell Willins, now 96 years old. All of them have what I would call "continuous goals." To work hard and be driven to always learn something new.

Now 93 years old, Al deals with eyesight issues and kidney disease, but is mentally sharp and a great conversationalist. He lives in the clean well-kept home he built with his own hands years ago after the war. He lived there with his wife, Esther, who passed away a few years ago from Alzheimer's. I can see from the home, and his involvement in his church, that Al Schumacher completes his missions.

The time we had together flew by, and, standing to leave, I shook his hand. He had one or two more stories to add as we stood. and I loved the detail of his recall of events now over 70 years in the past. I thanked Al for his time and his service and stepped out on the porch to head to my car.

"I need to go. You can go to your church meeting … thanks again and have a good day," I said.

Al grins as I step off the porch and onto the driveway and says,

"Everyday is a good day, some are just better than others."

They traveled far overseas
And applied their expertise
Their work was prolific
In the South Pacific
You could always depend on the Seabees.

Al George

US Navy

64th Construction Battalion CB "Seabees"

World War II 1944-1946

US Navy Destroyer USS Sproston August 1950 to December 1952

Boatswain Mate 3rd class

Chapter Eight

H-Bomb on the Enewetak Atoll

I WATCH THE SUN SETTING ON THE HORI-zon as its effulgence seemingly extinguishes, sinking into the breadth of water as far as the eye can see. The remaining glow exposes the impressive expanse, massive enough to cause some first European explorers in the 1600s to surmise they had reached China. Standing on its sugar sand shoreline and staring out at the ocean-like horizon, Lake Michigan can be very inspiring. Its mass caused the native Americans in the region to simply name it "Mishigami" meaning "large lake." One of the Great Lakes, it's the fifth largest lake in the world in area and the largest lake contained within one country. A treasure trove sought world wide of liquid riches we call fresh water.

I run the shoreline from south of Kruse Park, along the "dog beach" and north to Pere Marquette beach, culminating my run at the breakwater and the lighthouses of the Muskegon Channel.

As the waves lap the shore, I begin to walk and reflect on the conversations I had with Al George. Now 93 years old, a Muskegon native born in August of 1925, Al was inspired by this same lake and these same beaches years ago. Years before I moved there, Al "patrolled" the area as a young man. It was the "large lake" that caused him to choose the Navy as his branch of service when his name was called to serve. To serve in two conflicts, World War II and the Korean conflict.

When the Japanese struck Pearl harbor, Al George was a junior in high school ... too young to go to war. At that time, you had to be 21 years old to be drafted. As the world plunged into war, that soon changed to 18 years of age to be drafted for active service. His senior year in high school he tried to join the Navy Air Force on the V-5 program, also known as the Naval Aviation Cadet Act. It was a volunteer Naval reserve class (NavCad) program to send civilian and enlisted candidates to train as aviation cadets.

There was one big problem. They informed Al he was color blind. Inspired by the great lake, when drafted he chose Navy, but could not be on the surface fleet because of his color perception. They signal with color flags and lights, so they test for color blindness. He would instead be assigned to the "Seabees" and eventually earn his rate as a boatswain mate. Al George would be a "Seabee."

Seabee is an acronym (CB) for construction battalion. The name of the "Seabees" itself was created by Frank J. Iafrate. He had a drawing talent for caricatures. Frank was working as a file clerk at the Naval Air Station, Quonset Point, Rhode Island. A Navy lieutenant asked Iafrate if he could draw a caricature insignia that would represent a new battalion. He explained to Iafrate they were not an offensive attacking group, but would be trained to defend themselves, their unit and their project without hesitation. The Seabees would know how to build a small city and defend themselves while doing it. They were carpenters, machinists, plumbers, heating and cooling technicians, electricians, earth-moving excavators, barbers, cooks, pest controllers, metal workers, telephone and communications experts to name some of the skill set. Building dry docks, warfs, causeways, airplane runways, housing quonset huts and buildings. They would transport equipment from ships to shore on barges, clearing beachheads for incoming troops and making airstrips for fighter planes. They were very much needed in the Pacific in the island-hopping campaign and march towards mainland Japan.

I smile to myself as I research the work done by these hard-working patriots. I think this goes way beyond "Jack of all trades." The term's origin goes back to when Jack was used as a generic name for any general representative of the common people. Usage of the phrase dates back to the 14th century Middle English. They were "common" Americans like you and I, but they were doing uncommon duty heroically. I would coin the phrase and rework the adage as:

"They were jack of all trades *and* masters each one."

Iafrate at first thought a caricature of a beaver would be a great choice, knowing their propensity for building. He then, however, considered that when a beaver is threatened it runs away. So, the beaver was out. He then thought of a bee. Brilliant. A busy worker, who doesn't bother you unless you bother him. Provoked, the bee stings. It seemed like an ideal symbol. Bees are always busy working and won't bother people unless they are bothered first, at which point they retaliate with a sharp sting.

With a chosen insignia, the US Navy would recruit, enlist, and train young men like Al George as Seabees, organize them into battalions and logistically support them in their operations. With the exigencies of war, they would work hard and quickly to establish a forward base in the Pacific, and the South Pacific road to victory.

Seabees motto:

Construimus Batuimus; "We build. We fight."

"CAN DO"

"The difficult we do now, the impossible

takes a little longer."

His service began with boot camp at the Great Lakes Naval training center. "We got physically fit," says Al. He credits his fitness now at the age of 93 to being active his whole life.

Boot camp was November of 1943 to February of 1944. When assigned as a Seabee, he was sent to Camp Perry, Virginia to the US Navy Seabee center, then he joined his group, the 64th battalion Seabees, at Camp Endicott in Davisville, Rhode Island in February of 1944. There he had boat training known as LCVP (landing craft, vehicle, personnel,) a landing craft used extensively in amphibious landings in World War II. He took a navigation course. When assigned to the 64th battalion, they trained on the firing line with small arms to learn self-defense, and he specialized in small boat training. Later he earned his "rate" as boatswain mate.

The Navy's Boatswain's Mate rating is one of the two oldest ratings or "Navy jobs" dating back to 1794. Boatswain's mates train, direct and supervise personnel in ship's maintenance duties. They learn to use a marlinspike, a tool used in marine rope work. They care for the deck, painting, upkeep of ship's external structure, rigging, deck equipment and boats. Boatswain's mates are involved in loading and unloading cargo, ammunition, fuel and general stores. Essentially to be described as a wide variety of functions that help the Navy do what the Navy does. The Navy describes boatswain's mates as the "backbone of every ship's crew."

After boot camp and training, Al was sent overseas for his first assignment with the 64th Construction Battalion, 3 months in Hawaii building and repaving airfields. He was assigned to operating the Mauna Loa Ridge telephone switchboard. He enjoyed the three months his Seabee crew had to work in and see the sights of Hawaii before shipping out to the South Pacific war zone.

Their next stop was Tubabao, a little island off the island of Samar in the Philippines. It took 30 days to get there on the LST, known as a "landing ship tank," also monikered by sailors as a "long slow target." The LST was loaded full of all their equipment. The 64th Construction Battalion was assigned to make a naval station and causeway to the main island of Samar.

It was April 28, 1945 when the 64th battalion disembarked and went ashore at Tubabao Island just west of Guiuan Samar. As the final battles of the European Theatre of World War II and the German surrender to the Allies took place in late April and early May 1945, Al and the Seabees of the 64th battalion headed ashore on Tubabao island to build a US Naval receiving station.

Tubabao Island, a triangular shaped island in the Leyte Gulf, lying west of Guiuan and separated from Samar by a narrow strait, was selected as the site for a receiving station. The job ahead would be to build something like a small functioning quonset hut city. The huts got their name from the location of the first manufacturing facility, Quonset Point near North Kingstown, Rhode Island. More than just huts, construction included mess halls, recreation facilities, and utilities for 10,000 men from scratch that had to be erected.

Emblem for 64th Construction Battalion "Seabees"

It was a place with outdoor plumbing and "oil can" showers, mud, rain, heat, and insects. They were told to take their salt tablets every day and don't forget to take your atabrine as malaria prevention. Atabrine was the trade name for Mepacrine (also called quinacrine). Mepacrine was initially approved in the 1930s as an antimalarial drug. It was used extensively during the second World War by US Marines fighting in the Far East to prevent malaria. When you consider environmental conditions like rain, heat or mosquitoes, it is important to note that the Seabees lived in tents while building quonset huts for the Navy.

Route of the 64th Construction Battalion Seabees

They were working 9- to 10-hour days, 7 days a week on the island. The job of the Seabees on the island needed to be done NOW! Supplies were unloaded. Roads were built. Sanitation and refrigeration were needed for what accounts to be a small city they were building. A mess hall. Chow. Beans for breakfast, and lunch and supper. Chipped beef on a shingle. No wonder the Navy calls this "mess."

It's amusing to note that during World War II GIs became weary of Spam: a mixture of chopped pork shoulder, ham, salt, water, modified potato starch, and sodium nitrite, or, as ad campaigns coined it, "Miracle Meat." Spam became both the boon and bane of troops because it was so easy to transport in large quantities and had a long shelf life.

Now Jackson had his acorns
And Grant his precious rye;
Teddy had his poisoned beef —
Worse you couldn't buy.
The doughboy had his hardtack
Without the Navy's jam,
But armies on their stomachs move —
And this one moves on Spam.
—Anonymous World War II poem

Al and the 64th Construction Battalion worked very hard regardless of what they were eating. It was said that "the only reason Rome wasn't built in a day was that the 64th didn't have a hand in it."

Al George (far left)

Within 4 months the 64th battalion had built six areas, accommodating 1,500 men each. Galleys, mess halls, quarters, roads, walks, post offices and any necessary facilities like laundry, sick bay or recreational facilities. No sooner was the last nail driven … the Navy moved men in.

While on Tubabao, Al George started on a bulldozer as an operator clearing palm trees for the base. He then helped carpenters assemble buildings. Once the telephone system was set up, Al was assigned to the switchboard and PA system. They were able to even construct a ballfield for the troops.

There was news of the surrender of Germany. Men hardly paused to cheer, because there was still the Japs to be licked. Then came the bombs dropped on Hiroshima and Nagasaki. There were debates in Congress about how many men to release from the service and who to release. Rumors were swirling as to what happens next.

"We thought we were going to Japan or China," said Al.

There was talk of the 64th going to Japan to build quarters for an occupation Army after the Japanese surrender. There were also rumors that the outfit would leave for China. For Al and the 64th neither happened.

JOURNEY TO TRUK ISLAND AND LAGOON

When the war ended the 64th was dissolved and Al George was assigned to the 32nd battalion heading for Truk island in the Caroline island group. It was August 14, 1945 that Japan had surrendered unconditionally to the Allies, effectively ending World War II, known as VJ day or Victory over Japan day. On September 2, 1945, the same day that formal surrender ceremonies took place in Tokyo Bay on the USS Missouri, the Japanese naval and air base at Truk also had officially surrendered.

Located in the Caroline Islands, Truk had served as a key island of Japan's central Pacific power during the first two years of World War II. It provided anchorage for its large fleet and coined by some as "the Gibraltar of the Pacific" or "Japan's Pearl Harbor." After reconnaissance flights, it was recognized that the tiny atoll was the largest Japanese military base in the Pacific theatre. By mid-1945, however, it was a shell of what it had been early in the war. US Navy attacks in 1944 had pounded the island into an increasingly unsustainable forward base of operations for the Japanese. By the time Al George and the Seabees arrived, there was no resistance, only rebuilding to do. The Japanese that remained on the island were living off the land on a semistarvation diet.

They went to work on Truk, dredging coral to use on the air strips. Al describes it as big scoops, dragging coral for use on airstrips and loading it on trucks. The airfield was potted with bomb holes. Their assignment was to repair and extend the airstrip and build a small base. Once again, he was in charge of telephones and PA. And, yet again, they lived in tents during the construction phase.

The Japanese equipment and vehicles on the island were without fuel. The Japanese stuck on the island were willing to work and help them with some of the rebuilding.

"They were in great shape," said Al. "We put them to work to help us." There were over 20,000 stranded Japanese on the island. "They were cooperative," said Al. The Japanese were only there a month or two before the US Navy was able to help them evacuate on ships back to mainland Japan. Al collected a samurai sword, a rifle, pistol and binoculars surrendered by the Japanese to take home with him.

It went well except communication was difficult. There were some friendly missionaries from Germany on the island, but they couldn't speak English. They used hand talking and motions to communicate.

"We didn't see many of the natives of Truk Island," says Al. "I do remember the bananas; they were big and good."

By May of 1946, Al George was on his way home and honorably discharged, thinking if there was a war within the next 4 years he wanted back in the Navy and not the Army. So, on his way out, to preserve his rating as Boatswain Mate, he joined the Naval reserve. He proved visionary, and it would come to impact his life a few short years later.

Sure enough, as history would have it, the first military action of the Cold War would come in the form of an invasion. On June 25, 1950, the Korean War began when some 75,000 soldiers from the North Korean People's Army crossed the 38th parallel. This breached the line between the pro-Western Republic of Korea to the south and Soviet-backed Democratic People's

Republic of Korea to the north. American troops entered the war on South Korea's behalf.

When the Korean conflict came along, Al was married with one child and buying his Dad's moving company. He was called back into the service as part of the Naval reserve with his rating as a Boatswain Mate to serve on a destroyer. Al George reminded them he was color blind. This time it didn't matter. By August of 1950 he was back on active duty destined for the destroyer USS Sproston.

Al George

It created a dilemma for Al. He had to quickly get on a train from the Great Lakes Naval Center to Milwaukee, then fly to Muskegon. He had to sell the business and be there to sign the papers. Now with no business and married with a child, Al was off to serve again, this time on a destroyer in the South Pacific.

H-BOMB ON THE ENEWETAK ATOLL

WITH COMMUNIST FORCES NOW IN SOUTH KOREA IT WAS all hands on deck. The US Navy destroyer Sproston was re-commissioned on September 15, 1950. Al George would be on board the Sproston as it departed San Diego in early 1951 for the Enewetak atoll, Marshall islands to participate in the hydrogen bomb test "Mike Shot" Operation Ivy.

Both spelling and pronunciation of the atoll is a struggle for some folks. The US Government referred to the atoll as "Eniwetok" until 1974, when it changed its official spelling to "Enewetak." It was done to more properly reflect the pronunciation by the Marshall Islanders. Even today you will see references to "En·i·we·tok" [en-uh-wee-tok, uh-nee-wi-tok].

Al and crew of the Sproston were assigned to "guard duty" surrounding Enewetak, an atoll in the Pacific Ocean, as part of Operation Ivy, to keep others away as the US Navy was engaged with atom bomb testing. At Enewetak, Al George would have a front row seat to personally witness the first test of a full-scale thermonuclear device, in which part of the explosive yield came from nuclear fusion. Ivy Mike was the code name given to the first United States nuclear test of a fusion device. He would see the detonation of an H-bomb with his own eyes, a bomb which gets its power from nuclear fusion, much more powerful than the atomic bombs dropped seven years before on Hiroshima and Nagasaki, Japan. Imagine the yield of 10.4 megatons of explosive power. They would patrol and keep others away from the Enewetak atoll during testing, more specifically the island of Elugelab as part of Operation Ivy.

The area has a storied history. Enewetak was 190 miles west of the famous Bikini Atoll nuclear test site. Ironically in October of 1529 the area was "patrolled" by Spanish explorer Alvaro de Saavedra, a relative of Hernan Cortes and "burn the ships" fame. It was not so much a voyage of discovery, as other explorers such as Ferdinand Magellan had patrolled the Marshall Islands a few years before, as it was a search. The Marshall Islands are about halfway between Hawaii and Australia and are seated on ancient submerged volcanoes rising from the ocean floor. The purpose of the expedition was to find new lands in the South Sea or as we call it the Pacific Ocean and to bring back spice plants. Saavedra called the islands "Los Jardines" (The Gardens) and "Islas de los Reyes" (Islands of the Three Wise Kings) probably because Christmas was coming, and he was inspired.

Al George and those serving on board the USS Sproston

would patrol the area to keep others away from "Mike Shot." A huge bomb housed in a covered structure, impractical and undeliverable as a portable weapon, seated on the island of Elugelab.

Ivy Mike was the code name given as part of Operation Ivy. Armed with a hypothesis on what *could* transpire, no one exactly knew what the man-made thermonuclear explosion result would look like. Soon the detonation would elucidate to the world the destructive power of a thermonuclear bomb.

It was November 1, 1952. Al George and his other shipmates are on board the USS Sproston a mere 65 miles down range from the anticipated H Bomb detonation.

"I didn't have black glasses on the deck," says Al. "They told us to turn our backs to the blast."

"Weren't you worried?" I said.

"I didn't worry, no one was concerned," said Al. "They told us once it blasted to count to 10, then you could watch it."

"Did you?" I said.

Al sits across from me and looks up to ceiling to mimic how he looked up at the mushroom cloud in the heavens that day.

> *"Now 30 seconds to Zero Time*
> *Put on goggles or turn away*
> *Do not remove goggles or face burst until 10*
> *seconds after the first light.*
> *Minus 15 seconds*
> *Minus 10 seconds*
> *Niner*
> *Eight*
> *Seven*
> *Six*
> *Fiver*
> *Four*
> *Three*
> *Two*
> *One"*

A bright flash and an enormous ball of light filled the sky followed by a gigantic mushroom cloud darkening the heavens. The almost 11-megaton explosion created a fireball 5 kilometers or more than 3 miles across, and a mushroom cloud that climbed to 57,000 feet within 90 seconds, eventually stabilizing at 120,000 feet reaching into the stratosphere. Ten minutes later, it had spread out to about 100 miles. Radioactive coral debris rained down on ships positioned over 40 miles from ground zero.

When the bomb was detonated Al George and crew were only 65 miles away. That's less than the distance from his boyhood home in Muskegon to Milwaukee straight across Lake Michigan. They turned the ship right into it, heading into the blast site to check damages. Helicopter flights over Eugalab reported that the island was completely gone, disappeared from the face of the earth. All that was left was a deep crater. It looked like a dark-blue hole in the ocean, and, almost 2 miles across, it was deep enough to hold a 17-story building.

The creation and detonation of the first hydrogen bomb on the Enewetak atoll had allowed the United States to temporarily step ahead of the Soviets during the arms race.

Al George had seen with his own eyes the culmination of an announcement made by President Harry Truman a couple years earlier to support the development of the hydrogen bomb. It was the "hell bomb," as it was known by many Americans. On January 31, 1950, Truman had announced publicly the pursuit of the H-bomb development. This was due in part to the Soviet Union having tested an atomic bomb in Kazakhstan during 1949 and eliminating the US nuclear supremacy. What had accelerated the evolution of the bomb and its eventual testing was the discovery that Klaus Fuchs, a German-born British scientist was passing top secret information about the bomb to the Soviets. Fuchs had been brought to America to work on the Manhattan Project, the code name for the American effort to build an atomic bomb in the early 40s. Fuchs clandestine meetings with Soviet agents revealed a spy ring. The US now knew, that the Soviets knew what they knew, about the hydrogen bomb. By November 22, 1955, the Soviet Union had detonated its first hydrogen bomb in Kazakhstan. The world, forever changed, and would exist with the threat of thermonuclear war.

After the H-bomb test, Al and his shipmates headed back to Hawaii to dock and clean the ship due to concerns for radioactivity. They had to wash the ship down three times. That's not all that got a bath. The crew was stripped down, and they hosed them down too. Fresh clothes before dinner. A Geiger counter was used on each man before they could go to dinner that night.

"You're good or safe is all they would say," said Al, when checked on their way in to eat.

He flew out of Hawaii in December of 1952 and was back by Christmas 1952, discharged for good from military life. Living in a small house next to his parents, it was time for Al George the Seabee to build his own future, and he did. He was a salesman for office supplies for a while and worked for a freight company. He stayed in touch with the moving industry. He and his wife raised six children, 18 grandchildren and 33 great grandchildren as part of a post-war generation that raised the huge "Baby Boomer" generation, causing the urban sprawl and renewal that fed the moving and storage business he went on to own. Later, he would co-own a record management company that stored business records.

He didn't necessarily "retire" just like the other veterans I became acquainted with, the modus operandi for them I learned is they stayed active. They stayed involved. Al was a lot like the other veterans I had talked to about their experiences in World War II. They didn't fight for recognition; they served because it was "the right thing to do." They all have a matter-of-fact response that "You do what you have to do." Like the Seabees of World War II, they knew how to work long and hard. They had traveled to the other side of the world for their country, and returned to build lives, families and businesses in a place we all call home. The home of the free because of the brave who did what they had to do.

OPERATION RUMINATION

I STOP AND STAND ON THE SHORELINE ON ONE OF MY runs, looking out over the water of Lake Michigan. It's a cold day, no one on the beach, I'm alone with my thoughts. I stand there thinking about what Al George experienced, and all that he saw while serving his country between the age of 19 and 27 … much more than I did at that young age. During his service in the military, and then later in his life's work, business ownership, partnerships and as an entrepreneur, he fit the description of a reoccurring adjective I've had for him and the other World War II veterans I've spent time with this year.

Operose (OP-er-owss)
Adjective: Industrious; diligent

It's almost the perfect word, because not only does it *sound* like some kind of military jargon, code word or mission, it fits the character of these people. There is a lesson to be learned. I met Al when I gave a speech to a YMCA service club luncheon. He was there. Now 93, still serving, still industrious, still diligent.

If you're willing to take risks and outwork everyone else, you'll get somewhere in life. "We build. We fight. We can do."

I turn to continue my run down the beach and smile, thinking … what if we were all to employ the Seabee spirit everyday, "the difficult we do now, the impossible takes a little longer" but … we'll get it done.

My, what we could accomplish for good.

He learned their dialect,
Then on missions would direct,
Through a number of military tours
Many moves his family endures,
His service I greatly respect.

Bill "Old Man" Alverson

US Army

2nd Lieutenant 1st Cavalry Division Korean War

Major (Thieu Ta) Army Ranger Vietnam 1966 Pleiku Air Base South Vietnam

Colonel at Can Tho Army Air field Base Vietnam 1972-March 1973

Chapter Nine

Wet Toilet Paper and Cold Coffee

THE POET **W.B. YEATS WROTE IN** his poem *The Second Coming* that, "Things fall apart. The center cannot hold." There is a lot of truth to that. It takes resilience and determination to hold things together. Part of the process is learning from mistakes. Other people's mistakes are your homework. Most have a lifetime to make them. We together learn in the journey. Also, a sense of humor doesn't hurt, as an essential characteristic of a resilient person. And leadership principles taught at a young age tend to stick for life.

Bill Alverson taught me in short order that after 30 years of active duty and 32 moves with his family, he has had a sense of humor in the journey. Laughter can be our best ally in keeping us hopeful and sane. When "under fire" humor will help us see the positive aspects of a situation along with the negative. When it comes to laughter in the midst of struggle, I admire Bill Alverson for that ability. He also has ingrained leadership principles he carries with him his entire life.

"I was lucky to have a good man as a platoon sergeant in my rifle platoon," said Bill about his experience when first arriving in Korea during the Korean War. When he first arrived in Korea, Bill had basic principles engrained in everything he did, principles that guided him from his ROTC training as an officer and confirmed in basic course.

Leadership principles (follow me)

Knowledge of small unit tactics

Weapons capability

Ground navigation or map reading

And most important … integrity.

Upon arriving in Korea and the Korean War, he approached the company commander who had "the battle rattles" or shakes, and, pointing, sent him to "the knob up there." Scared of the big guns firing, Bill knew it was time for him to enter the fight. He was told to "go down that dry creek bed and find your platoon." With eyes large in fear and amazement, he traveled the dry creek bed, which was about 15 miles west of Seoul and 1 mile south of what would become the "DMZ" or 38th parallel. As a young 22 and a half year old man, he was armed with an M1 carbine rifle and *no* ammunition, an empty canteen, lots of questions and core principles. He met Platoon Sergeant LeBleu, hoping to make a good first impression. "Everyone, including LeBleu, knew I was a scared, green lieutenant," recalls Bill. Despite that, Alverson and LeBleu hit it off from the start.

His name was platoon sergeant Ernest LeBleu from Louisiana. He showed Bill the ropes and never embarrassed him. He knew what needed to be done and got it done. Communication within the platoon, especially when under attack, could at times be difficult.

"We make a good team LeBleu."

"How is that sir?"

"When you get excited and things are tight you start speaking French, and when I get excited and scared my lips are moving, but I'm not making any noise," said Bill laughing heartily. "They couldn't understand you and they couldn't hear me."

The biggest difficulty at platoon level was *communication* for the 3rd division. The division integrated three regiments, consisting of Korean soldiers, the 65th infantry composed of National Guard Puerto Ricans from New York and English speaking GIs. Bill told me, "When things got tight out there, communication became challenging." I had to put my coffee down and we laughed out loud over his recollection. Even in the face of combat and fear, the thought of Korean, Puerto Rican and English-speaking GIs, with a sergeant that spoke French when excited, is the perfect example there is always humor to be found, regardless of the situation. It certainly would have left me speechless.

"Everyone understood profanity," said Bill. "It doesn't matter what language you speak, you knew the difference between a compliment and profanity."

They also understood they were in this together, and they had each other's back. Bill painted a picture for me of him walking through a rice paddy in Korea. A Korean man, part of his 3rd division, walked towards him, knowing he had orders to leave the division. Years later the memory of hugging that man in tears was clear in the mind of Bill. Duty, honor, camaraderie, respect circumvented any language barriers. They were in this together. He recalls for me, "The man was a light machine gun loader, 'John the Rock' a Korean who would fight." On one occasion the enemy charged their position repeatedly and John the Rock hollered, "Ammo have a no, plenty of targets" says Bill, laughing now in recollection. They stood their ground as the enemy came in waves, five distinct waves, picking up ammo and rifles from dead combatants on their way up. It was an all-night fight. Bill and his men stood their ground. This experience taught Bill's two sons, Larry and Gary, who both also served in the military, lessons on life and the military: Success on the battlefield depends on, and evolves from, learning and applying key military truths. Lead by example. Know those who serve with you. Know their capabilities. In this attack on a hill and out of ammo, his men looked at Bill Alverson and asked him what will you do? "We will not surrender," said Bill. The men stood by him saying "we are with you." Prepared for a knife fight, even picking up rocks if necessary, the incessantly charging, stubborn combatants fortunately and finally withdrew.

WET TOILET PAPER AND COLD COFFEE

BILL ALVERSON WAS COMMISSIONED IN JUNE OF 1951, and retired from active military service in September of 1978. I sat there thinking, *this man had served my own time and the time of a number of others over the course of his lifetime.* He served in the National Guard in college and ROTC while "broke" going to school at Washington State University in Pullman, Washington.

"I thought I was an athlete, I played football and ran track in high school which helped me in the Army," said Bill. However, he kept the end of the bench warm in college.

Upon graduating in 1951, as a distinguished honor ROTC graduate, he got a regular Army commission as a second lieutenant and went right to Fort Benning. Fort Benning straddles the Alabama and Georgia border and was named after Henry L Benning, a brigadier general in the Confederate states during the Civil War. Bill called Fort Benning a place for "wayward boys."

As a second lieutenant, you are considered an entry-level commissioned officer rank in the United States Army. A second lieutenant is generally placed in command of a platoon, consisting of 16 to 44 soldiers, including two or more rifle squads lead by a senior non-commissioned officer.

"There are lots of jokes about second lieutenants," said Bill.

"There was a saying that *second lieutenants, wet toilet paper and cold coffee are all the same.*"

Known for making dumb mistakes and taking advantage of

their rank and position, there are a
lot of jokes about them. "Most of them are deserved," said
Bill … "except of course in my case," as we laugh hard at his
perspective.

KOREAN WAR

THE STORY BEGINS WITH 4 MONTHS IN BASIC TRAINING AT
Fort Benning. They were primarily ROTC graduates, but some
West Point and National Guard were there also. From there he
had orders to go to the far east with the 1st Cavalry Division
as a second lieutenant to Hokkaido Island, Sapporo Japan, and
was assigned to 7th Cavalry Regiment in late 1951. He spent 5
months there, before going on to the Korean war. Young and far
from home, we talked about how some people early in life can
have a big impact on you. Bill said he was "extremely fortu-
nate" as rifle platoon leader, because his commander, William F
Braun, was tough and fair. "He was very tough yet always fair
and would chew your tail out if there was something he didn't
like. I didn't like it at first, but came to respect it as something
that molded me in my early twenties. It made a huge impact on
me, more than he could have ever known."

Bill recalled that infantrymen in Korea would be paid for
combat duty, but you had to be on the line and fired at for 30
days. "I'm not sure who kept score, but someone did." It was $65
a month for being "shot at" and he sent the pay to his wife. They
had one child and another that was born while he was gone. His
son was 1 year old before he finally saw him for the first time.
Once his pay was 2 days short and that sticks out in his mind.
"You buy a beer and maybe a dinner outside of the supplied rations, but the rest went home." Once asked about combat pay,
he replied "Whatever they are getting paid it's not enough when
getting shot at," said Bill. Regardless of who kept score he pack-
aged the money and sent it home to Anita.

Halfway through college, Bill Married Anita. They were flat
broke. Anita worked as a secretary to help support them, earn-

ing $125.00 a month. That was a lot of money at the time, and the result of her choice to forego a college education to help the family. I can clearly see the pride and respect Bill and the family have for her humble strength throughout the years. While enlisted in the National Guard, Bill earned $100 every three months, provided he made the drills. "When you don't have anything, and you have a dollar in your pocket, it's a lot of money," Bill laughed.

They left for their honeymoon with $25 and a tank of gas. They stayed in tents while on the road, and, when they returned, he still had $10 left. When you are flat broke, frugality is a discipline and Bill and Anita had that discipline from a young age. Born in June of 1929, he learned at a young age how to be frugal. He had just turned 89 at the time of our interview, celebrating a 69th wedding anniversary with Anita, the young lady who got him through high school by letting him copy off her English paper. With two boys and a "rowdy husband," Bill credits her with persevering through 32 moves. "She got very good at packing," said Bill.

With Anita at home with the boys, Bill found himself far from home in Korea and at war. When Japan's colonial hold of Korea ended with their defeat in World War II, by mutual agreement the United States entered the South and the Soviet Army occupied the north, divided by the 38th parallel. This became a stalemate when agreement could not be found in the UN general assembly, and by 1948 the Republic of Korea with its capital as Seoul was established south of the 38th parallel, and North Korea established and proclaimed the Democratic People's Republic. A stalemate ensued which was broken by an armored invasion by the North on June 25, 1950,as they crossed over the 38th parallel and captured Seoul. A three-year war that no one wanted then ensued. When a ceasefire was declared in July of 1953, a demilitarized zone or DMZ was established along the 38th parallel, which still stands today. After 3 years of fighting and thousands of casualties, the line in the sand remained the same. A stalemate. Since then thousands of US servicemen and women have served in South Korea. 36,914 US deaths occurred in that war, defending the dividing line against communist intervention. This was made poignant yet again as recently as the summer of 2018 when, on July 31, a US Air Force plane carrying what are believed to be the remains of US troops killed during the Korean War some 65 years ago arrived at Osan Air Base in South Korea. Fifty-five cases of remains of these American heroes were finally laid to rest on American soil.

That crossing line, boundary, source of conflict, was a contentious seesaw of struggle made transparent to me in a story Bill shared. Stationed just below the 38th parallel, one night he was ordered to take 55 men across the line. They hadn't had a recon or aerial flight over the area, just a map, and "how do you read a map at night?" Bill said. Even though he questioned the wisdom of those orders, he followed them. When they got through the line into the North, a Chinese sentry fired in their direction. One of the men in Bill's group was hit and died. "I know he didn't aim at anything, because he couldn't see," said Bill.

Having to carry him back across the line, Bill decided they needed artillery cover and fired a red star cluster flare into the air. The battalion commander came on the radio and said, "What did you fire that for?"

Bill replied, "I am aware of the meaning and that is exactly why I fired it."

He had shot the flare to let his guys know that he needed help, that he was in trouble out there. He did it to alert them because they would be coming back through and didn't want to die by friendly fire. Bill wanted them to put some artillery fire out there to keep the Chinese heads down as they headed back through the line. As a result, they got artillery cover which kept the noise of their movement down and kept the enemies heads down.

They were primarily fighting the Chinese. I thought of the conundrum and how at that time the fight with the Chinese would play back in Washington. I thought how eventually the riff between President Truman and General MaCarthur, who wanted to press the issue, would result in MacArthur's firing. I can only imagine Truman's thoughts and fears of a war-weary world and the potential of a third world war with China. "Very true," says Bill laughing, "but second lieutenants were not entitled to that level of thinking."

"You shouldn't have got yourself in that position," the battalion commander said.

Bill radioed back, "You SOB you sent me out here." He aborted the mission and turned around to head back across the line.

It's hard to get back through friendly lines when there has been a fight out in front. The men are now on alert, and it's dark. Trying to cross back over the line was precarious with nervous troops. The password that night was **"Icy"** and the response was **"Summit."** Those defending the line challenged with **"Icy"** and you had to come back with **"Summit."** "How is a Chinaman going to say something like that," Bill said laughing.

They were scared to death and carrying the body of their fallen comrade. When they crossed the line, there was a messenger there asking "Where is Lieutenant Alverson?" Bill identified himself and was told to report to the battalion commander. A lieutenant colonel was there to give him a dressing down.

"We'll talk later," said the lieutenant colonel, "but do you have anything to say?"

I can only imagine how upset Bill was, having only just moments earlier experiencing fear out in the field and losing one of his men. Heart-in-throat fear is how Bill described it to me, which is a fear I have not experienced, because I have never been shot at. But he realized he was in charge and had to maintain some measure of civility and ability to escape their predicament.

"No sir" said Bill, "except they taught us at Fort Benning that anything said over the phone or radio is not admissible as evidence in court martial." This "endeared" Bill to the lieutenant colonel forever.

"I was on his S list but I didn't get court-martialed," said Bill.

Instead Bill was transferred to I & R or Intelligence and Reconnaissance, also known as the cavalry, the forward eyes and ears of the infantry who tried to actively engage the enemy and get information. They traveled with jeep-mounted 30 caliber machine guns to be the forward eyes and ears, engaging the enemy lying in wait. Their job was to make contact with the enemy. He recalls leading a team of 11 jeeps and reaching a crossroads without "contact" from the enemy. As leader of the scout platoon, forward of the regiment, he felt it was a good time to break out C rations and have some lunch. This was a big mistake because they were soon fired on, forcing them to the let C rations fly as they quickly repositioned the jeeps beyond a ridge for good firing position. This was a leadership learning moment for Bill … don't let down your guard, not even for a moment when responsible for the lives of other men.

I asked Bill what it was that drove him, kept him going despite difficult conditions? The question brought tears to his eyes and his response was, "Personal pride and the good Lord. I was responsible for some 40 to 50 men and had to take care of them," Bill said, quickly adding, "And they took care of me." I felt the sense of duty he had when Bill said "The orders I gave affected their lives." I said to Bill, "You had a sense of duty, responsibility, you had to be sharp." In a self-depreciating way he commented, "Yes you had to be sharp. And how do you make a round rock sharp?" I quickly learned that Bill used self-deprecating humor back then, as he does even today, to deflect attention from himself. He has a very strong sense of duty and honor ingrained in him.

Bill and I sat across from each other at a dining room table as he recalled leading his team through the Chorwon Valley, which is in the Gangwon Province of South Korea near the border of North Korea.

Their assignment was to track north until making contact with the enemy. They headed north, parallel with a railroad track. It was dark and 2 o'clock in the morning. He asked Sargent LeBleu to cover him while he and one other man checked the other side of the berm they'd been paralleling on their move north. When they crested the berm in the darkness, they made contact with the enemy. Instantly a fight broke out. A Chinese soldier shot at him, but Bill shot him first. LeBleu brought up the ranks in support and a skirmish broke out. They had "made contact" as instructed. Fortunately, no one was lost from his platoon in this fight. After every firefight, it was their job to search the casualties for information that might aid in the fight. He searched the man he had hit and found a picture in the man's jacket. It was too dark to view, so he shoved it in his shirt. Later, when debriefed at the main lines in a tent with a lantern, he pulled out the picture. It was a family portrait of a Chinese lady, holding a baby, with a little boy standing beside her. With tears in his eyes, Bill thought of his own son, Gary, only 6 months old at the time, in the arms of his wife, Anita, with 2-year-old Larry standing by her side. Bill fought back tears as he told me, "When you kill someone you never forget it."

While in the IR or Intelligence and Reconnaissance platoon, he had the opportunity to provide armed escort for General Dwight Eisenhower on a visit during the Korean War. Eisenhower, a few short years later, would become President of the United States. It was February and Korea was cold ... winter, bitter cold. The winters were unbearably harsh and severe on the Korean Peninsula during the war. In addition to the enemy, American soldiers fought the frigid, biting cold. It is said the arctic winds blowing down from Siberia turn the country into a frozen wasteland. Frostbite was the worst malady, but there were also the frozen rations, icy terrain, jammed weapons, and a shortage of cold-weather gear.

Eisenhower said to Alverson, "Is it cold out there? And you should stand at attention lieutenant."

Bill answered the general, 'I am standing at attention sir. I have on everything I own to try to stay warm.'

Eisenhower got a "good snort out of it," said Bill as he laughed heartily.

A Second Tour of Duty …
Bill's First in Vietnam

AFTER THE KOREAN WAR, BILL SPENT TIME WITH THE 44th Division 9th Infantry Regiment in Washington at Fort Lewis as a 1st lieutenant. His second tour of active duty would be in 1966, again to Southeast Asia, however, this time to Vietnam. He volunteered. At the time he was stationed in San Francisco "shuffling papers." With two boys, one in the 8th grade and one a sophomore in high school, Bill was off to Asia again.

There was a stop at Fort Bragg and Bill was ordered to learn Vietnamese.

"Sir you must be making a mistake. I flunked Spanish in school and my wife got me through English class in high school," said Bill.

"You're not using this to get out of going to Vietnam, Alverson," his instructor said.

He passed. No one flunked.

Bill got to Vietnam where he served from January to Christmas day 1966 as an Army Ranger and an advisor to a

Bill Alverson

119

Vietnamese Ranger outfit. Upon arrival, they were picked up by a Vietnamese bus driver. Bill, fresh from language school, volunteered to talk to the driver who replied in perfect English, "When were you in Hanoi?" It appears Bill had obtained an accent and his language instructor back in the States had given him a "Hanoi accent."

It was on to Pleiku, Vietnam as an advisor to a Vietnamese Ranger platoon. This assignment proved difficult, due to the cultural and training experience they had. Any similarity between a Vietnamese Ranger unit and a US Army Ranger unit was purely coincidental recalls Bill. "One shot and the Vietnamese Rangers would run," said Bill laughing. They also weren't very good to their own people, stealing from them and treating them poorly. Again, the ingrained leadership principles, this time, integrity, gave Bill the tools to be an example and lead others.

THIEU TA

ONE DAY BILL'S GROUP LEFT THEIR BASE IN PLEIKU IN THE central highlands of Vietnam. They were warned to be aware they might get ambushed on their right flank. Bill was a major, or, as the Vietnamese called him, "Thieu Ta." It was his role to advise the Vietnamese Rangers. Their work was patrolling and pacification in the region. They went into a village, and Bill sensed there was trouble brewing. He knew from fighting in Korea that there were always kids and dogs present, and if there weren't … it was trouble. They blustered in, and, sure enough were whacked from the right, just like they'd been forewarned. His advisory team and Bill were always up front and they dropped down, using their M-16s to return fire. He was trying to tell the Rangers to just shoot in Vietnamese. "Just Shoot!" Lost in translation and under fire it was again humor in the face of duress. A Vietnamese lieutenant tugged on his shirt and replied in English, "Thieu Ta, you're telling them to 'shoot your friend on the table' in Vietnamese!"

As they lay on the ground under fire, Alverson and Sargent

Abuduski made contact with the enemy. The word "contact" is, in my mind, an insipid description of what was really going on there. Contact is the military term for firing on or being fired upon by the enemy. Listening to Bill's stories it occurs to me he had been shot at numerous times in his life. I've never been shot at, at least not that I'm aware of. If I was shot at, I think I would use different vernacular than "contact." Instinctively based on his training, Bill applied the leadership training principle of "awareness."

John Miner, his radio man, tapped Bill on the heel from behind him.

"Yeah, John what is it?"

"Sir I think we need to get out of here."

Bill sarcastically replied, "You got any ideas?" Bill decided that his radio man and Abuduski would run 20 yards, while he provided fire cover from a kneeling position. After they ran, they would then drop down and provide cover fire for Alverson to run. This is a process called leap frogging. Bill remembers saying, "Whatever you do don't hit me." Disciplined training had taught Bill that we don't just all stand and run away. There was a discipline of ordered retreat to follow. You fire and move, fire and move, navigating the terrain that lies ahead.

The men engaged in their leapfrog routine, and after about the third leapfrog, Sargent Abaduski, while running, did a flip in the air and landed on the ground.

Abuduski cursed the roots he thought he tripped on and Bill told him to give them space, "you're too close!" Sergeant Abaduski again tried to run and once again went down in a heap.

"Sir I think I'm hit," he said.

"Can you run?" asked Alverson

"Damn right I can run!" said the sergeant.

But he couldn't. The sergeant was hit right in the knee. "Bam" just like that. Bill picked him up and put him in a fireman's carry, and while running was hollering at him, "Abaduski, you eat too much!" He carried his sergeant out of the line of fire, and the men made it out of the ambush alive.

I asked Bill why that experience stuck out in his mind. He said it was because once again it was one of those moments that was humorous while they were scared to death at the same time.

Bill recalls that a short time after that experience, he received a call from the hospital.

"Are you the commanding major of Sergeant Abuduski?" said the voice on the other end of the line. "I need to report he has left the hospital and is AWOL," said the nurse.

"I can assure you Abuduski is a good man and would never go AWOL," said Alverson.

While Bill was still on the phone speaking to the hospital representative, Abaduski hobbled up the sidewalk. With his mouth wide open Bill told the nurse "I'm looking at him right now." Ever faithful and resilient, Sergeant Abuduski had left the hospital of his own accord, and hitch-hiked back to his fighting outfit.

A Second Tour to Vietnam

Bill's second tour to Vietnam was in 1972 to the Can Tho Army Airfield Base along the Mekong Delta. He was in line to be promoted to full colonel, but for some reason it was delayed. Bill took a trip to Washington to determine what the delay was. It turned out to be due to a misunderstanding. In the interim, Bill's old track coach got him into graduate school at Washington State University. While in grad school for guidance and counseling, he was finally promoted to full colonel. After 10 months of grad school, Bill was on his way back to Vietnam. A colonel is the senior field-officer grade commissioned officer rank, directly above lieutenant colonel and below brigadier general. Colonels typically command a brigade-sized unit, consisting of 3,000 to 5,000 soldiers. A pretty big deal, and far more than the 40 to 50 men he'd lead as a second lieutenant back in Korea. In typical self-deprecating humorous fashion, Bill tells me he figures the Army felt as an infantryman he needed some polishing.

Bill is assigned as base commander at Can Tho responsible for logistics like fuel, loading of planes and other day-to-day needs of the base. Now this was not an easy job. Along with the natural challenges the Vietnam jungle imposed, the Delta and the Mekong river often, at high tide, would put the runways underwater. In addition to those who served there, aircraft and boats were the life-line and life-blood of the day-to-day operations on the base.

His reputation was cemented with the troops the first day he arrived. Again, applying the leadership principle of 'do it right the first time,' he personally inspected the entire perimeter of the base the first night. "That practice and discipline *always* paid off," said Bill. He approached a concrete barrier wall that adjoined a canal that ran under the perimeter of the base. The waterway or canal naturally breached from outside the base into the interior, leading to an area where aviation fuel was stored. In that area a soldier was sleeping with his head down. Colonel Alverson quietly approached the guard, and, when close, shouted in his ear. The startled soldier of course jumped to his feet. Ironically and fortuitously due to the shouting a VC or "sapper" as they would be called was also startled and surfaced in the water of the canal. "Shoot him!" Bill ordered, "shoot him!" When the clandestine VietCong was retrieved from the water, they discovered he was wired with explosives, his motives obvious with the aviation fuel as the target. The very next day, all around the base, the word was "the new colonel is so good he can smell them.'

One of the colonel's assignments was to oversee the management of the five large generators used to provide electrical power to the base. Large generators on wheels, it was power to the people, or in theory to the right people: military personnel and their operations on the base. The generators were running all the time, and, in most cases, at max load every night. One of the generators was overused and about to burn up. "I had a good man, a non-commissioned officer overseeing the generators," said Bill.

This non-commissioned officer made an observation. He reported, "Sir someone is stealing power from our generators."

Once again Bill was applying the leadership principle of management by observation and inspecting the perimeter. There were floodlights around the perimeter of the base, which bothered Colonel Alverson. The floodlights helped ground troops spot the enemy before they breached the camp's perimeter. Bill applied leadership principles by asking the question: Is the defense really a defense? Even though light around a perimeter sounded good on paper, the reality was it gave the enemy full view of the compound for mortar targeting.

Bill and the generator manager got in a jeep and drove the perimeter of the base. Upon inspecting the perimeter, they found a Vietnamese Ranger unit had bivouacked in that area and tapped into the generator, selling power to the surrounding communities. They were running a less than honest, yet entrepreneurial operation. Bill could see the lights on in the villages in the distance. Using the process of elimination, one by one, they shut down the generators. They eventually reached *the* pirated generator and shut it down. The entire village went black. They then turned it back on and the lights went on in the village. The less-than-honest, but, entrepreneurial Vietnamese Rangers, were in the business of selling pirated power to the people. Shutting it down made Bill an unpopular guy with the surrounding villages, but a good manager of resources and logistics for his "charge" at the base.

The loss of life during war and the leadership principle of "follow me" in reaction to that loss are evident in the integrity of Alverson even today. His countenance quickly changes and he fights off tears in telling the story of a helicopter shot down on his watch. I sit in silence with Bill's son Gary as he composes and recounts the incident. He pushes through the story, describing the 15 men who lost their life when a CH-47 Chinook helicopter was shot down. It was their job to recover the bodies and secure the Chinook from enemy hands. It was a delicate operation and "a bad deal," says Bill. Since it was first put into service in the early 1960s, the Boeing CH-47 Chinook helicopter did most of the heavy lifting as the US Army's soldier and supply transport aircraft. When shot down, the bodies of those who lost their lives are to be recovered. Keeping equipment from enemy hands is also a priority. To avoid further loss of life, those who go in need to be disciplined and on guard, knowing they will come under enemy fire. Bill recounts returning to the base, hearing cursing and shouting. A sergeant major and a newspaper reporter were going to toe to toe. They were fighting over an article written by the reporter, questioning hesitation, and unwillingness to go out and retrieve the Chinook and crew. The reporter made assumptions and didn't understand the delicate operation involved. Colonel Alverson quickly backed up his sergeant major, poking the reporter in the chest as they argued. Bill said, "Get six men and throw this SOB over the fence." They did said Bill laughing, he didn't go out the door. His ingrained leadership principles to support his men was on display for all to see.

Final lessons are learned. Success on the battlefield depends on, and evolves from, learning and applying key military truths.

Lead by example
Know those you serve with and their capabilities

Bill lived those key military truths in a long and distinguished military career where he served his country and his men. Bill saw it through to the end. March 1973. Two months after the signing of the Vietnam peace agreement, the Paris Peace Accords, the last US combat troops left South Vietnam, as Hanoi freed the remaining American prisoners of war held in North Vietnam. America's direct eight-year intervention in the Vietnam War was at an end. For Bill Alverson it was a ride on a C-123 to Tan Son Nhut Air Base located near the city of Saigon in southern Vietnam. The United States used it as a major base during the Vietnam War, stationing Army, Air Force, Navy, and Marine units there. A chartered commercial airliner, Braniff airlines, flew them out of Vietnam and sent them home. The stewardess told Colonel Bill Alverson that if he didn't tell anyone they can serve alcohol. Bill laughed. "I won't tell anyone," he said. The officers on the upper deck enjoyed a glass of champagne. "I'm sure the guys down below enjoyed some beers," he said.

PAYING THE PRICE AND
INVESTING IN THE FUTURE

THROUGHOUT VIETNAM, AGENT ORANGE WAS USED around the perimeter of bases. In pictures and video I've seen, I immediately noticed how the perimeter was not at all "jungle-like." A US program, code named *Operation Ranch Hand* sprayed millions of gallons of herbicide called Agent Orange to eliminate forest cover and crops to expose North Vietnamese and Viet Cong troops. Herbicides were also used along the perimeter of bases to provide a distant and clear line of sight for oncoming trouble. Most of the chemical was dumped in orange streams from aircraft, but were also sprayed from trucks and hand-sprayers around US military bases. Agent Orange contained Dioxin, a highly persistent chemical compound that lasts for many years in the environment, particularly in soil, lake and river sediments and in the food chain. Dioxin accumulates in fatty tissue in the bodies of fish, birds and other animals. I am told some military personnel would joke "Only you can prevent a forest" which was a sarcastic spin on the popular US Forestry service firefighting campaign that featured Smokey the Bear.

At retirement in his late 60's Bill had prostate cancer. Like many other veterans of Vietnam, he paid the price of "chemical warfare" due to Agent Orange. He had surgery, and was fine until recently, and is having some trouble again, taking two Chemo pills daily to control its growth. Still he looks fit and his recall of events years ago includes a lot of detail. Bill credits health and mental awareness to being active. You can tell by sitting with him, even now at the age of 89, that he has led a physically active life. During the war, the C rations they had in the field always had four cigarettes in them. Bill didn't smoke, because his Dad had died of lung cancer. You can't be a good athlete and smoke, stuck out in Bill's mind. So, he would trade his cigarettes for the candy bars.

"The chocolate bars were so hard they would break your teeth," said Bill. "And I wonder what they did to your innards.

C-rations were good hot or cold, but whoever said that didn't eat them."

He always prided himself in being in good shape and said the Army keeps you active. I've learned from correspondence with young men currently in basic training, that, the army hasn't changed in that regard,. Always a runner or a biker, he now has to take caution being outdoors with sun exposure due to skin cancer.

Bill and I stood shaking hands and laughed at the fact we are the same height, build and size despite our separate paths. I commented on how sharp his recall was of experiences during wars and training. We talked about the benefits of being a life-long runner, especially the ability of running to boost brain power. We both agreed that, as neuroscientists have found, running stimulates the brain to have an impact on mental ability. As he stood talking to me, I thought, *how can someone who has gone through years of war, prostate cancer, skin cancer and heart bypass surgery be so sharp with such a great sense of humor at the age of 89.*

OPERATION RUMINATION

I PERSONALLY AM CONVINCED THAT RUNNING CAN strengthen brain cells, recall and other cognitive tasks. I am convinced moving forward that aerobic exercise and running can slow the deterioration of mental ability that happens with old age. I have personally witnessed example after example, including Bill, in the formulation of my thoughts. Wishful thinking I'm told by others. However, in real life, I have witnessed that exercise can be healthy for brain function no matter the age. Is it possible that fresh brain cells could be grown with repetitive healthy exercise? No excuses, just positive energy and exercise. Moving forward. I personally think it brings clarity and empowerment. I feel empowered after a long vigorous run.

I sat there listening to Bill recall details, and thought there is no question the connection between physical exercise and cognitive skills at any age especially in "old age" like Bill "Old Man" Alverson. When reaching the point that running is a "relaxing" process, the answers seem to become obvious, the activity happy and exhilarating and the imagination is nourished. Is it possible his efflorescence of memory was enhanced by a lifetime of physical exercise and activity? It caused me to believe, that despite life circumstances, running and vigorous exercise was the real-life prescription for depression as I had learned long ago. I was renewed and inspired in our conversation that I was on the right track.

Bill served a little over 30 years on active duty. When he got out, he worked for a short time for a credit bureau, then went to work for a friend that sold Piper airplanes in Boise, Idaho. He was selling airplanes in his sixties and doing quite well! The problem was, when Jimmy Carter became president, and interest rates went through the roof, selling airplanes became quite difficult. He ended up in Olympia, Washington driving a school bus and involved in the district maintenance. When kids would swear on the bus, "Old Man Bill" made them walk. This "old" military man got their attention. It rains a lot in Washington state. A few times kicked off the bus, and they learned who was in charge. The second lieutenant turned Thieu Ta, then full colonel, with a lifetime of experience and service could command a busload of teenagers.

As I left my conversation with Bill and stepped out on the porch, it was a gorgeous summer day. I walked to my car, munching on a brownie he gave me to take along. I sat down in the car and looked up. Bill had stepped out on the porch, standing next to the American flag, flapping in the breeze against the blue sky and fluffy white clouds. He straightened his back and I could see the "military" in him, as I imagined him as a young man risking his life as a GI in Korea. I slowly back out the driveway and reach the road. As I turn to leave, standing straight and tall he raises his right hand and gives me a crisp salute. I look down at my arms holding the steering wheel and I have goosebumps. I thought, when it comes to service for one's country, my opportunity to talk to those who have served is a personal blessing for me. A learning experience. Serving others and self sacrifice, all while seeing both purpose and humor in this life we live.

I thought ... leadership lessons learned.

The typewriter he would thank
As his means to get out of a tank
He sang acapella
A handsome fella
A crooning American Yank!

Sergeant Sidney J Helder
United States Army Europe (USAREUR)
Director ESCO Choraleers

Chapter Ten

The Singing Soldier

THE FILM FLICKERS ON THE SCREEN and Sidney Helder, a young man already with a flair for entertainment is where he wanted to be. The cinema was the place to be on a Saturday night in the 1940s and 1950s. For a little bit of pocket change, friends could take the bus downtown to be entertained at the movie theatre.

It was a former opera house built in the 1800s and as most cinemas of its day was ornate and unique. Many cinema theatres back then did not have cup holders but instead ashtrays and heavy curtains. Now dinosaurs of days gone by, it was known as the Foto News, and, in his town, would open in 1944, the place to be on a Saturday night. Folks would line up to watch the news, cartoons and a feature film. In the pre-television and internet era, people saw the news every week in their neighborhood movie theaters. Newsreels were shown before every feature film, with a few cartoons thrown in for added entertainment value.

Breaking news was supplied by radio or the daily newspaper. But neither one of those sources provided the intrigue of a moving picture. Newsreels were played prior to the main feature and were the only way most people first saw actual film footage of news.

"It's how we saw the news from the European, Asia-Pacific and North Africa fronts during World War II," says Sid.

One of the most dramatic newsreel stories was the Hindenburg explosion May 6, 1937. Newsreels had photographers in New Jersey at the time as well as recorded eyewitness radio reports.

President Roosevelt understood the potential impact of moving pictures and established the Office of War Information (OWI) by Executive Order 9182 on June 13, 1942. The silver screen would be used to make the motion picture an indispensable tool for morale, communication and the rallying point for a democracy that had many serving overseas. By the late 1940s television news would already begin to supplant the newsreel, and, by the late 1950s, television was a ubiquitous in home newsource for how people viewed news events. But for a period of time, the cinema was how we visualized history in the making.

At the time Sid's brother Diemer was in the Navy during World War II. He was ready to be shipped to the Pacific theatre when VJ day came along ending the war. His sister was dating someone in the Navy influencing Sid Helder to serve as well. During High school he joined the Naval reserve; it required training once a week locally and 2 weeks of the year advance training at the Great Lakes Naval Center in Illinois. He graduated from high school in 1950, and, by 1952, he and his friends would become active duty as the Korean conflict ramped up.

They didn't think much of it. Sid said, "It seemed like everyone was going into the service. It was the thing you do."

In 1952 Sid headed to basic training or Navy boot camp and he said it was what he expected. "Rigid" as he put it. What he did not anticipate, however, was to fail the physical examination due to asthma. On January 2 of 1953, he received a letter from the Commandant of the Ninth Naval District of the Great Lakes Headquarters, transferring him to "suspended status." It was a physical disqualification and suspension until he would

Sid Helder

receive an honorable discharge. He was to go back home. He was disappointed and discouraged … all his friends were now gone. His asthma condition was real, as a little child he had almost died. He recalls sitting on his Mom's lap struggling for breath. It was hereditary, his mother too had asthma and had always struggled for breath.

It would be years later that Sidney Helder would be able to claim an honorable discharge from *both* the Navy and the Army. Six months after his discharge from the Navy, by order of the draft board, he was to report to Detroit, Michigan for a physical to enter the Army. He told them he had failed his physical with the Navy. Their response was, "You're warm and breathing … you're in the Army now. You passed."

It was off to Fort Knox for 16 weeks of basic training in the 3rd armored division. The first night of basic training Sid experienced an asthma attack. Reporting to sick bay the next morning he was checked out by the doctor. He was fine and *never* had an asthma attack again from that day forward.

I asked Sid, "What was it? The calisthenics? The running? A miracle?"

"They scared it out of me," he said.

His previous military experience in the Navy gave him the rank of an E-2 training platoon sergeant. Now freed from the effects of asthma he had three hash marks on his sleeve and would call the cadence for 15 to 20-minute forced marches when his company messed up with an infraction. It was summer and it was hot. They stayed active to the point it was tough to keep your pants up as you trimmed down to a lean and trim physique.

With the Korean War in progress, Sid and others had the thought in the back of their mind they would be sent to Korea. Taking a train to Camp Kilmer in New Jersey, it gave him the opportunity to visit both New York City and Washington DC. But there was anxiety after basic training, the Korean war was on the minds and radar of those facing the next step in their service.

When he had taken armored training, he thought it would be "cool to drive big tanks." He quickly changed his mind about wanting to be in the armored division operating a tank. There was a blind spot while seated inside the turret of a tank. He saw how a foot soldier could sneak up behind a tank and strategically place a hand grenade on the engine. "You would be a sitting duck," says Sid. In addition, they were shown the armor-piercing shells that could be fired at them. The shells would burrow into the tank, creating white-hot metal as they breached the tank. "It would be nice driving tanks, but, after seeing that, I thought get me out of here," he said. Helder didn't want to be a sitting target inside a tank turret, and his desire to operate a tank quickly waned.

Instead of orders to Korea he received orders to go to Europe. "I can type," says Sid. "I didn't do well typing in high school and had wasted my time, because I was distracted by the cute typing teacher," he said. He got a second chance. Sent to typing school he ended up as adjutant to Chief Warrant officer Meade typing orders and correspondence. He wanted out of the armored division. "I don't like tanks and I'm out of the tanks!" said Sid with a smile on his face.

He was also able to enlist an additional skill. Singing.

Prior to entering the military, he and three other high school friends had formed a quartet called the Grand Rapids Christian High Quartet. After high school they became "The Extension Chords." The Chords got their name early on, while practicing for a contest in a corner of a room so dark that they couldn't read the music. Someone found an extension cord, and it wasn't long before they turned the name of the group into a play on words.

The Army decided in the 1950s that culture and entertainment would be important to the morale, welfare and recreation of US Soldiers stationed in Europe as an occupying force. Even

First place Singing Platoon USAREUR finals November 1954. Sid Helder (right) receives trophy

with the Korean War raging, the Truman administration and Department of Defense placed a high priority on the post-World War II Europe presence of American forces.

Sidney Helder was stationed in Germany in a little town called Hanau, east of Frankfort at an Army base near the Iron Curtain. Many Americans would serve in the 50s along the Iron Curtain from the port town of Bremerhaven south to Frankfort. Soon his entire outfit was transferred to Orleans, France and Maison Fort. They were Special Services Division United States Army Europe (USAREUR) Communications Zone or

"Com Z." One of the benefits of this deployment was a roughly 134-kilometer drive (83 miles) from Orleans to Paris. This made a weekend trip to Paris feasible from time to time. Sid's friend, Stuart, had told him, when you get to Paris you have to go to Frank's American Bar for sandwiches and a beer. They got to know Frank and even though it was in a "seedy" part of town, it was a little bit of Americana and home in faraway Europe.

He soon would have the opportunity to see much of France as the conductor for the United States Army Europe champion ESCO (Engineer Supply Control Office) Choraleers "Singing Platoon" and "Battalion Level Chorus." Noted for their harmonious singing prowess they, entertained and lifted spirits and were recognized with awards in the process.

USAREUR 1954 Singing Platoon Champions,
Director Sid Helder

Singing Christmas Carols Christmas Eve 1954 Orleans
France by the Joan of Arc statue

Sid had applied *both* his typing and singing skills in service to his country. He received an honorable discharge and headed back to the States in the spring of 1955 to begin his civilian life. Yes Sid Helder, the singing soldier, had received an honorable discharge from both the Navy and the Army.

It was time to dive into the family business, and his Dad was glad he was back to help him run the printing business. On November 27, 1959 he married Jeannie Betten, and they raised a family of five kids together. *(Authors note: We shared a good laugh. November 27, 1959 was the day I was born).*

"Typing skills never came in handy," said Sid laughing.

Sid and "The Extension Chords" had won the Barbershop Michigan district state contest in 1952 before they went their separate ways to serve in the military. They were back together again after 1955 and went on to compete internationally.

Sid looks at me with a grin and says, "In Grand Rapids we were the 4th chapter of the national group SPEBSQSA."

"What?" I said. "That acronym just popped out of your head, and not very memorable."

"The Society for the Preservation and Encouragement of BarberShop Quartet Singing in America," he proudly recites. That's a mouthful. As he digs through a box of memorabilia, it is easy to see how music was a big part of his life, from the Extension Chords performing in *The Music Man* at the Civic theatre, to his work as conductor for the Holland Windmill chorus. A box of printed programs and pictures, recollections of days gone by, including singing with the Grand Rapids Great Lakes chorus and numerous church choirs. It made me think that a conductor has the front row seat to a collaborative adventure. Long after the sounds have drifted away and everyone has gone home, the pictures and programs document the adventures as a score for our memories.

Now years later we flip through photos, old programs, letters and newspaper articles together. I listen to the music of the Extension Chords, and pick out the fluid pitch perfect tones of Sid Helder's tenor voice.

The Extension Chords left to right Sid Helder, Cal Verduin, Don Hall, Don Lucas

I see how the box of memories unpacked and the questions jogged his memory, how the music and memories are now words of his story. As said by French poet and novelist Victor Hugo of *Les Miserables* fame, "Music expresses that which cannot be put into words and that which cannot remain silent."

It's important to stay active and keep the faith says Sid Helder. He has been tested and experienced times of doubt like all of us. He, like I, had a friend die young at the age of 42. Don Hall, the bass singer of the quartet, died suddenly at the age of 42. After a sudden attack he had been revived but died on the operating table. Sid also lost his wife Jeannie 18 years ago. We talk about those events in our lives and their impact. You want the world to slow down. There is anger and disbelief, a range of emotions as you deal with your grief.

Myke Lucas later joined "The Extension Chords" as their bass singer and the "Chords" have entertained over seven decades. As we sit and talk over pie and coffee, I can see my questions bring back a flood of memories. Later that day

I look up the song *That Old Gang of Mine* and smile as the lyrics seem so fitting for Sid Helder at this point in his life.

> *I've got a longing way down in my heart*
> *For that old gang that has drifted apart*
> *They were the best pals that I ever had*
> *I never thought that I'd want them so bad*
> *Gee but I'd give the world to see*
> *That old gang of mine*
>
> *But the war is all over and last night as I stood.*
> *On the same corner back in that old*
> *neighborhood*
> *I couldn't help brushing a tear from my eye*
> *For I knew not a face in the crowds that went by*
> *Gone forever are the pals that I love*
> *There isn't a trace or a sign*
> *Of that regular honest to goodness old bunch*
> *That I call that old gang of mine*

In addition to entertaining audiences with songs like *I'll take you home again Kathleen, My Wild Irish Rose* and *Sweet Adeline,* their fame grew when they signed a contract to sing for Archway Cookies. Archway cookies began in 1936, baking soft oatmeal cookies and doughnuts in a garage in Battle Creek, Michigan. With baking ingredients in short supply during World War II, the company concentrated exclusively on baking cookies. Archway is best known for its variations of oatmeal cookies. Sid and "The Extension Chords" recorded jingles for radio and TV:

> *"Dear old girl, your cookies just don't taste*
> *the same ... Dear old girl, it's Archway sets my*
> *heart aflame"*

The Barbershop genre came into being in the 1800s, and to while away the hours on his feet, the barber would start crooning a tune. Patrons added their harmonies. What about the colorful and flashy patterned jackets and vests synonymous with quartets? It started with vaudeville. While other acts backstage set up, Barbershop quartets entertained the crowd in front of the curtain. In order to be seen by those in the "cheap seats" or "nose bleed seats," they donned flamboyant costumes.

The Extension Chords garnered a lot of attention when they did the Archway cookie gig. I look at a Barbershop record album from the 60s and realize they were good. The back of the record album says, "In 1966 a quartet known as The Extension Chords made several singing commercials for a food advertiser. Sales went up, which was hopefully expected, but quite unexpected was response in the form of letters, wires and phone calls asking the identity of the quartet. TV and radio announcers coast to coast dubbed them the mystery group. Their style is no mystery however, it was perfected singing for wakes, weddings and just for the pure pleasure of making beautiful sounds."

Sid Helder never drove a tank through a battle-scarred landscape. He never had to beat asthma again for a doctor in sick bay. He never got to serve in the Navy as he had intended. He served his country behind a typewriter and with his vocal chords. You never know where life may lead you, but Sid Helder, the singing soldier, served his community with the printed word his entire life, and he did it with a song in his heart and on his lips.

OPERATION RUMINATION

I ruminate on how we all go through uncertainties, disappointments and struggles in our lives. It's not whether we have them, but how we deal with them. I've realized a lot of the older veterans have a very real and distinctive sense of humor. And whether or not you can "carry a tune," a song on your heart or your lips can carry you through.

I noticed research done by the University of Frankfurt, interestingly enough a short distance from Hanau, Germany where Sid Helder had served. They reported research that singing boosts the immune system. They tested the blood samples of choir members participating after an hour-long rehearsal to those who were passively listening and found differences.

Maybe it's because singing is known to release endorphins, the feel-good brain chemical that I experience when running or exercising. Maybe, just maybe, singing a song can reduce the levels of the stress hormone cortisol in our blood stream.

If you think about it, improved blood circulation and oxygen affects the brain in a positive way *and* just may increase your circle of friends. It certainly will influence them. I believe that was the case for Sidney Helder, the singing soldier, and I'm glad to call him a friend in my circle.

Our lives are influenced and affected
By those who as leaders are selected
She answered the call
And she stood tall
A true leader who is respected.

Colonel Jill Morgenthaler
US Army
Battalion Commander in the 88th Regional
Support Command Division
Brigade Commander 84th Division

Chapter Eleven

Fake it until You Make it

T HAD BEEN A LONG WEEK, I WAS ON the road facing a 45-minute commute to work that morning. I was tired of the traffic reports, the gloomy weather forecast and the dreary news stories on the radio. I really didn't feel like going to work that day, my impetus for timeliness was lacking and liquid motivation in the form of coffee had cooled and didn't taste well anyhow. I reach for my phone and decide a good podcast could remedy my en route doldrums because coffee isn't going to cut it.

I settle on a Ted Talk entitled "Fake it until you make it" and a public radio 'Moth Radio Hour' podcast entitled 'Hope and Glory.' I engage the bluetooth in my car and chuckle to myself thinking *I could certainly use a little hope this morning and glory is optional but I'm good with it if the occasion arises.*

The first speaker in the Ted Talk is Colonel Jill Morgenthaler. "Hooah!" She captures my attention as I roll down the road and I "Hooah" myself as she explains to her audience that a "Hooah" response means, "I got it, I'm with you." Jill would later explain to me in conversation, that when she steps on stage and "Hooahs," the audience it is met initially with 98% of the crowd responding with giggles and inquisitive faces. She remedies the situation as she engages her audience. Soon the audience responds with a confident "Hooah!"

Now retired from the Army after 30 years of service and a professional speaker after her military years, Jill knows how to lead and get the job done.

When thrown into a leadership role, the learning to lead might take a little time, so she applies the mantra "Fake it until you make it."

First you have to learn from Colonel Jill that "leaders are not born, they are grown," and she explains how on the speaking circuit and in her book *The Courage to take Command: Leadership Lessons from a Military Trailblazer.*

I pull into the parking lot at work inspired by the podcast, the 45-minute commute has flown by and I'm ready to head into work that day and lead the troops. At the very least I was prepared to fake it until I made it and make a difference. Upon arriving to my office, the very *first thing* I did was pen what I hoped to accomplish as I scribble at the top of a legal pad on my desk, "email Jill Morgenthaler."

Colonel Jill Morgenthaler knows something about firsts. She was a trailblazer. She was one of the first women to enter an experimental class for women in the US Army ROTC and train as an equal with men. In 1972, at the tail end of the Vietnam War, the draft had ended and a volunteer army was sought to fill the ranks. It was at that time the Army decided to try an experiment of treating women as equals and leaders in the ranks. Jill joined the ROTC for officer training with a 4-year ROTC scholarship at Penn State University. After ROTC boot camp she went on to be the first woman Battalion Commander in the 88th Regional Support Command Division, the first Brigade Commander in the 84th Division and rose to the rank of Colonel, serving in both peacetime and war. She was also the first woman to run homeland security for the state of Illinois. A recipient of the Bronze Star and the Legion of Merit for her lifelong leadership, she would eventually find herself standing toe to toe with Saddam Hussein in Iraq. In 2004 Colonel Morgenthaler was sent to Baghdad to coordinate all the public affairs and media issues for the multinational forces under the command of General Ricardo Sanchez. Her moment with Hussein occurred during a judicial hearing for crimes against humanity.

I email Colonel Morgenthaler the day I was scheduled to take my APFT (Army Physical Fitness Test) and received a response the same day. We would interview later in the week. She, also true to form, as a person who encourages audiences to identify their abilities because "you are not empty handed," encouraged me in my impending PT test.

The day arrives for our interview and I open my laptop, turn on my recording device, and I set it on the desk near the phone. I put the phone on speaker and dial the number thinking as I dial, and already knowing, her's is a story of resolve, courage, strength and life lessons.

I ask Colonel Morgenthaler where did she get her drive? She had to be driven to achieve what she has in her lifetime.

"Both my parents were involved in competitive sports and academically were honor students. My dad was a Marine ," said Jill. "They put pressure on us four kids to achieve. My parents did not accept excuses. Unlike my siblings I was not naturally an athlete, but the Army turned me into one. And being a woman in the Army, I had to overachieve."

It was in boot camp, just as her Dad had predicted, she found out that being a woman serving in the Army was going to be one of the toughest challenges of her life. She would be called a "bitch, bimbo or butch,"..... "And those were just the B words," Jill says. Many male soldiers were angry to see women coming in as equals and leaders. Every step and turn was filled with obstacles and hurdles, but Morgenthaler's father (a Marine veteran) and mother raised her to believe quitting was not an option.

"In addition to the verbal abuse, I'm sure there were physical challenges in basic training too?" I asked her.

Jill Morgenthaler (far right)

"Basic training was not what I expected," said Jill, "because the strength things were focused on the upper body instead of strong legs. I had strong legs and had to work on the upper body conditioning."

Back then they would make it difficult for the female recruits and she cites an example.

"When we would go out to run they would deliberately put the women in the back of the formations. The people in the back are at a disadvantage, behind from the start and we would lag further behind as we ran up and down the hills. At one point I got mad and stopped in my tracks. I knew they had to turn around and come back. So, I waited until they turned around and I joined the front of the pack."

We laugh together as she tells the story. She would continue to demonstrate to her peers that she was there for the duration and resolved to succeed. I think to myself that *little did they know at that time she was in it for the "long run" and would complete 30 years of military service eventually rising to the rank of Colonel.* She more than "survived." By the end of boot camp, her peers gave her a 100% score of confidence in willingness to follow her into combat as a leader .

I know these "stories" become much more than stories at face value. They are life lessons. Morgenthaler would carry life lessons with her over the "long run," including the strong penchant for fitness, and agrees with me that physical activity is a key to staying young. We laugh as she shares with me that she and her sister on vacation in Ocean City, Maryland had a tarot card reading. This psychic tarot card reader wasn't on her game. At least this day.

"You need to work out more."

"I work out every day," says Jill.

"You've been divorced."

"I've been married 30 years. I want my money back."

THE STING OF DISRESPECT

BACK IN THE 1970s, EVEN THOUGH SHE HAD DONE ALL she had been asked by the Army and passed boot camp with flying colors, the sting of discrimination and abuse because she was a woman did not stop. Jill shares the story on the Moth Radio Hour broadcast called 'Hope and Glory' and you can hear the audience has her full attention. She had mine too, it is an amazing story and lesson that she presents with expert delivery. In the broadcast she details how, just prior to graduation, Commander Captain Mitchell announced that because there were now women at boot camp there should be a "beauty contest."

"I don't want to participate in a beauty contest," said Jill, "I am here to serve as a soldier."

Jill's friend, private Mussgorsky, who she had helped in boot camp, because he couldn't swim, had her back. He quickly raised his hand and volunteered to be in the beauty contest.

"OK fine Mussgorsky, you're in," said Captain Mitchell, "But so are you Morgenthaler, that's an order."

As you listen to her on the Moth, you can feel the emotions ranging from disbelief, laughter, hurt and anger. Jill Morgenthaler felt betrayed by the Army. She had done all that was asked of her and was about to graduate. There would be 5,000 men in the audience and an outdoor stage for the show. She was backstage wearing a blue cotton dress, the only dress she had packed with her when she had left for boot camp weeks before. Mussgorsky was in drag wearing an evening gown he had been loaned by Mitchell's wife.

There were catcalls and obscenities shouted as she stepped on stage, her legs were grabbed and she quickly felt as though she went from being "part of the team to merely body parts." There was no way she was going to dance or sing as she stepped to the front of the stage.

"So I flipped them the bird," said Jill, "I flipped off 5,000 men ."

"I felt so betrayed and had given the Army everything, taught to leave no one behind," says Jill. She exited the stage to head back to the women's barracks. She was quickly surrounded by her squad of men who surrounded her saying,

"We told Captain Mitchell, don't put Morgenthaler on stage, sir, you don't know what she will do!"

They were soon joined by Mussgorsky still in his evening gown who exclaimed, "They crowned me Miss Foxhole 1975."

As hard as it was, it taught her never to leave anyone behind. She had pioneered a pathway for future female recruits. There never was a Miss Foxhole 1976 or future contests from that point.

Morgenthaler was mastering a can-do attitude that would stick with her for life. "The Army slowly became more accepting of women, and their opinions and knowledge started to matter to our superiors," she says.

It wasn't easy. As a second lieutenant in 1997 at the DMZ in Korea she had to prove herself as an officer to those she commanded. At that time, because of the volunteer enlistment, there were a lot of men who were illiterate, uneducated or troubled. They weren't very accepting of a female officer. They were not going to listen to a woman.

"One of my advantages was my unit was comprised of primarily military smart soldiers. We were a military intelligence unit engaged in electronic warfare, and they were professionals.

I also lucked out that my commanders wanted me to succeed," she said. They bought into her vision as a leader, that they were there to "save lives and bring freedoms."

Even today as Army retired, she brings that motivational message in her presentations, using the acronym "MAKE" in her speeches.

The letter **M. Me**. It's about your vision. Jill recommends your vision be in 140 characters or less which makes a lot of sense in this Twitter age. Her vision and motivation was to "save lives and bring freedoms." It's about something bigger than yourself. Her motivation and vision got her team to rally around her.

The letter **A. Abilities**. You are not empty handed. You possess abilities.

The letter **K. Know** your people. A leader gets to know the strengths of an individual and puts them to use.

The letter **E. Emulate**. Emulate those that you respect. For her an important influence was her Dad. Jill Morgenthaler's dad was an influential Marine and well respected. She knew that because she heard it. Jill's father passed away at the age of 63 and never got the chance to see her make the rank of colonel, but his influence lives on. She would hear of how people liked and respected her father and that he was "funny." In her service as an officer, she got the opportunity to hear people talking about her around the corner, and, when she would hear "she is kind and funny" it was a reflection on the influence her dad had on her development.

"When I would hear people say 'she is kind and funny' I thought ... Oh, I did it," says Jill.

I said to her, "E for emulate works in the reverse too." I know people in their 60s and older that I look at and think *I don't want to be like them when I get to that age*. She agrees and recalls a difficult major and general she had to deal with in Iraq. She calls them "Major Hulk or General Miserable." I chalk it up to the old adage that 'we can learn from the mistakes of others.' But those that demonstrate good leadership make a lifelong estimable mark on their understudy often without direct intention. Jill proceeds to wrap up that portion of our conversation with the consummate observation from someone who would know something about the subject:

> "The key to leadership is showing respect before asking for respect."

> -Jill Morgenthaler

I ask Jill what is it about the selfless service I have seen in the veterans I have spent time with this year? I have questioned myself seeking answers. Is their sense of service innate or is it created or taught? She pauses and answers, "It is cultivated by family, community and the military training to do something bigger than they are." She says she has passed that value on to her kids when they, for example, on Thanksgiving day deliver meals to shut ins.

"It is a taught value to do something bigger than who they are," she says. "It is a value. And teamwork is the best way to teach selfless service."

She recalls, during a military exercise, a finger pointed at her and being told 'you are dead, someone else has to step in.'

"We are replaceable Morgenthaler."

"You are not the only one," she reminds me. "There is continuity and no arrogance or the military would never succeed."

WHEN TRAINING KICKS IN

THE REALITY IS, PEOPLE ARE PUT INTO LEADERSHIP POSItions every day, in business without the leadership training. It's the cart before the horse kind of thing. Without training you are making it up as you go. With training, in a difficult situation, the training received hopefully kicks in. I have been in difficult situations before as a leader, however, I have never been shot at ... at least not that I know of. It caused me to ruminate on courage and handling fear, not truly knowing how I would react until tested.

"Whether under fire in Bosnia or the bombing attacks we went through in 2004 in Iraq, your training kicks in," says Morgenthaler. "When caught in the crossfire your training comes first, fear is something you deal with later," she said.

Caught in the crossfire in Iraq she recalls jumping out of the Humvee on the ground and instantly "locked and loaded" with 9mm pistol in hand, later wondering *how did it get there?* The training kicks in. "Even though the 9mm is no match for the M16," she says laughing.

Colonel Morgenthaler in Iraq

She recalls an ugly scene in Bosnia in 1997 that could have easily gotten out of control. She and a general, without bodyguards, were surrounded by an angry mob with sticks and stones. Her training kicked in. She identified the mob leader. "If you don't stop now I'm shooting *you* first," she says. It worked. He dispersed the mob.

"But fake it until you make it … doesn't apply to all professions right? Like an airline pilot or doctor?" I said tongue in cheek.

"What I'm saying is, people get good at their job and one day the boss says 'you're in charge'," says Jill. "Without training you are thrown in as a leader and you have to fake it until you make it."

Morgenthaler's training and resolve kicked in when she had a face-to-face confrontation with deposed Iraqi despot Saddam Hussein. On December 13, 2003, US soldiers found Saddam Hussein hiding in a six-to-eight-foot-deep hole, nine miles outside his hometown of Tikrit after living months on the run. Colonel Morgenthaler was sent to Baghdad to coordinate all the public affairs and media issues for the multinational forces under the command of General Ricardo Sanchez. Her job was to get the coalition and international media into the courtroom hearing. In a tiny courtroom in Baghdad, Hussein was scheduled for his first judicial hearing for crimes against humanity. Jill Morgenthaler was stationed outside the courtroom as she waited for events to unfold inside.

Flipping from coward to tyrant, the hearing was contentious as Hussein, wearing a suit and shackled in chains, was arrogant and self-righteous.

"It blows my mind I got to meet one of the most famous evil men in the 21st century," says Jill.

After the hearing, Hussein was escorted from the courtroom. He took notice of Morgenthaler standing against the wall. The US Army Colonel and Saddam Hussein were less than three feet apart. "Hussein stopped and started to check me out from head to toe," recalls Morgenthaler. "I felt like I was being undressed by his eyes, like I was some blonde bimbo to him."

The State department had asked her to wear civilian clothes, because they were actively downplaying the role of the US military, and starting the transition to the Iraqi government. "When Saddam Hussein saw me, he just saw a blonde woman in a blouse and a skirt," says Jill Morgenthaler. "He had no idea I was a colonel. His look was like 'what are you doing here Bimbo?' I thought to myself *you don't stare at me that way.* I stared right back, using all my nonverbal skills to telegraph to him, 'yeah dude you have no idea I'm a colonel in the US Army.' He's checking me out and I think *I am looking at a dirty old man.* All of a sudden, he wasn't this evil monster, he was just a dirty, pathetic old man who was going back to the jail when we are done with him. I looked him in the face and it was bring it on."

The dictator had met his match in Jill Morgenthaler. In the early 1980s, Saddam involved his country in an eight-year war with Iran, which is estimated to have taken more than a million lives on both sides. He is alleged to have used nerve agents and mustard gas on Iranian soldiers as well as chemical weapons on Iraq's own Kurdish population in northern Iraq in 1988. He then invaded Kuwait in 1990.

Little did he know that in a hallway in Baghdad he would lose a stare-down with a woman who stood her ground. Jill Morgenthaler, as taught by her dad, wasn't faking anything. She had made it **her way**, and did it with a lifetime of lessons in leadership that now benefit us all.

OPERATION RUMINATION

I WANT SOMETHING TO RUMINATE ON, AND I KNOW I'M talking to the right person in Jill Morgenthaler. I wind up and fire a final question to her, a respected decorated veteran with an amazing history and story. I can't wait until Hollywood decides to develop a screenplay for a movie about her story. With a background of years of military leadership, I ask Colonel

Morgenthaler for personal advice I can take with me now approaching the age of 60.

"I believe we are meant to reinvent ourselves many times throughout our lives and especially during our 50s and 60s," she said.

Jill had to reinvent herself when she was in charge of Homeland Security for the State of Illinois and her boss, former Governor Rod Blagojevich went to prison. Blagojevich has been serving time in a federal prison in Colorado since March 2012 on a 14-year sentence. He was impeached and then convicted of numerous corruption charges in 2011, including allegations that he tried to sell, trade and solicit money for President Barack Obama's old Senate seat after Obama won the presidency.

"My boss went to prison and I couldn't get a job interview," said Jill. "What I did get is time to write my book and speaking gigs, which is now a full-time job and I'm loving it. I was so glad I was forced to reinvent myself again."

She explains to me that, when she wrote her book, all of a sudden her life made sense to her. "It was so disjointed until I put it together and looked at the themes and realized ... *Oh that's why I had to go through that.*"

I personally have seen people flounder trying to move forward. They have dreams, but that is where it stays, in the dream stockpile. The primary annoyance, for me personally, is people with a penchant for excuses and those who have transitioned to a state of apathy. I guess that's why Jill Morgenthaler's story resonated with me. Colonel Morgenthaler teaches us that you set goals, figure it out, and then take the final important step ... YOU DO IT! I had that with my first book. I took the advice of noted author Anne Lamott to heart. She answered the question I have often been asked, "How do you write a book?" Her answer was ... you park your rear end in a chair and you write it. End of story. Jill says to me that in her consulting, when people say my dream is such and such, she says take a class. Do something. Move forward. "The military was always educating us," says Jill.

I thank Colonel Jill Morgenthaler for her service. She is still serving. Regardless of whether we have it figured out or are floundering, she is an inspiration, and her story helps all of us, young and old, male or female, if our heart is in the right place, to 'fake it … until we make it' and make a difference for us all.

He softened the harshness of war with sweets
Each day for the kids he had treats
The rations were handy
He gave them all candy
And a smile for all that he meets.

Chapter Twelve

Run the Mile You're in

FOR SOMEONE WHO HAD NEVER BEEN any place else but Michigan, the change of scenery for 18-year-old Bill Hardiman happened swiftly and almost matter of fact. Drafted and sent to 6 months of basic training in San Antonio, Texas in 1967, he was now told to "come to attention and to step forward."

"Private Hardiman, Southeast Asia."

With a salute that is all that was said. In short order he was on a boat for Vietnam. It was Easter 1967 when he left, and he recalls people dressed for Easter going to church. "That's where I wanted to be" he said. Instead, he would travel to southeast Asia to serve as a medic for a line battery artillery unit in Vietnam.

Bill and I settle into our booth at a restaurant to share a meal and conversation. About to dig into his plate of salad and salmon, Bill pauses and puts his fork down. He remembers the day he arrived at the Chu Lai Base Quang Nam Province in Vietnam. He was one of six in a tent with other medics, each had been there for differing amounts of time in their tenure. For young "Doc" Hardiman he had not yet had the experiences the other medics had shared, and his introduction was to be explosive.

The Vietcong would shell bases from a position not far away then attempt to escape unscathed. A sudden mortar attack was not unusual and served as Bill's introduction to life in Vietnam as shells rained down on the base.

"Hit the deck!" Someone yelled.

Hardiman, who just moments before had been listening to the other medics and trying to figure out what he was doing there, instinctively complied with the warning. Falling to the ground, he hit the deck hard.

"I was so afraid. I was trying to get as low as I could get. There was nowhere to go. I felt as though I wanted to dig my fingers in the ground, clawing the ground out of fear," said Bill.

He looked through the curtains of the tent as the ground shook and thought to himself, *I just got here ... is it always this way?* Far removed from what must have been a terrifying introduction to life in Vietnam, he now chuckles over lunch and says, "It looked like the 4th of July." The Vietcong shelling had struck paydirt. They had hit the ammo dump. For Bill it was a baptism by fire. Howitzer shells and other munitions in an ammunition storage dump are inherently dangerous in themselves. But when an ammo dump is hit by incoming VietCong or "VC" shells, the results are dramatic, incendiary, explosive and deadly.

Shell-shocked and on the ground everything changed in a moment. Someone ran past the tent yelling "Medic!" Instinctively the other medics jumped to their feet, grabbed their bags and ran out of the tent. Bill got up and ran too. His determination to run out like the others and seek someone to help was a realization that, doing his job was greater than the fear. "Courage is not the absence of fear," says Bill, "it is the experience of fear but overcoming it to do one's job and fulfill one's purpose."

Bill started running. He knew why he was running and where he was running. He was running to help someone and fulfill his purpose there. He ran to the perimeter "looking for someone to help." The perimeter is a dangerous place as enemy snipers lurked outside the base, looking for human targets. At that moment, a startled soldier in a fox hole yelled at him, "What are you doing?

Get in here!" Bill dove into the foxhole, ending his introduction to his new surroundings at Chu Lai.

Basic training as a medic had taught him how to be very good at making beds, Bill said with a chuckle. Serving as a medic, when he first arrived in Vietnam, they offered him a firearm. He refused because he was a conscientious objector. However, after some months, he realized he was always trying to figure out how he would protect himself or patients in his care if they were attacked and soldiers around him were hit. That's when he realized he believed it was right, in his conscience, to protect himself and others and accepted a side arm. He was young and trying to figure it out, as an 18-year-old in a foreign and dangerous country; there must have been a host of conflicting and contradictory thoughts and emotions. I had always pictured medics in previous wars wearing a bright red cross on their helmets and not carrying weapons. Not the case. Vietnam's jungles and ambushes made carrying a gun necessary. Medics would wear sidearms. A .45 caliber semi-automatic M1911A1 gun was issued and worn by the medics.

FOGGY RECOLLECTIONS

LIFE IS ABOUT EXPERIENCES AND RELATIONSHIPS. THEY stay with you even after the fog of years and time. I sat at lunch with Bill as he recalled his experiences in Vietnam and I thought, *You never realize how thick your fog is until it lifts.* He does remember very clearly the road to a village and the gate at the perimeter where the kids would gather for candy. Bill collected candy from other soldiers sent from home and distributed it at the gate to the kids, clamoring for a treat in the midst of a war-torn environment. He passed out boxes of candy every month and they never ran out. "Take it Doc," the other soldiers would say.

"Same time everyday" says Bill, "but the crowds would get bigger" he says with a smile.

His practice caused and organized other soldiers to also "adopt" kids. It was a sense those children didn't choose to be born and live in that environment. I focus on a picture of Bill and a young

Bill Hardiman

South Vietnamese girl who brought her little brother for help. He had been hit by white phosphorous. Known in Vietnam as "Willie Pete" and similar to napalm, the chemical substance is used in shells and grenades, igniting spontaneously to produce an intense heat. Used to light up enemy positions, white phosphorous is also effective when used to firebomb opposing forces, causing severe chemical burns and melted skin. This boy was injured on his face and forehead, and Bill had helped clean and care for his wounds.

He remembers an officer was skeptical and cautious of the practice of "adopting" kids or passing out candy. You better be careful they could be "bombed up" the officer said as word of warning to Bill and the other soldiers. Bill blew it off and thought "I can't live like that. I still want to do it." Bill feels in a war-torn environment they needed someone to love, to help them make life better.

"I'm still doing that years later but on a bigger scale," says Bill. "Not only were we helping those kids, but the *giver* is receiving. It's more blessed to give than to receive."

Bill the medic was called on to serve then just as he has served his entire life. It's not always easy, but you do what you have to do with a purpose. He recalls a visit by a 2nd lieutenant. The lieuten-

Bill "Doc" Hardiman

ant had suffered an eye injury requiring stitches.

"Sew me up, Doc," the lieutenant said.

Reluctant as a new medic and inexperienced he said, "Let me call you a *real* doc."

"No, said the lieutenant, "just sew it up."

Bill remembers breaking the needle in the process, but did what he had to do. He laughs as he recalls later the 2nd lieutenant walking by and with a thumbs up saying, "See, it's healing. Nice job, Doc."

You learned to do things you didn't know you could.

Bill smiles as the memory comes back to him. "You are able to do much more than is imaginable."

As a medic, he may have been trained how to make beds, but instinctively knew his job was to serve others and "rush to it in the name of the Lord. He had something for me to do." That "life lesson" was learned in basic training one day. He and the other re-cruits were resting in the field, weary of sergeants yelling at them. Bill recalls they had been crawling under barbed wire with sore elbows and knees as bullets whizzed above them. One recruit had the nerve to speak up to the drill sergeants, asking why they are always yelling at them. He says the response not only made the barbed wire drills more motivational and tolerable (he attacked the course with renewed vigor) but also became a life lesson he applied to his life.

The sergeant told them, "We're getting you used to instinctively obeying orders. It's orders or it's your life. Your life depends on it."

Bill sipped from his water pushing aside his lunch. "Life is tough," he says. He recalls a young man who didn't listen, a young man who didn't follow orders in handling land mines and witnessing the end result. "Tough situations require perseverance and obedience. I've made my share of mistakes in life. But I've learned to obey. I listen to my heavenly Father and I obey his voice. He has my best in mind and knows what I need."

WELCOME BACK

YEARS LATER WHEN INVITED TO A BALLPARK TO SPEAK TO Vietnam veterans to "welcome them back." he was part of an effort to welcome these men in a way they had been denied in the late 60s and 70s. A large group of Vietnam veterans arrived on their motorcycles wearing leather, an imposing group with a common past. As a Senator, now feeling like a "fish out of water" while wearing a suit and arriving in a car, what he said resonated with the men who had gathered. It connected them despite their various walks of life.

Bill said to them that together they had faced three things. Inside each of those tough leather wearing rough exteriors, was an 18 year old boy. He could see in their eyes the reality was that years later they still all had three things in common.

THEY EXPERIENCED *FEAR*

THEY HAD ALL FACED FEAR.

"I was an 18-year-old kid. What did I know?"

Today we know there are times when a past fear might re-emerge, even though the present situation does not truly warrant the need to be afraid. We hear of some veterans experiencing

PTSD when a situation or their mind prepares them for the worst to happen. The power of emotional memory is a real and complex reality. Today Bill helps those who suffer from this condition through faith-based connections.

I asked Bill how he dealt with the fear of how, at any moment, personal disaster or trauma could strike. He talked of being out in the field and on patrol, wondering if the individual working there would set down their rake and pick up a weapon, if the person shaving him with one simple stroke could cut him. He and everyone in his division were targets ... every day. Danger was all around.

"When you're in a helicopter being shot at you can't move."

I thought about that comment Bill made as I watched a video of life on the base at Chu Lai. He described it as a hill with big guns on it, a perimeter fence with a road to the village and a gate. Danger was all around even if you didn't go outside the perimeter fence. Mortar attacks on the base were frequent, and if you were in the wrong place at the wrong time, there was nothing you could do. I paused the video and read a large sign hanging from a post inside the perimeter on the base. In large red letters, on a dirty, white background, complete with spelling errors, the sign said,

"Danger Helicopters can kill you. Never approach from direct front or rear. Keep down to 5 feet or lower. Approach all planes right middle section door. Stay clear of the chopper's rear! Don't lose your head use it!"

Bill had arrived at Chu Lai, his base, but spent most of his time as the only medic at an artillery line battery at one of the outposts, near Duc Pho with the Americal Division. He recalls watching, with his battery, the plunging jets on their strafing runs. "You would see the tracers before hearing the sound of the jets and the explosions," said Bill. This would be followed by the Huey Cobra attack helicopters strafing the area for "Charlie." The name Charlie, for describing the VC or Vietcong, comes from "Việt Nam Cộng-sản," which just means "Vietnamese Communists." This, in turn, was shortened to just Việt Cộng. From there, "Viet Cong" was further shortened to "VC," which in the NATO phonetic alphabet is pronounced "Victor-Charlie," which gave rise to the further shortened, "Charlie" designation. Once the strafing raids were done, it was time for the artillery battery and infantry to do their work. "Unlike previous wars in our history, this war was an introduction to guerilla warfare for us," said Bill.

In answering my question on fear without hesitation, Bill said, "I turned to the Lord." In addition to his faith, Bill had a practical reoccurring thought that he carried with him wherever he went. He played it over and over again in his mind.

"In ten to fifteen years this will be a distant memory," he said. The repetition of that thought, in addition to his faith, seemed to give him the resolve and the courage to face his fear. Bill then set down his fork, and, with a serious look in his eyes, seemed to make a point with emphasis, looking me in the eyes as he said it.

"Courage is not the absence of fear, it's doing what you have to do despite the presence of fear."

THEY HAD EXPERIENCED *LONELINESS*

THEY WERE LONELY. HE DESCRIBED IT AS PHYSICAL PAIN due to loneliness in a faraway, foreign place. The kind of loneliness that hurts physically. I could see the emotion in his eyes as he talked about "being so lonely, missing his family, missing his country."

As we talked enjoying lunch together, I could see him digging up memories and the emotions he had experienced as a young man far from home.

"My sister would send me popcorn. It was stale."

Pausing from working through his salad, a big smile broke out on his face.

"Yeah but it was good!" he said, tilting his head back in laughter.

I could see we had dug up a simple memory from the recesses of his mind. The thought of something so simple as popcorn many years later, invoked a moment of joy and laughter. A simple gesture that had embedded a lifetime memory was suddenly harvested for our benefit. It caused me to think of the many ways we can make an impact on someone's life with just a simple gesture, smile or word at just the right time.

THEY RETURNED HOME TO A *COLD SHOULDER*

BUT WHEN THEY CAME HOME, THEY WERE NOT WELCOMED by their own country. They were welcomed by their families, but not by their country. Styles had changed, but there was no ticker-tape parade like WWII.

I asked him if he was glad that he served. Without hesitation he said that he was both glad and proud to serve his country. Bill says, "I found out I could do things I didn't think I could do. You are able to do much more than is imaginable."

I asked him if the pardon of draft dodgers by President Jimmy Carter bothered him today. On January 21, 1977 (the year I graduated from high school) President Carter fulfilled a campaign promise, and, on the second day of his presidency, pardoned draft evaders to the Vietnam War. Whatever you did whether right or wrong, pardon meant you were forgiven for it. Bill said to me it does not bother him today. He was drafted to service and he served his country. We learn forgiveness through the many mistakes we all make in life.

OPERATION RUMINATION

As I drive down the road after having lunch with Bill my rumination focuses on the difference between fear and anxiety. We've all experienced anxiety which to a large extent is self-imposed. Some anxiety is warranted while some is not as we enjoy life living in a free environment of choice. Freedom is a gift paid for by the sacrifice of others. Anxiety can be rumination gone wrong, if it is perpetual without resolution. But to truly experience fear, loneliness and rejection, like Bill had, is something I have never experienced. How would I react? How would I deal with facing true fear, true loneliness and rejection?

I ruminate as I think of his story about running outside the medic's tent, not knowing where he was running when the ammo dump had exploded. I thought of a phrase that a running friend had shared with me in the past year, a friend my same age who understands the trials and disappointments of life we all experience. I've run in long-distance races with him.

"Run the mile you're in."

When told to stand at attention, Bill had been ordered to go to an embattled foreign country. Sometimes in life, you do not have control of the position you are in. You do, however, have control over how you will react to it, experience it and the impact you will make on others as you journey through.

You Run the Mile You're in

I listened intently to Bill as we shared our stories of the impact we each experienced while visiting the Vietnam Memorial in Washington DC. In my research, the Vietnam Veteran's Memorial wall lists 1,404 Army medics and 692 Navy Corpsmen who died in the service to their country and are memorialized on that wall.

Bill described the tears he experienced as he stood by the bronze statue called the "three servicemen." In order to portray the major ethnic groups that were represented in the ranks of US combat personnel that served in Vietnam, the statue's three men are purposely identifiable as European American, African American and Latino American. And I recalled the impact that statue had on me when I stood by it. It seemed to me as though the placement purposefully had the three soldiers looking on in tribute to the rows and rows of names imprinted on the wall of the memorial, fallen comrades who died in the service to their country. They stand to remember.

I picture Bill in my mind, standing there alone with them, experiencing tears as he gazed on the three soldiers and recalling what he had seen and experienced in his time serving his country. *Today he stands to remember.* Many of these things he today does not want to talk about, but carries them with him and they ground him in a life of public service. Bill served as mayor of the city of Kentwood, Michigan from 1992-2002. He was elected to the Michigan Senate in November 2002, representing the cities of Grand Rapids, Kentwood and Lowell and the townships of Cascade, Lowell, Vergennes and Grattan. He served in the Michigan Senate until 2010 when he reached term limits. Today, Bill serves as director of the Office of Community and Faith Engagement for the Michigan Department of Health and Human Services with an emphasis on veteran's needs.

Bill and I have a common trait. We both love history. He shared that a historical figure who is a hero to him was William Wilberforce. Mr. Wilberforce reached a point in his life where rumination and reflection on where he had been and where he was going reached a poignant juncture. It changed his life. William Wilberforce won election to Parliament in England in 1780. He began to see his life's purpose as a public one of service, and no other cause was more important to him than the abolition of slavery. Introducing multiple resolutions against slavery, the pathway to abolition was repeatedly blocked by vested interests, parliamentary filibustering, entrenched bigotry, international politics, and political fear. He would not let the issue die, and he was vilified in the process. In his faith he persevered through defeat, debilitating illness and depression. His antislavery efforts finally bore fruit in 1807 when Parliament abolished the slave trade in the British Empire. He then worked to ensure the slave-trade laws were enforced and, finally, that slavery in the British Empire was abolished. William Wilberforce heard three days before he died that the final passage of the emancipation bill was ensured. Historian G.M. Trevelyan says that the results of the perseverance of Wilberforce was, "one of the turning events in the history of the world."

Many years after the death of William Wilberforce, as we end our lunch together, Bill slides out of the booth and concludes our conversation with these thoughts.

"We have to persevere … perseverance," Bill said. "God has given us a purpose. I have to get it done."

With cathode ray tube qualifications
He would fine tune amplifications
With a Kodak instamatic
And recordings pragmatic
He had mastered telecommunications.

Ron "Alphabet" Konyndyk

9th infantry Division Spec 5

MOS 32D20 Fixed Station Technical Controller

Dong Tam My Tho Vietnam

Chapter Thirteen

A Picture is Worth

a Thousand Words

THE NEWSPAPER EDITOR ARTHUR Brisbane is said to have given a speech in March of 1911 where he used the phrase, "Use a picture. It's worth a thousand words." Others have been credited with the phrase, including its consideration as a Chinese proverb. The American short story-writer Eudora Welty is quoted as saying, "A good snapshot keeps a moment from running away."

Many snapshots or pictures taken during the Vietnam War were not taken by professional battlefield photographers, but rather by young men barely out of high school. Kodak instamatic cameras with film cartridges were nothing like today's digital photography. They were, however, pocketable, portable and easy to load. This opened the door for many poignant photographs of real life in a distant war to be sent home. Instead of professionals shooting pictures from the outside looking in, this war, thanks to the Kodak Instamatic photos, were shot from the inside out. Far more portable than the original work of George Eastman in 1888, an instamatic could be placed into a front pocket ,and, if kept dry with a plastic bag, could capture the moments in the field.

The 1960s were the days of small parking lot Fotomat booths that popped up in parking lots in the mid to late 60s. You could drive up to drop off film and pick up your photos or slides the next day. For a soldier in Vietnam, like Ron "Alphabet" Konyndyk, the cartridge could be mailed home for processing. He would also send recordings on tape instead of letters home to Mom and Dad. His former life, now residing in a box, on a shelf in a closet … untouched but not forgotten. Of the 600 slides Ron sent home … 150 remain.

If a picture is worth a thousand words, can a word be worth a thousand meanings? The word that came to mind for me as we rummaged through his photos and recordings was "poignant." They were poignant, because they could evoke emotions when taken off a shelf. Poignant, because they were very personal, very real, from the perspective of one in the moment.

Born the day before D-Day, June 5, 1944, he, like many other soldiers in the Vietnam War, had a father that served during World War II. Ron's Dad had served the US army in Belgium, in Luxembourg, had landed in Le Havre ,France about an hour northeast of Normandy beach, and was in Germany when the war ended. But his Dad did not tell or share his story. Now Ron would live *his* own story in the middle of the Tet Offensive, along the Mekong river about 40 miles southwest of Saigon.

Seeking a glimpse of Ron's story, we sit in the basement as he loads a carousel of old slide pictures into the Kodak Carousel projector. There are boxes of slides in the large Tupperware container he has pulled from the closet. A chain with his dog tags and can opener jangle as I pick them up to read the words imprinted on the surface. There are old army fatigues, a helmet, C-rations and documents. A rejection letter signed by former president Gerald Ford from October of 1967 catches my eye. Ron attempted as a college graduate to enter Air Force officer's school. He was told the class was full and the letter from then Representative Ford said, "with regret we cannot have a more favorable answer due to a long delay in response from the Air Force."

At the time, Gerald Ford was house minority leader in the House of Representatives in Washington. Ford, as minority leader, was a critic of the Johnson administration and questioned whether the White House had a clear plan to bring the war to a successful conclusion. When Ford criticized the plans for progress in Vietnam from the floor of the House, an increasingly frustrated President Johnson accused Ford of "having played too much football without a helmet at the University of Michigan." The press tempered the salty language for which Johnson was notorious, changing comments like, "he's so dumb he can't fart and chew gum at the same time" to "he's so dumb he can't walk and chew gum at the same time." Only a few short months after the date of Ron's letter from Gerald Ford, LBJ, the man who won a landslide of epic proportions in 1964, stepped away from the office he had spent his life pursuing. In late March 1968 Johnson stunned the nation.

"Accordingly, I shall not seek, and I will not accept, the nomination of my party for another term as your president."

President Johnson was highly frustrated by the Vietnam war, and criticism was coming from every corner. It was a tumultuous period in time, and young adults like Ron were drawn into rapidly unfolding and tragic historical events. Young Americans were dying in Vietnam. Only days after Johnson's announcement Dr. Martin Luther King was assassinated, and a couple months later Bobby Kennedy, one of Johnson's critics and opponents for the nomination, was also killed by an assassin's bullet in June of 1968. Gerald Ford himself had dates with destiny a few short years down the road, becoming Vice President in 1973, and eventually the 38th President of the United States in August of 1974 with the resignation of Richard Nixon.

Meanwhile, Ron's destiny for the next couple years was set. His draft number was up. Entrepreneurial in nature, having worked as a realtor and a production controller at Keeler Brass while going to college, his heart sank when he received the letter in the mail that he had been drafted.

"It felt like I had been sentenced to jail for 2 years," Ron said.

Drafted at the age of 23, he would be 25 when he got out. Ron smiles and says he didn't realize until later that the best part of the whole thing was, it would eventually lead him to his wife Mary upon his return from Vietnam.

While the nation roiled in politics, tragedy and turmoil, the start of Ron's journey was a bus ride from Grand Rapids to Detroit

Ron Konyndyk

to be inducted into the Army. On the ride to Detroit, he sat next to a friend who tried to convince him to cross the border to Canada.

Draft dodgers were often college-educated sons of the middle class who could no longer defer induction into the selective service system. I have seen estimates of how many dodged the draft vary wildly from 20,000 to as many as 100,000. In the 60s and 70s Canada was a country that opened its doors to ambitious, young people. During the Vietnam War, the liberal prime minister, Pierre Elliott Trudeau, welcomed American deserters and draft dodgers, declaring that Canada "should be a refuge from militarism." Americans who arrived were generally able to obtain legal immigrant status simply by applying at the border, or even after they entered Canada. The process today is more onerous and secure than it had been during the Vietnam Era. In the 1960s, prospective immigrants could complete their application form at the border, through the mail, from within Canada, or at a consulate. Canada's point system, introduced in 1967, evaluated applicants according to their education and training, occupational demand, occupational skill, age, knowledge of French or English, family connections, and employment potential.

In other words, Ron Konyndyk was a prime candidate to run for the border. Instead, Ron chose to be inducted and take the trip to Fort Knox. I asked him why, and he said his duty was ingrained in him. Serving his country was the right thing to do. In addition, he was counting on his college education to help him out with a better assignment. He never saw his friend again, and said his friend did not make the trip with them to Fort Knox. He assumed he crossed the border into Canada and was pardoned along with the other draft dodgers 10 years later by President Jimmy Carter. Ron's journey didn't take him north, instead it was on to Fort Knox and Fort Monmouth, New Jersey, then on to Vietnam where he Xed the days on his calendar during that tumultuous year.

It all happened so fast. A letter in the mail, a bus ride from Grand Rapids to Detroit, a physical and then a flight to Fort Knox, Kentucky just south of the Indiana border. He was in the Army now. During boot camp that year, Fort Knox experienced one of their coldest winters on record during January and February. Upon arrival to basic training, Of the 180 in his group, Ron was shocked to discover that, after a show of hands, less than half had completed high school. He was one of only four that had completed college. He felt like a "fish out of water" and was so uninterested in the mitigating, self-medication of marijuana, that he then and there re-established his goal in singleness of mind that "he was going to make it home."

Ron's journey took a surprising turn due to a high-vacuum tube in which cathode rays produce a luminous image on a fluorescent screen, used chiefly in televisions and computer terminals. The cathode ray tube.

One day, the captain who was in charge of testing new recruits, entered his barracks at Fort Knox. This in itself was un-usual, but what happened next changed Ron's course in military service. The men at attention heard the captain say,

"Ron K....Ron Kon.....Ron Knen"

Ron knew this was about him. The flustered captain, trying to pronounce his name said, "Hey Alphabet." Ron stepped forward and the captain said, "Come with me." They went to another room where the Captain bought a coke from the pop machine and set it in front of him. The Captain went on to say, that in all the years of testing, they had never had someone draw a better diagram of a cathode ray tube. It was there the captain made his offer. We'll send you to radio school if you sign on for an extra year of service. You'll go to Fort Monmouth, New Jersey instead of Fort Polk, Louisiana "with the other grunts."

Ron said no to signing on for another year, and later wondered if he had made a mistake. As fate would have it, his cathode ray tube diagram must have been impressive, as they still sent him to 8 months of radio school at Fort Monmouth. Little did they know one of the last classes Ron took at Ferris State University, prior to being drafted, was a physical science class requiring diagram of the cathode ray tube. It was still fresh in his mind. Ron attended radio school after all without having to agree to an extra year of service. That's where his luck ran out. One half of the class was assigned to Vietnam, the other half to a tropospheric scatter base in Aviano, Italy, a small, sleepy town located in a non-touristy part of Northern Italy about 45 miles from Venice. Because Ron's last name started with a K and was in the middle of the alphabet, just one person flunking out would shift assignments under the half-and-half proposition. Ron "Alphabet" went to Vietnam.

Ron was stationed at a base called Dong Tam, which ironically means singleness of mind. This was his home for the next year. The Mobile Riverine Force MRF (MRF) comprising the 2nd Brigade, 9th Infantry Division and the US Navy River Assault Squadrons 9 and 11 were established at Dong Tam. By the time Ron arrived, the base occupied 12 square kilometers and included a 500m runway and a loading basin for boats. Ron's focus, his

Ron Konyndyk

personal *cri de coeur* was to make it home. He honestly shared with me that was *the* goal … "to make it home." Not a hero. Not bitter. He "did what I had to do" and the "objective" was to make it home.

At My Tho in the Mekong Delta, the job of the base was to help stem the flow of weapons from Cambodia down the Mekong River. An area of vast agricultural resources, their job was to secure the delta from the communist insurgency. Looking not to displace South Vietnamese residents with the establishment of a base, Army engineers developed an area about eight miles west of the delta town of My Tho. Engineers had dredged river sand and silt into an abandoned rice paddy, to provide a foundation as a base for American soldiers. Engineers raised the height of the area 5 to 8 feet to limit the effects of flooding in the rainy season. The Navy used the area to repair riverine patrol boats or PBR (Power Boat, River) that would run on Detroit diesel engines with power jet drives. The 9th infantry used the base as headquarters for operation in the Mekong Delta.

Keeping a diary, he noted the base was subject to 183 mortar attacks while he was there. He can still hear the sirens, not knowing at times if it was outgoing or incoming shellings. The Vietcong harassed the 9th infantry stationed there with mortar fire. I thought, *it must have felt like there was no place to hide within a confined area, surrounded by water and wetlands with shells falling from the sky.*

After shellings, they cleaned up the debris, loading it on to a truck to take to the "dump" outside the base. We view slides on the old slide projector of curled tin on the barracks and blown out screens, due to the concussion of mortar attack blasts. Ron recalls the force of an attack that hit the ammo dump, the concussion throwing him and his friend into the safety of their bunker.

As we enjoy a breakfast conversation and the aromas within the restaurant sipping on coffee, I can see that even today Ron can recall the "aroma" of the dump. "Stench" is the word he used. Taking an M16, the standard issue automatic assault rifle used by American forces in the cab for the ride, the "dump truck" would be filled with mangled screens, tin and two-by-fours wrecked by the Vietcong harassment shelling. Whether going to the dump or on patrol at night, you could be shot at and not know where it was coming from. Generally, the debris never made it to the dump. South Vietnamese kids and women jumped on the back of the truck en route to the dump, throwing their treasure off the back to be dragged to Grandma who would guard it. One man's junk is another man's treasure sort of thing. By the time they made it to the dump the truck would be empty.

Ron prodded his pancakes with his fork and looked up at me from his breakfast. "It kind of inspired me," he said, "The South Vietnamese were just trying to survive the situation like me."

At Dong Tam, as well as around the world, technology was rapidly changing. Hand held radios and night vision equipment, called starlight scopes, were being used. A starlight scope was a night observation scope that used light reflected from the moon and stars. Looking through a starlight, everything looked green, but you could see at night. Available light is intensified so you can see through the darkness, peering through a binocular-type device. Ron didn't watch the historic moon landing of Armstrong and Aldrin and Apollo 11 that July. He listened to the event step-by-step off the LM (pronounced "Lem") via the tropospheric attenuation. The borderless blue marble photos of earth, taken by Apollo astronauts and the technology being developed to "land a man on the moon and return him safely to the Earth" within the decade, had escalated the pace of technological invention never to look back.

As the crisis in Southeast Asia deepened, communication methods between the United States and South Vietnam remained extremely vulnerable. A single undersea cable linked the Pacific Command in Hawaii with Guam, but this connection did not extend to Southeast Asia. The Army depended upon high-frequency radio, a medium that could be easily jammed. To improve communications, the Army called upon a new technique, known as scatter communications. The method worked by bouncing high-frequency radio beams off the layers of the atmosphere, which reflected them back to earth. One type, tropospheric scatter, bounced signals off water vapor in the troposphere, the lowest atmospheric layer. A second method, ionospheric scatter, bounced the signals off clouds of ionized particles in the ionosphere, the region that begins about thirty miles above the earth's surface. Using special antennas, both methods provided high-quality signals that were less susceptible to jamming than ordinary radio. Scatter communications did not require a line of sight between stations. Tropospheric relay stations could be as much as 400 miles apart, compared to about 40 miles for microwave stations, a decided advantage when operating in hostile territory.

During the Tet offensive the Vietcong targeted many signal sites. Communication was vital. Riverine operations in the Mekong Delta presented yet another set of problems, as the 9th Signal Battalion of the 9th Infantry Division discovered. Here, swamps and heavy jungle made ground combat virtually impossible, and the Viet Cong controlled the few roads in the region. Hence, tactical units conducted operations afloat. While supporting the Mobile Riverine Force, a joint Army-Navy endeavor, they faced the challenges posed by communicating from shipboard.

Ron Konyndyk

While in motion, operators had to constantly rotate their directional antennas to maintain a strong signal with command. On the base, they faced the constant lobbing of shells by the Viet Cong, attempting to do damage to the communications structure, as well as other infrastructure.

I read the job description given Ron under the guise of MILITARY OCCUPATIONAL SPECIALTY CODE (AR 611-201). He "must know" the operating characteristics, capabilities, limitations and use of voice, teletype, facsimile, data video, cable and wireless, VHF, microwave, scatter, satellite, and narrow or wide band systems. The use of the word "must" was repetitive in the job description, leading me to believe that communication is vital in war. Take for example in the Civil War in the mid 1800s, spies (called scouts if they were in military uniform) were important for providing intelligence to the officers. The spies or scouts rode through potential battlefield areas, observing troop movement and talking to townspeople to pick up any information the locals had gleaned as to the plans of the enemy. Now, a little more than 100 years later, communications and information were just as vital to a war effort. The job description, however, had changed markedly in a century, particularly in the jungles of Southeast Asia.

The Kodak carousel vents a hot and musty aroma as it flips through memories long past: pictures of Bell Huey helicopters on the base. Ron talks about being "secured" to communication equipment and being shot at in a helicopter en route to Vung Tau for repairs. While in basic training, the Army was checking with his high school instructors and employers, granting him a secret security clearance. Responsible for communication equipment repair and safe return, they were targets in helicopters en route. When a "secret" piece of equipment ,like a piece of encryption equipment ,left a secured area, it was attached to the person who carried it in a manner which was classified. If Ron or anyone else tried to detach it, an incendiary device would engage to destroy the piece of equipment. Ron said they called it a grenade, but is sure it was not. Fortunately, nobody knew of anyone who had ever set one off to test this theory.

We flip through more slides projected on the screen in his basement. He recalls a sign in the hospital at the base that said, "If you can read this sign your chance of survival is 95%." More slides, more memories. A small refrigerator in the barracks. Beer bought at the PX for 10 cents a can and stored in the fridge. During mortar attacks the price rose to $1.00 a can. Slides from Christmas in 1968, showed Bob Hope and Ann Margret visiting the base.

More slides of soldiers filling sandbags. The "bunker" was simply barrels filled with sand and timbers, covering the distance between the barrels. We view soldiers on the beach. "China Beach and the South China sea," says Ron. We laugh as he recalls soldiers paying South Vietnamese kids one dollar a day to fill sandbags, so they could lay out on the beach. Watching the slides, I comment that it seems all they did was fill sandbags. Ron leans back on the sofa. "We filled a lot of sand bags, always needing more, they would deteriorate" he says.

Slides bring back memories of going months without a shower, "River rats" in the dirty Mekong River. Slides of tanks on the roof of constructed shower houses, where, with the pull of a chain, the water heated by the hot tropical sun afforded an occasional shower.

A slide is projected of Ron in his guard post. Wearing a flak jacket they had perimeter duty once every 10 days. If the Navy out on the river detected trouble it was the job of the 9th infantry to go and root it out.

The screen, now blank, the slide carousel has made a complete circuit. Grainy colorless pictures told the story of days long since passed. We look at the boxes and postage used to mail pictures and tape recordings to his family back home. The small packages sent to the US, Ron could mail them for free. His parents spent 30 cents in postage to send them back.

MISSION ACCOMPLISHED

Ron REMEMBERS THE CHEERING ON THE PLANE THE DAY they left over South Vietnamese air space. They were going home … his goal from the start. They were told "not to wear the uniform" upon returning to the United States but most, himself included, did not have any other clothes to wear. In addition, they would find that in the late 60s clothing styles had dramatically changed.

Landing at the Army processing center in Oakland, California, they found the center personnel were off for the weekend. They were not informed that the plane was scheduled to arrive. There was no cheering, no welcome home. It was Friday of Labor Day weekend 1969, and no one was there to greet them. No food, no physical, no medals, no cheering. Two days with nothing. Finally, on Sunday, a few Army personnel showed up doing a "half job" to process them out. Just the paperwork to get them on their way, the result of one soldier getting a hold of his congressman. Ron doesn't remember the details, other than recalling they were not "happy troops." Finally discharged, after a long and lonely weekend to a San Francisco airport, he remembers them holding the door open for him on a commercial flight to get him back to

Chicago where he could call his parents. Soon his mission, his goal, would be accomplished … he would "make it home."

Today, his Vietnam experience was in a large Tupperware container taken off a closet shelf and sitting on the counter. His life in a box … the past, and he didn't look back. Not bitter, "not a hero," today in his 70s he looks healthy and fit despite the effects of Agent Orange used at the time as a weapon of war for crop destruction and defoliant to expose enemy positions. As we had looked through his slides on that old Kodak Carousel, I could see far beyond the guard position he would take on the perimeter. The "jungle" or vegetation was cleared for line of site well beyond the perimeter.

Agent Orange contained Dioxin and was a toxic chemical herbicide and heavily doused throughout Vietnam during Operation Ranch Hand. Agent Orange is 50 times more concentrated than normal agricultural herbicides. Aerial flights dumped millions of gallons over forest, brush, agricultural areas and jungles defoliating everything. Tanks and trucks were used to spray it along base perimeters to clear the area. Many took the effects of Agent Orange home with them, and Ron was no exception. After a visit to the doctor for a physical at the age of 60, the evidence of highly elevated PSA numbers brought that home to him.

"Cancer is something you deal with," says Ron. "You do what you have to do."

BOOTS ON THE GROUND

RON SAID, "I STILL HAVE MY BOOTS, DO YOU WANT them?"

Suddenly, I realized they were wearing boots in training, not the advanced state of the art running shoes I wear today.

"What?" I said thinking I'm not running in those.

I realized I might have to change my training plan to Plan "B" … as in boots.

This was reinforced by a friend of mine in the locker room

at the Y. Johnny is a veteran who served as a drill sergeant in the 70s and saw me in my Army physical fitness shirt training at the YMCA.

"I would make you wear the boots instead of those things," he says laughing, while pointing at my running shoes. "We didn't have shoes like that back in the 70s."

Ron's boots sit on the counter along with the other memorabilia. We unpack some of the remaining contents of the container together, not knowing what we would find. We debate trying to eat some leftover C rations of Chili Con Carne, but decide against it when we notice the cans are leaking. Mary, Ron's wife, unfolds a brittle and faded, long and folded piece of paper found in the memorabilia. Spread out on the sofa, the 6-foot-long banner is printed in some sort of IBM 1960s computer print, and Ron surmises it was hung in their communication bunker trailer at some point. We slowly together read the words of the banner and break out into laughter when its message sinks in …

> *"Jingle Bells, Mortar shells,*
> *Viet Cong in the grass,*
> *Take your Merry Christmas,*
> *and shove it up your a--"*

OPERATION RUMINATION

I RUN ALONG THE BEACH TO THE BREAKWATER, THEN TO the lighthouse at the end to do my push-ups and sit-ups. My basic training is quite basic this morning. I push myself to complete it and am glad that I do. The sunrise eclipsing the tree line make the water sparkle. A slight breeze causes ripples on the lake as a few fishermen cast their lines into the water. It's peaceful and quiet. We all need moments of peace and quiet in a world that moves at a hectic pace. After running, the quiet moments when you slow down reward you for your effort. You breathe it in, and your mind seems clearer.

Walking on the breakwater, I begin my journey back, ruminating with a clear mind in the process. I reflect on how many of the veterans I've met had just a few *tangible material* possessions from their experience. Many had physical bodily realities, that became evident later in life like Ron's exposure to Agent Orange, or others struggling with PTSD, nightmares or injuries. All veterans brought back a plethora of memories with them. The physical possessions are put on a shelf in a closet somewhere, and, in most cases, forgotten. The memories, if the story is not told, are carried by the veteran but forgotten by others over time. Just like the leaking ration of Chili Con Carne in the box of tangible physical reminders on the shelf, the memories spill out as we dig through Ron's "time capsule" in a Tupperware container. I realize the veterans I had spoken to all brought *something* back with them.

I'm amazed at how many, like Ron, quickly assimilated back into everyday life and closed the door on that chapter in their life, and are now surrounding us in our daily lives. They put the experience on a shelf of a closet, close the door and are there with us, at the grocery store, the mall, at work, at church, on the streets. You wouldn't know what they experienced unless you asked, or they said something.

The word "sonder" comes to mind. The realization that each random passerby is living a life as vivid and complex as your own ... an epic story that continues invisibly around you. I chuckle as I think "sonder" or later you would think they would share their story. Maybe it's up to us to get the story, to ask the right questions, to share those stories. Lessons are waiting to be learned. Some never share their stories and that's OK; it's to be understood and respected. For those that do tell their story, our experience, side-by-side with them, as we live our daily lives, are enriched by their service and their memories.

In the case of Ron "Alphabet" Konyndyk, his box on a shelf was a picture worth more than a thousand words.

An influence in our life provides
The course one ultimately decides
Something stays
Is there always
In great things something abides.

Robert Bowyer

Sergeant US Army

173rd Airborne Brigade

2 tours to Afghanistan Operation Enduring
Freedom

MOS 92 Romeo Parachute rigger 11 Bravo Infantry,
Airborne CIB Combat Infantryman Badge
Active duty 2002-2008 Reserves 321st
Psychological Operations 2009-2017

Chapter Fourteen

In Great Deeds Something Abides

I WALK ALONG THE DOCKS IN THE HARBOR as row on row of white glistening pleasure craft are parked in their slip on a beautiful sunny evening. Millions of dollars of boats are floating on the water in the Muskegon harbor, but one boat stands out from the rest. Not by its size, it's not as long and tall as the others. Not by its color, in stark contrast to the polished white yachts; it is USMC forest green semi-gloss, the basic US army dark olive green. It has hardened armored steel with dual machine guns on the port and an imposing mortar, 60 mm, Mk4 Mod 0 and M60D medium machine gun on the stern dedicated to the men of River Division 593 Iron Butterfly. It is an understatement to say its position and appearance in the harbor is distinct and conspicuous from the rest.

People mill about in light, airy clothing, oxford shirts, shorts and loafers. A wedding party walks by with women in colorful dresses and heels and young men looking uncomfortable in their suits. There he stands on his boat, a PBR Patrol Boat River, wearing olive green and a cap with dark-black sunglasses. A colorful sunlit American flag flaps in the breeze. I greet Sergeant Robert Bowyer and thank him for his service. "Don't thank me," he says, "thank you for paying your taxes." He shakes my hand and welcomes me aboard.

We sit on the Patrol Boat River he is restoring as the "flagship" of his Operation Black Sheep project. A PBR boat in Vietnam was versatile with dual Detroit diesel engines and Jacuzzi jet-powered pump-jet drives, allowing it to move quickly and operate in weed-choked rivers. They were used to stop and search river traffic in areas like the Mekong Delta to disrupt weapon shipments by the "VC" or Viet Cong. They frequently engaged in firefights with enemy combatants, both in boats as well as on the shore.

Robert knows that when veterans go to war and come home, they are different. Sometimes it is for the good; but, often times, things that were once easy become a struggle. They, like Robert, are changed because of the realities of war, and sometimes feel like the general population does not understand them. Service members can be made to feel like the black sheep of the community. It is the goal of Operation Black Sheep to promote a sense of belonging, respect, and brotherhood among veterans and the general public alike. Operation Black Sheep offers a meaningful and engaging experience that recognizes the sacrifices, courage, and valor of all military veterans. It fosters a thorough understanding of the Vietnam Era; including, the political, historical, social, cultural and military aspects of the Vietnam War.

As someone with a keen interest in history, an education and a passion for history, Robert Bowyer is animated in his opinion on the topic of the Vietnam War. "If you interview Vietnam vets, they have something in common and that is they are proud of their service. Our country would rather forget it, vets want to celebrate it." Robert backs up that opinion with his Operation Black Sheep commitment.

By maintaining and preserving the Mark II Patrol Boat River (PBR) in operational condition, it allows both civilian and military individuals to experience firsthand the thrill of riding on an operational PBR. Each month specific dates are reserved for veterans to take a ride in the boat. By riding, touching and experiencing one of the few remaining PBRs, veterans suffering from PTSD can benefit from the experience on the lake.

Military service began with basic training for Robert Bowyer at Fort Knox. From there it was on to Fort

Lee, where he was taught the basic fundamentals of being a parachute rigger (92R). After being a rigger at Fort Bragg for two years, he then reenlisted to be an infantryman (11B). I said to Robert that he looks like he's in great shape. Robert laughs and says he was back then. They ran him hard with backpacks of heavy gear weight. "We used to go on runs called Jurassic Park on difficult terrain, if that tells you something," he says with a grin. He looks fit but chuckles when he says, "the guys in the reserve are a little chunkier than active duty."

His first deployment was to Afghanistan to fight the Taliban. Firefights or as Robert called it "TICS" or Troops in Contact. Essentially patrolling villages and being shot at or avoiding IEDs. They would patrol villages and be involved in firefights. It was a search for "HVT" or high-value targets. Robert explains an example of what "psychological operations" are. They would rank Taliban individuals as high-value targets. The Taliban would blend into the population. I can see with Robert it's personal. He speaks of the Taliban cutting the fingers off women or performing circumcisions with rusty scissors with a grim and serious look on his face.

"We would put out a bounty on the #2 high-value target and distribute leaflets in a 100-square-mile area. In an act of twisted psychological competition, the #1 target would be mad about the attention given the #2 target and kill him for us."

He stands near a steering wheel and panel of gauges on the boat. On the shelf above the gauges is a bobblehead figurine of JFK. I ask why and Robert tells me the Lyndon Johnson bobblehead flew out of the boat and Nixon's head fell off. "The Vietnam Presidents," says Robert with a grin.

He leans against the metal plate partition, resting his arms on atop

Robert Bowyer

the plate, exposing colorful tattoos to the sunlight. Behind him on the boat I read a phrase "In Great Deeds Something Abides." I ask Robert about it. He peers at me through dark sunglasses, but I can see I've struck a chord.

Robert explains to me that he served in active duty from 2002-2008. When he was an infantryman "grunt" he said he was treated like garbage. "I learned the hard way," said Robert, "I went from one who prayed, didn't drink, didn't smoke to a hardened, toughened person out of necessity. The world is a harsh place." It was his second tour of duty to Afghanistan that he was awarded the distinction of Sergeant of the Guard or Cordon Rifle Sergeant at Bagram Air Base, responsible for the transfer of casualties headed back to the US. There are military personnel on hand to render honors—standing at attention and saluting—at each transfer point when a casualty in active duty returns home.

In my interactions with Robert he was kind and respectful, but I could also tell "hardened" from the experiences. After active duty in 2009, he volunteered for the reserves as a sergeant in the 321st Psychological Operations until 2017 and attended Grand Valley State University. It was in 2009 when he'd had enough with life, and, as Robert put it, "life sucked and people sucked so what's the point?" It was at this point his wife convinced him to take a history class at Muskegon Community College, where he was introduced to the story of Joshua Lawrence Chamberlain. The story of Chamberlain, a hero in the Civil War, defending the Gettysburg Union flank at Little Round Top, gave Robert new life.

"Chamberlain, despite what he went through, did not have a pity party," said Robert. "He didn't go through life drunk, angry or with an attitude of boo hoo me. Though a hero, he didn't want to talk about his heroics in the Civil War after it was over, he wanted to talk about education and being productive in life."

It is from Chamberlain the quote "In Great Deeds something Abides" originates.

> *"In great deeds, something abides. On great fields,*
> *something stays. Forms change and pass; bodies*
> *disappear; but spirits linger, to consecrate ground*
> *for the vision-place of souls ... generations that*
> *know us not and that we know not of, heart-drawn to*
> *see where and by whom great things were suffered*
> *and done for them, shall come to this deathless*
> *field, to ponder and dream; and lo! the shadow of a*
> *mighty presence shall wrap them in its bosom, and*
> *the power of the vision pass into their souls."*

-Joshua Lawrence Chamberlain

I owned a DVD of the 1993 movie *Gettysburg* adapted from the historical novel *The Killer Angels* by Michael Shaara and I wore it out I watched it so many times. The inspirational life and death improvisation of Joshua Lawrence Chamberlain imploring his men to "fix bayonets". Running out of ammunition and exhausted from protecting the Union flank on Little Round Top, he led the 20th Maine down the hill, using the slope to surprise the Confederates on their charge up the hill.

I once met Jeff Daniels, the actor who played the role of Joshua Chamberlain in the movie. He was amazing in that role and depicted well the passionate, compassionate, principled leader I believe Joshua

Chamberlain was in the Civil War. Daniels, at the time, seemed frustrated with most people recognizing him for his role as Harry Dunne in the movie *Dumb and Dumber* released in December of 1994, a box office success that developed a cult following in the years following its release. I think of Joshua Lawrence Chamberlain and the amazing acting job Daniels did in reprising the role of Chamberlain in leading his men on that hot, July day of 1863 on Little Round Top.

After graduation from Grand Valley, while drinking bourbon with his friend, Chris, the idea of a PBR river boat restoration was birthed. His thoughts of Operation Black Sheep and its goal, to recognize and help veterans, was conceptual. Robert says when he reached out, "most people laughed." His friend Chris didn't laugh. "You should do it, Rob, if anyone could do it you could do it." It was July of 2016, after tracking down a PBR, that he drove a trailer to Chicago, Illinois. "It was the worst part of town," laughs Robert. He pulled the boat and his dream north to Muskegon and has been working on it ever since.

With a bachelors degree from Grand Valley State University in history, with a focus on American military history, Robert hopes to go back at some point for his masters. He currently works for L3-CPS Combat Propulsion Systems, specializing in tank engines and transmissions.

OPERATION RUMINATION

I THOUGHT OF THOSE WORDS BY JOSHUA LAWRENCE Chamberlain when visiting Gettysburg and walking the field of Pickett's last charge and the area surrounding Little Round Top. "This now deathless field, to ponder and dream ... the shadow of a mighty presence ... the power of the vision pass into their souls." I sat in the middle of the field and closed my eyes to ruminate. I could feel the shadow, the power and vision of what had taken place there. By focusing while closing my eyes, I could feel the footsteps walk past me towards the Union position. Granted, the day I sat in that Pennsylvania field it was August with record temperatures of over 100 degrees. I still contend I felt the shadow of a mighty presence in

Sergeant Robert Bowyer on board the restored Operation Black Sheep Mark II Patrol Boat River (PBR)

now a deathless field. I took out a pad of paper and penned a song at that very spot.

> *For the ages we'll never forget, never will our*
> *memories fade*
> *For in that high-water moment, stood a brave and*
> *valiant brigade*
> *Along the stone-stacked walls of war where the fire*
> *no longer rages,*
> *Are peaceful breezes and memories, of three days*
> *that last … for the ages*

After meeting Robert Bowyer, I reflected on his experience, and concluded that, to a large part, you are what you are today, because of what you've been through. However, it is ***what you do with what you've learned about yourself*** that can make the difference for your future and benefit others. You can be bitter about struggles and do nothing, or you can use your experience to better others. **Bettering others gives one purpose.** It is true that in great deeds … something abides.

Each in diverse directions
Today see in their reflections
Army was one's course
The other Air Force
Brothers with strong connections.

Gregg Larabel
US Air Force October 1962 to March 1984.
Aviation electronics and USAF recruiter
E6 Technical Sergeant

Doug Larabel
US Army 1965 to 1991
Vietnam 3 tours 1967, 1969 and 1971
Army E7 Sergeant First Class (SFC) Airborne
Infantry
101st Airborne and 173rd Airborne Brigade

Chapter Fifteen

The other Side of the Coin

The Larabel Brothers

I WALK INTO THE RADIO STUDIO ON THE 9th floor on a cold, January day. I've done that for 25 years, but today feels different. The forecast is foreboding with arctic temperatures and blizzard conditions. The Polar Vortex is loose, and on its way to wreak havoc on travel conditions. I am asked by the program director to remind people of its potential. It brings to mind days past … specifically the blizzard of 1978 when I was fresh out of high school and 18 years old. I decide to run with it and open up the phone lines for recollections of that life-threatening epic winter event.

It was on January 24, 1978 a moisture-laden Gulf Low, developing over the southern United States, and a unrelated separate low-pressure system, were about to collide in the upper Midwest. Within 24 hours, the merger of the subtropical jet stream, with high winds and the polar jet stream with equally impressive winds, would lead the low-pressure system to explode into winter reality. The great blizzard of 1978 had formed and paralyzed the Midwest. It was a legendary weather event and I'll never forget it. Neither had my listeners.

By Thursday, January 26, 1978 it was snow, wind and cold in a "storm of unprecedented magnitude" according to the National Weather Service. It was categorized as the most severe of winter blizzards. Winds gusting up to 100 miles per hour, along with heavy continual snow, caused drifts that buried neighborhoods like mine. The wind chills were deadly as much as -50 degrees below zero.

The phone lines filled with people wanting to share their experiences. We heard from people picking up prescriptions from the pharmacy with plow trucks, and telephone operators who could not leave work stranded for days unable to go home. Others were drinking beer and skiing behind snowmobiles. There were also heroes delivering expectant moms to the hospital on snowmobiles. One caller, Gregg, caught my attention when he said he remembered the weather event. At the time he was serving the US in the Air Force in warm Okinawa, hearing about the stories of snow drifts, wind chills and blizzard conditions back home from his parents. I put him on hold, knowing I would want to talk to him during a commercial break. We agree to meet the following week. Gregg would bring along his brother Doug who had served in Vietnam. In 1978, I was busy starting a career, working full time and going to college, while these guys were serving their country in the military. By the time of the great blizzard of 1978, Gregg had already served 16 years in the Air Force, and Doug had served three tours in Vietnam.

I meet with Gregg Larabel, who had called me on my show, and he brings along his younger brother Doug. They were so different ... yet ... connected. Gregg now 74 and Doug 71 had divergent life paths obvious from the start of our conversation, yet bonded. I smile as I think "bond of brothers" as we talk. These two brothers had taken very different courses, and had served their country in very different ways. Gregg leans in and tells me he served "free of combat." That certainly was not the case for Doug in the jungles of Vietnam.

"I thought I had an exciting job and he had a cushy job," says Doug. If you want a hot meal, a cold beer and a nice place sleep, you go to the Air Force base. The Air Force base even had a PX post exchange where you could buy what you wanted," he says laughing.

"I volunteered for Vietnam in 1965 but I was getting married to Penny right after I volunteered so I withdrew my volunteer statement. We all have a job to do," says Gregg. He was needed for aviation electronics, working on planes like the F-100 Super Sabre jets used for close support and counter-insurgency missions in Vietnam. They were the US Air Force's first production airplane capable of flying faster than the speed of sound in level flight.

The similarity with Gregg and Doug is they both served for a long time. Gregg was in the US Air Force from Oct 1962 to Mar 1984. Doug was in the US Army for 23 years, from 1965 to 1991. After 3 tours in Vietnam, Doug went back to Fort Campbell, Kentucky in 1974, then various posts, including Germany, Panama, Alaska, Fort Benning, Georgia and finally Fort Bliss in El Paso, Texas until 1991 when he retired.

Their Dad was a "bah humbug" smart and hard-working World War II veteran who worked for the C&O Railroad. He worked long hours, talking of the industrial middle class "Bourgeoisie" of get by, make do and work hard existence ... the type that shakes your hand but doesn't hug. He was smart in that he built his own ham radio station. Mom had to take care of the six kids. Mom was always moving, industrious and goal oriented. The boys remember her taking them to the beach in Grand Haven and camping in an old Army tent. They were both an influence on Gregg and Doug; they epitomized the mid-20th century hard-working adults that never complained and never explained. They did what they had to do.

Gregg's basic training took place at Lackland Air Force base in San Antonio Texas. "I didn't know what was coming. They are there to break you down then build you back up. It was beneficial. I was only 17 years old," says Gregg. He remembers that because he was on the cross-country team in high school, and he was showing up the other guys on the obstacle course. His drill sergeant didn't like that. The senior master sergeant at Luke Air Force base in Arizona said, "19-year-old Airman Larabel is too fun loving," on his performance report and "always joking around." It didn't help he was an old crusty World War II and Korean War veteran chief master sergeant. I'm sure he couldn't relate to teenage Gregg Larabel and people like his high school friends, Fran Nawrocki, Jim Krzewski and Bob Julian, who were "always screwing around."

Doug's basic training was at Fort Knox, Kentucky beginning in September of 1965. Again, Doug says the purpose was to break you down then build you back up. Everything was rush, rush, then hurry up and wait. He remembers a tough drill sergeant by the name of "Youngs" who was from the deep south. For a teen who had lived only in Michigan, he found the southern accent difficult to understand. Doug needed the tough guidance. "I was the rebellious sort," says Doug. "Of the six kids in our family I was the trouble maker." Basic training set his mind and served a purpose.

After Basic training Gregg's path in the Air Force turned out to be very different from his brother's path. Gregg served the Air Force as both an avionics technician and an Air Force recruiter. It all started at Lackland Air Force Base in San Antonio, then on to Amarillo Texas for Automatic Pilot Training. Gregg served at

Luke Air Force Base in Arizona for one year to work on F-100 aircraft. As part of the build-up in Vietnam, the United States began expanding the number of F-100 squadrons in Southeast Asia. By then, most F-100s were distinctively painted in the green-brown camouflage color of the Vietnam jungles. He was transferred to Eglin Air Force Base in Florida for a year to work on the F4 Phantom jet that was adapted by the Air Force from the Navy to replace the aging F100. After a short year and a half stint at Lear Siegler Instrument Division, it was on to Keesler

Gregg Larabel

Air Force Base in Mississippi to study INS (Inertial Navigation Systems).

Gregg's next stop was Osan Air Base in Korea. In Korea he worked on the Convair CT-29 aircraft that flew recon missions along the DMZ. He remembers clearly an orphanage while stationed in Korea.

"Once a month some of my friends and myself would go out to the village off base and visit an orphanage," says Gregg. "While we were, there the children would put on a dance performance for us and lay out a table of fruits and sweets. Some of the orphans were placed there until the parents could afford to raise them. Others were simply orphans turned over to the orphanage. They were very loving, happy children."

From Korea it was a short stint at Langley Air Force Base in Virginia, before he came home to Grand Rapids for 4 years as USAF recruiter. Next, it was Little Rock, Arkansas to work on the C-130 Cargo aircraft, a four-engine turboprop airplane used for troop, medevac and cargo transport.

At the time of the great Midwest blizzard of 1978, Gregg was stationed in warm Okinawa at the Kadena Air Base Okinawa, Japan. He served there for three and a half years on KC-135 tank-

Gregg & his girl -
Amarillo AFB - Texas
January 1963

ers, also known as the "Stratotanker". This aircraft provides the core aerial refueling capability and airlift for the United States Air Force. The workhorse airplane serves the Air Force's capability to accomplish its primary mission of global reach.

"One of my regrets while in Korea and Okinawa was that I didn't learn the language. I learned enough to communicate between their broken English and my broken Korean and

Japanese," says Gregg. "We always learned the bad slang words. I think every GI would admit that, no matter what country they were in," he says with a grin.

After Okinawa, and prior to retirement, he returned to USAF recruiting duty from 1980 to 1984. On the flip side of the coin, his brother Doug's military journey would take a very different path.

Doug's journey began when the state sent him to a Lansing boys training school, where he worked in a greenhouse. That was his initial introduction to a plant called cannabis. "I didn't know what it was," says Doug, "until I was in Vietnam and saw it growing there." Doug's path had started down the wrong road at a young age. He was in trouble with both his dad and the law. After boys training school it was "go to jail or go into the Army," as Doug put it. A young man like Doug would have difficulty enlisting because of his police record. That's where President Lyndon Johnson's Defense Secretary Robert McNamara comes in to the story. Doug was an example of what eventually became the "McNamara 100,000" serving in the Vietnam War. He needed discipline and polishing and had a record with the law. It came down to jail or Army for him. The Army infantry gave it to him and more. The reality is that most of McNamara's 100,000 recruits ended up in the infantry and the killing fields of Vietnam. Doug Larabel was no exception.

In 1966 Defense Secretary Robert McNamara had an idea, a plan to get more desperately needed troops in Vietnam. They would widen their reach for enlistees by lowering the standards for entry into the armed forces. If the standards for passing the Armed Forces Qualification Test could be lowered, tens of thousands of previously "unqualified" young men and women would suddenly be available for military service. When the idea was hatched and launched in October of 1966, they called it "Project 100,000." That was their goal for the number of recruits in the first year. The reality is, that by the end of the war, more than 350,000 entered the armed forces due to this plan.

McNamara promoted the plan by saying recruits would gain valuable skills and self-confidence, which would help them get good-paying civilian jobs when they got out of the service. The US Senator from New York, Patrick Moynihan, argued that drafting the hundreds of thousands of young men and women being rejected annually as unfit for military service would transform them into hard-working law-abiding citizens. They, in turn, would teach their children, breaking the generation-to-genera-

Doug Larabel (left) Vietnam 1967 Army 101st Airborne

tion continuity of crime and poverty.

With the Johnson administration plan in place, military recruiters were backed by an aggressive public relations campaign, some ads using the verbiage "Vietnam...Hot, Wet, and Muddy. Here's the place to make a man." They promoted it as a good career choice. Pressure was put on recruiters to sign up more "volunteers" for the program.

Doug Larabel was one of those recruits, one of those volunteers. I asked him if he was scared when he arrived in Vietnam. "Yeah we were scared, "he says. "I remember getting off the air-conditioned jet, walking down the ramps into old school buses waiting for us. They had mesh wire over where the windows would be. It was hot on the drive from the airport to the Long Binh Post and it smelled." That stench, I heard from other veterans, was noticeable on arrival.

He was in a difficult and dangerous position in Vietnam. One of his jobs was as a Jeep "TC" or truck commander. With 106mm M40 recoilless rifles mounted on the jeeps, they travelled down two tracks into the jungle and formed defensive positions for an engineer unit tearing up and excavating foliage and brush. They were there for the engineer unit's protection, rousting out and engaging the VC.

"The one recurring thought that I have about Vietnam, is operating at night, in all three tours," says Doug. "For days, sometimes weeks, all our patrolling and setting up ambushes was done at night. These were some of the most frightening times. It seemed that the darkness was what God intended when he created night," he says.

"At night in the jungles, there were rotted sticks or trees that had some kind of a phosphorus growth on them. They would

Doug Larabel in Vietnam

glow and it looked like lights or eyes; it was scary. We would strain our eyes to try to see the man in front of us. At times we would grab hold of the ruck sack of the man in front and stumble along, hoping we would not get separated. It seemed like every time we would stumble or fall there was a tree with thorns to grab ahold of. We called them black palm with long thorns like a sea urchin."

Doug pulls a curled old photograph from his pocket. He's sitting in an excavated area with lifeless limbs of trees all around him. I comment on the "Viet War" headband he's wearing. "We all wore them," says Doug. "We called them hippy bands," as he laughs at the recollection.

There were times when he felt it was the end. At one point he wrote a letter to his parents on the inside cover of a C-ration box. He wrote it as his "last letter." His Dad was upset with him for sending pictures of the conditions, including pictures of Vietnamese war dead. It wasn't until years later after the war Doug's Mom gave the C-rations cover letter back to him. He still has it today.

I struck a chord with Doug when the conversation turned to John Honrath, a close friend of his in his squadron. John was killed in Vietnam. Doug's squad leader always wrote a letter to the parents and families of those who died. In the letter to John's parents Doug's name was included. The Honraths who lived in California sent a letter of condolences to Doug's parents in Michigan. I can't imagine the confusion and grief it caused his parents.

Years later Doug got the letters his parents had collected. When his Dad, who did not say anything about it, had died, his Mom gave him the boxes of letters and correspondence. John Honrath's brother Joe lives in Las Vegas and they began to correspond. A few years ago, Doug was able to travel to Las Vegas and meet with John's brother, Joe. He hopes to someday travel to California to visit John's gravesite. The memories surface emotions that are, I'm sure, deeply imbedded in Doug's mind and heart. Talking about it brings those emotions to the surface.

After his military service, Gregg did some aviation electronics work for Lear Siegler in their environmental lab testing equipment. He also sold real estate. He bought a bowling center called "Paragon" and sold it after 16 years. Gregg says, "While in Okinawa, my love for bowling carried over from bowling back home, so I became the secretary/treasurer of the Okinawa Men's Bowling Association. I was responsible for traveling around to the seven different military bowling centers for their annual certification inspection of the lanes and bowling pins. I would also inspect the lanes after an honor score (300 game/800 series) was bowled. I bowled in five different leagues and was secretary of those leagues. My wife Penny served as president of the Okinawa Women's Bowling Association. I was also a

Doug Larabel 1971 with 173rd Airborne Brigade

Junior Bowling Coach. When I returned to the states as an Air Force recruiter in Grand Rapids I was a Director of the GR Men's Bowling Association and later the secretary/treasurer. The military has competition throughout the services in all sports. Some of the Olympic competitors come from the military such as boxing, diving or biathlon. My daughter Michelle was All-Events Bowling Champion for her command while she served in the Air Force."

He is one of those "continual goals" guys so he had a "year of depression" without anything to do after selling the bowling business. He went to work again, this time for Spectrum Hospital nutrition services for 5 years. It was Doug, however, who drew Gregg back into retirement to pursue their first love, metal detecting. Ring finders international, metal sleuths who go out and find jewelry and other lost treasures. Their services are free, they do it for their "book of smiles" which is fun to read.

They both got the bug for finding lost treasure and metal detecting, when for Christmas 1972, they got a Bounty Hunter Red Baron metal detector. Their dad got them interested in metal detecting years ago. "Good exercise," says Gregg, "lots of squats." They haven't stopped since. Even today Gregg's cell phone rings often with requests to find lost rings, keys or other treasures. They're known as the "ring finders." His phone rings and Doug tells me the client calls keep coming. Gregg hands me a business card that says "have detector will travel." Always moving, always busy, just like their mom demonstrated to them years ago. I ask Gregg what he considers his best find. When serving in Okinawa he detected and found a blue star sapphire gold ring. "I also found lots of bullets," says Gregg. "On the island during construction, from time to time, unexploded ordinance would be found, so when I found something big I left it alone," he says with a grin.

For most people, when they lose a treasured ring they are devastated. It's a big deal. Many will google "lost ring" and

The Ring Finders comes up. From there they find Gregg in West Michigan. I was reading how they heroically find lost and dear items, and the testimonials are touching and sincere. They don't charge a fee for their work, but many people are thrilled, and, in gratitude, will offer them a reward.

Jen and Mark were swimming at Pere Marquette beach in a cove where people park their boats and swim. I'm very familiar with that area. It's where Operation Rumination and my physical training took place. Mark's wedding ring had come off in about 4 to 5 feet of water. Jen called Gregg and he met her there at 8AM the next morning.

Gregg describes it this way. "The day was cool, dark and dreary. It stormed but we were never weary on our 45-mile trip to the lake. We met Jen, she showed us the area, and, in the rain, we started our search. The waves were rolling about a foot, which made detecting a little rough trying to keep our balance. I got a good signal out about waist level which turned out to be

Okinawa treasure finds

an old can top. Moving out deeper about up to my neck with the rolling waves, I got a great signal, and put my scoop into the sandy bottom several times. About the fourth scoop, I saw the white gold wedding band at the bottom of my scoop. We walked up to the beach and Jen was in her car out of the rain. I held up the ring and Jen got out of her car and asked if she could give me a hug. In my wet clothes we hugged, and she was one happy lady. She immediately called her husband to tell him the good news. Another day of making someone happy, I love my job."

A "Bond" of Brothers

Doug and I sit together sipping coffee as Gregg goes to the car to retrieve artifacts. He returns with a large Plexiglas box full of "treasures" found while combing the area when stationed at Okinawa. He was there more than 30 years after the massive Allied invasion in 1945. Gregg opens the box. Full of Japanese yen, coins, bullets like 50-caliber shell casings, locks, spoons, matchbox cars, lighters and more.

I look through the box thinking *these two brothers are like flip sides of the coins* I'm looking through. Their military and life experience and personalities are very different, contrasting, yet like the two sides of a coin they are one … bonded as brothers and in it together for the long haul. They demonstrate that a **"bond of brothers"** is a treasure. They come from a military family. Their father had served in the Army Air Corps during World War II. Brother Jeff served after the Vietnam War in the Army 101st airborne from June 1975 to 1978 at Fort Campbell, Kentucky as a field wireman in communications. They have three sisters, and their husbands all served too. Both Gregg and Doug have children that have served. For Gregg, a daughter who served in the Air Force 6 years and now even a granddaughter, who has just applied for officers training school in the Air Force. Doug has three children, two sons including a son who served in the Navy on the USS Bunker Hill, the ship that fired the first tomahawk missiles at the onset of Operation Desert Storm in 1991. He also has a daughter that served in the Coast Guard for 18 years.

Doug says to me, "Most of us made it out and were happy to be alive. I would not trade my time in the military for anything."

Gregg says to me, "I know it's a phrase many others have used, but I wouldn't take a million dollars for my experiences, and I wouldn't take a million dollars to do it again."

He turned his young life around
In service his purpose he found
With tools to apply
He helped others to fly
He served proud with his feet on the ground.

"Pontiac" Pete "Wintergreen" Gorter

Air Force Structural Maintenance Technician

Spec 5

Lakenheath Tactical Air Command Base Suffolk,
United Kingdom

1987–1991

Chapter Sixteen

Right Place, Right Time, Right Tools

IF ART IS DEFINED BY THE CLASSICS, Picasso, Monet, Van Gogh, then most of us would struggle in meeting the standard. But art is in the eye of the beholder. The beauty of art is that it's subjective; it allows you to develop your own meaning and your own connection. Art is culture and the rivet was an important historical symbol in American culture. Certainly, Norman Rockwell's painting of Rosie the Riveter was artistic and enduring from the time it appeared on the cover of a May 1943 issue of The Saturday Evening Post.

The simple rivet joined not only sheet metal together, but it spurred an American military cultural change, beginning in WWII and how aircraft were used in war efforts. Today Kevlar and carbon fiber are used in high-tech composite aircraft, but the rivet still plays an important role in aviation. Sheet metal work, riveting, and repair of military aircraft involved in sorties, are susceptible to wear and tear and metal fatigue, making riveting and repair of aircraft an art in the eye of the beholder.

"It was like a sleek, beautifully crafted work of art sending F-111 Aardvarks up into the air, and it was very satisfying," says Pete Gorter with a smile. Pete served as an artist (his art) of sheet metal, rivets, framework and Kevlar composite repairs on what I describe as a "turbo-fan-powered maximum speed of Mach 2.3, at altitude bunker busting work of art and defense of freedom" otherwise known as the F-111 Aardvark. The F-111 Aardvark participated in the Gulf War (Operation Desert Storm) in 1991. Pete watched live on CNN in real time as the technician's "flying works of art" delivered munitions to Iraq in sorties and safely returned the US airmen back to the base. "Riveted" to the TV they watched as superior American airpower, thanks in part to those in support on the ground, kept the F-111 Aardvarks up in the air to make short work of Operation Desert Storm. F-111s dropped almost 80% of the war's laser-guided bombs, including a penetrating, "bunker-buster" ordinance, and were credited with destroying more than 1,500 Iraqi tanks and armored vehicles in Operation Desert Storm. Their use in the anti-armor role was dubbed "tank plinking." The crews of F-111s from "medium altitude" used guided munitions in Operation Night Camel during Operation Desert Storm with bombs designated for entrenched, hard targets, as well as softer targets like armored personnel carriers.

THE EARLY YEARS

FROM A YOUNG AGE PETE ENJOYED MAKING MODEL AIRplanes. He recalls enjoying building remote control airplanes from start to finish, then flying them at the local remote-control flying club. A personal friend, I think Pete is amazingly gifted and creative. His early model days have come full circle as he is currently a craftsman with Waco Aircraft Corporation. This Corporation, founded in 1983 and located in Battle Creek, Michigan, is the world's preeminent manufacturer of sport biplanes.

In his high school years Pete struggled in his relationship with his Dad. Pete left home and headed for Anaheim, California on a motorcycle where, he quickly began hanging around the "wrong people." After experimentation with cocaine, his relationship and "partnership" with ex-cons resulted in some bad choices and dangerous situations. To his credit, he realized of his own accord that this was going to end badly, so he traded in his motorcycle for a Camaro and headed back to Chicago.

Working, yet ever restless, he soon quit his job realizing he needed "boundaries." Despite his dad's favor, Pete went to a recruiter to sign up for the Air Force. "I needed to straighten out and serve," says Pete. "To know my limitations and boundaries and to be able to mentally focus." He turned his life around.

Pete credits his turnaround to the time he spent in tech school at Chanute Air Force base in Champaign County Illinois. "I learned respect for authority and teamwork, as well as the ability to focus on a project," says Pete. "Standards are *crazy high* as a technician in the Air Force. They would have everyone muster in the morning. At parade rest the NCO would have lists of assignments where I would receive mine. We didn't goof off on the job. Always focused on the job at hand and working as a team."

It didn't start out that way. When first signed up by the recruiter, he was sent to basic training in San Antonio, Texas for 6 weeks. Riding to the base in a bus, Pete's thoughts were with his past and how this was going to be different. He was going to "toe the line" and conform to rules or standards, similar to standing poised at the starting line in a footrace. He wasn't going to call attention to himself and would be a shining example.

"I was going to fly under the radar," said Pete.

When they arrived at the base for basic training, everyone was herded off the bus to line up for roll call. Names were called out by the sergeant off a list of the new recruits. Pete stood at attention as the names were read alphabetically. He knew they were getting close to his name when they hit the Gs and, with a page turn, the sergeant struggled with his name due to the fact a staple covered a portion of his last name.

"Gor, Go, Peter Gort….Gaten?"

Pete spoke up. "It's pronounced Gorter." Big mistake.

Instantly T.I. or Training Instructors were in his face and screaming into his ears from both sides. "Who do you think you are!?" Along with a tirade of expletives they welcomed Pete to his new home. Welcome to 6 weeks of molding in San Antonio, Texas, Pete Gorter, better known as basic training. I laugh as he recounts the frustration of physical training drills and testing. Not that he couldn't handle it. It was because as a team on those runs you were only as good as the slowest struggling person in the group. You crossed the line together. Pete called them "chunky chickens" with a wry smile on his face. Pete was evolving from being a rebel without a cause into a focused, serving team player. Pete was finally learning the meaning of teamwork and service.

"I learned what I was capable of and also my limitations," said Pete. He was beginning to learn that, in life, it is often about "right place, right time, right tools."

RAF LAKENHEATH

TEAMWORK IMPACTED PETE'S ATTITUDE WHEN EARLY IN his military career he watched the US attack on Libya. He recalls the 1986 campaign when fighters left RAF Lakenheath on bombing sorties to Libya to punish the regime of Mohanmar Quaddafi in Operation El Dorado Canyon. On 5 April 1986, Libyan agents had bombed "La Belle" nightclub in West Berlin. It tragically killed three people, one being a US serviceman, and injured 229 people. The Western world was exposed to modern-day terrorism. West Germany and the United States obtained cable transcripts from Libyan agents involved in the attack. Influenced and motivated by an American serviceman's death, Ronald Reagan, on 14 April, ordered an air raid on Libya. For the Libyan raid, the United States was denied overflight rights by France, Spain and Italy, as well as other European continental bases. This forced the Air Force to fly around France and Spain, over Portugal and through the Straits of Gibraltar which added 1,300 miles each way. Refuelings of the flights along the way would be needed.

The distance did not deter them from their orders and their duty. It's been said "I would fly 8,000 miles to smoke a camel," Pete says with a wry grin on his face. Their job was to be efficient and with superior fire power help return US airmen safely to their point of origination. I asked Pete what motivated him in his time at Lakenheath. "My training," said Pete. He quickly added,

> *"We were trained to support missions.*
> *We joined to support a country.*
> *It was about pride in our work and a sense of*
> *duty."*

Royal Air Force Lakenheath is located in the United Kingdom, approximately 70 miles northeast of London. With a long and storied history, it provides worldwide responsive combat airpower and support. The Liberty Wing consists of more than 4,500 active-duty military members, as well as both British and US civilians. It is not immune to occasional controversy or protests. Surrounded by barbed wire, akin to a WWII compound, fence jumpers would, from time to time, make their presence known.

Jumping the fence, nuclear protesters would, at times, breach the perimeter and get on the base. Anti-nuclear activists would gather outside the base they believed houses nuclear weapons. From time to time someone would get inside the fence perimeter. Pete recalls working on a plane and hearing a banging noise. A protester who had made his way into the area was banging on a jet engine intake with a steel pipe and wrenches. The technicians were instructed not to take matters into their own hands. They were to radio the SP to come and diffuse the situation. "We were the guests in the UK," Pete said.

HOLD/HOLD SHORT

HOLD/HOLD SHORT IS A COMMONLY USED PHRASE TO keep a vehicle or aircraft within a specified area or at a specified

Pete Gorter

point while awaiting further clearance. "Hold/Hold short was a discipline Pete needed to learn in his younger days. In the Air Force he found that discipline.

One day all personnel were told not to enter a restricted area on the base. They were briefed whenever, as Pete put it, "The Commander in Chief" was in the house." Much to his surprise during that day Pete was assigned to enter the restricted area. "Are you sure?" Pete asked himself inquisitively, wondering what he was getting himself into. He was taken to a hanger and cleared. He remembers all the secret service agents. President Ronald Reagan was in town visiting Margaret Thatcher. Marine One, the helicopter used to transport the president had a problem. A broken latch handle on the door needed to be repaired and Pete was the right man for the job. He drilled out the handle and repaired the latch to Marine One. He was commended for his work, and, in a small way, had served his country unlike any of us get the opportunity to do.

"Right place, right time, right tools," says Pete with a grin.

It's a "how did I get here" moment we all experience at some point in our lives. We talked about how, in life, most people don't use "Plan A." Most people find themselves in Plan B, C, D or other in the twisting turns of life. But have no doubt, that whatever your moments are, when that moment arrives you've been equipped with the right tools for that time and place. Recognize and seize the moment.

A Pontiac was the first car Pete ever owned, and, even though they are no longer made today, he loves collecting them and restoring them. I think Pontiacs are like Pete ... one of a kind. They don't make them like that anymore. Anyone who paid attention on the road in the 1960s and 1970s took notice of muscle cars - those sleek, high-performance vehicles with V8 engines that could be heard from a mile away. A brand of General Motors, Pontiac made vehicles and muscle cars that defined an era with legendary models such as the GTO and Trans Am.

Though Pontiac was, at one time, one of the top-selling brands in the United States, its leadership was unable to formulate then execute a strategy that would allow the Pontiac brand to continue. In business since 1926, Pontiac was sadly discontinued in April, 2009. Whether a Pontiac or Pete, some things and some

"Pontiac" Pete Gorter

people, when placed in the right place at the right time, have the right tools … and are originals never to be duplicated.

Pilots and mechanics have a special relationship. Overall, the relationship between mechanics and pilots is a respected and well-revered one. Pete calls it "a real brotherhood of trust" as well it should be. If you're sending thousands of pounds of aircraft aloft with thousands of pounds of fuel and munitions, the pilot and mechanics share a vested interest with lives at stake and a pride in executing professional successful missions.

On April 5, 1989, an Air Force F-111 with pilot and WSO (weapon systems officer) took off from Nellis Air Force Base in Nevada for training exercises. Although the pilots are normally based at RAF Lakenheath, Suffolk, England, training exercises are performed at the Nellis bombing range as part of Red Flag 89 exercises. Tragically, the plane crashed about 60 miles southeast of Tonopah during a training exercise at the Nellis Bombing Range. The loss was due to the aircraft hitting the crest of a ridge near Tonopah, Nevada.

Located about 160 miles northwest of Las Vegas, the Tonopah Test Range is an immense area of flat terrain ideal for low-altitude, high-speed aircraft exercises. Situated between two mountain ranges, Tonopah's remote location and restricted airspace provides the perfect venue for training and testing flights.

On this April day tragedy struck. Eyewitnesses say they were flying below the mesas and turned into a box canyon, a narrow canyon with a flat bottom and vertical walls. They realized they couldn't pull up in time so they ejected. The F-111 went straight into the wall of the mesa. The capsule clipped the edge of the mesa and tumbled for a few hundred yards across the top of the mesa. A very sad and tragic loss of life.

It was shortly after that, Pete witnessed the missing man formation fly-by over his base, RAF Lakenheath, the home base of the pilots who perished in the crash. It was to honor the F-111 pilots killed during training exercises at Nellis AFB in Nevada.

"We were shocked and devastated back at Lakenheath," says Pete. "To see the jets come over the base and watch as one pulls up and goes straight up into the stratosphere like a rocket. I was directly underneath and watched the red-hot exhaust from the afterburners as taps played on the base loudspeakers. I still well up with emotion like it was yesterday. It was a very sobering experience."

WINTERGREEN

ONE DAY, AFTER ASSIGNMENTS ON THE BASE, A VAN picked up technicians like Pete, taking them to their various tasks. Pete was assigned to hanger 102 to make some repairs on equipment. He had picked up a coke and was seated in the front passenger seat. Pete placed his partially finished drink in the front console for retrieval later upon arrival to his designated assignment. The van looped the base, picking up the technicians upon completion of their assignments. This day Pete found the assignment to be relatively easy and completed his task in short order. Jumping back into the vehicle he grabbed his soda, taking a big swallow. As it reached his stomach, he quickly realized something was terribly wrong. Retching the contents out the door, he was physically ill from ingesting the swill. It was Jim Bob Howdy from Texas who admitted to using the soda container as a spittoon for his wintergreen chewing tobacco habit. To this day the smell of anything wintergreen makes Pete queasy to the point of being sick. Breath mint anyone? I suggested to Pete that the *original patriots* might take umbrage to his aversion, to the point of loathe, for the flavor and scent of wintergreen.

pa·tri·ot ˈpātrēət/
noun - a person who vigorously supports their country and is prepared to defend it against enemies or detractors.

Pete the patriot took one for the team, and, to this day, is reminded of it anytime the aroma of wintergreen is in the air. Mints, air fresheners, cleansers and the tree that dangles from the rearview mirror can bring back the gag reflex for him. The original patriots, aka colonists, by 1768 were consuming almost two million pounds of tea, and American wintergreen *Gaultheria procumbens* played an important role. Wintergreen was used by Native Americans to brew a healing tea, and, during the American Revolution, it became a go-to source as a tea substitute for English tea, which was scarce. A tax on tea and the ensuing revolt would form a nation … a call to arms or, at the very least, a tea party. After the Boston Tea Party, colonials rallied at local parsonages and organized the campaign to ban English tea from every household. They distributed petitions for signatures and circulated anti-tea pledges. Colonial America then searched the landscape for suitable herbs, and the mint family was popular. The "Liberty Teas" were born to stand up to King George and his tea taxation. In addition to the leaves of Monarda, also known as Bee Balm or Bergamot, and other herbaceous plants, spearmint, peppermint, and **wintergreen** were also favored in colonial times. Readily available, wintergreens in the genus *Gaultheria* contain an aromatic compound called methyl salicylate which gives it that minty flavoring. Pete might also want to bear in mind that wintergreen oil is an ingredient in some lubricants used in firearm maintenance to clean, lubricate and preserve metal surfaces of firearms.

COWPUNK

PETE MET HIS WIFE JULIE IN ENGLAND. HE PLAYED GUItar and wrote music for a GI Band called "At 10 Paces" that played "Cowpunk" in English pubs. Popular in the 1980s it was punk rock meets country music. Johnny Cash meets the

Pete Gorter performing with *At 10 Paces*

Ramones. They recorded in London and pressed out record albums with the band consisting of military maintenance troops. The genre started in England and existed in the US in the 80s as means for an MTV generation to make country music palatable. Cowpunk was perfect for Pete's musical prowess. It was again *right place, right time, right tools.* The audiences then seemed taken aback that the members of "At 10 Paces" were Americans.

"They assumed we were English punks, pretending to be Americans, playing English music on their turf," said Pete. "Our reception in the pubs around the air bases was a bit hostile. The more distance between us and the air bases, the more receptive they were, and they enjoyed it. We knew we were going to have a good crowd when I looked over to see a huge poster of JFK on one wall of the pub and a poster of the Stray Cats on the other. When in Rome, play what the Romans want to hear," he said.

Pete's creative mind combined with edgy behavior always was entertaining. When Pete and I were in a church band together, years later, more mature and settled down, the guitar Pete pulled out of the case had a bumper sticker on it that said, "Eternity. Smoking or Non-Smoking?" He always knew how to put on a show.

In 1991, with the threat of scud missiles and chemical war in Iraq and Kuwait, Pete was on the list to be the next in line to be sent to Bagram Air Base and the Middle East. The speed at which Operation Desert Storm concluded, made it unnecessary for him to go. With his wife Julie pregnant with their first child, it was off to Travis Air Force base in Fairfield, California for his final military assignment to work on C5 transport planes. The C5, with its first flight in June of 1968, has provided the United States Air Force with a massive airplane and heavy intercontinental-range strategic airlift capability.

At the end of Operation Desert Storm there was a large exodus of personnel that left the military, making civilian transformation and career opportunities in the aircraft industry slim. It made sense to move to Michigan to be near family and look for the next opportunity. Today, Pete lives in Middleville, Michigan with his wife Julie and two kids. Little did he realize that the military training and experiences he had acquired

"Pontiac" Pete "Wintergreen" Gorter

would prepare him and be just what he needed to build planes at WACO. He repairs and renovates Pontiacs in a pole barn, and travels to Battle Creek daily to work on Biplanes for WACO. Occasionally, he takes out his guitars to play. In his personal journey, no one could say he hasn't been creative or original, ever ready to practice his art and employ his creativity at the right place, in the right time and to use the right tools.

OPERATION RUMINATION

PETE IS ONE OF THOSE PEOPLE WHO CAN TAKE SOME-thing that already exists and develop creative solutions to improve it. The trick is doing that within the parameters of boundaries and being effective in what you do to serve others. And service is the key. Pete, through military service, learned how to harness that creativity within boundaries, the necessary parameters, boundaries and focus needed to serve. I once read of the person who mistakenly said, "I'll throw another log on the fire as soon as things heat up in here." Timing plays a role.

"Now that I have time to reflect on it, my life has a definite BM/AM, before military and after military," says Pontiac Pete. His service was a life-changing event, and now he can clearly see the difference in his outlook on life before, during and after his service in the military. He goes on to say, "I firmly believe our country should have a mandatory 2-year service commitment straight after high school. Why send juveniles to boot camp *after* they have gotten into trouble and have no direction or knowledge of their boundaries physically and mentally. There is no price you can put on the benefits and the rewards that you cannot experience in any other way."

Patience may be a virtue but sometimes you just have to make something happen. In life, one of my pet peeves is the comment, "We tried that and it didn't work." It is a discipline to find the right place, to recognize the right time, and then apply the creative tools you've been gifted in life. Sometimes you have to force the issue.

For me, as an author and someone in radio for 25 years, my ruminations drifted towards Earl Nightingale and 'The Strangest Secret.' Earl Nightingale was a radio host, speaker and author who focused on personal motivation and development. Earl Nightingale was on the USS Arizona at the bombing of Pearl Harbor. One of few survivors of the cataclysmic and tragic explosions of the Arizona that still today rests on the bottom of Pearl Harbor. Because of his position on the "aft mast" of the ship he survived saying, "it was a matter of being *in a lucky spot at the right time.*" If you listen to 'The Strangest Secret' he says,

"The opposite of courage is not cowardice, it is conformity. Doing it like everyone else without knowing why." His key point is, "We become what we think about."

A master at painting a picture with the spoken word he loved visual metaphors. One of my favorites is an apothecary scale and his viewpoint that, success in life is directly proportional to the number of people you serve and the quality of that service. The scale, with a cross-arm on top, two bowls on chains; a very honest mechanism. If one bowl is compensation and the other is service, his point was to focus on the service bowl side of the scale. A rich life of "compensation" will follow, tipping the scales in proportion to the service we offer to others. As you sow, so shall you reap.

I laughed, thinking Pete didn't need to worry about conformity, making his willingness to serve and enlist a courageous act. At a young age Pete was focused on the wrong bowl, but he recognized the need for change. He became what he thought about. He volunteered to serve our country. It was service that compensated him by changing his course and direction. He put himself in the right place, at the right time, with the right tools.

A moment's notice sent anywhere
For missions they prepare
Adapting to change
Their lives rearrange
They're ready and always there.

Colonel Mark E. Tellier
National Guard
Chief of Staff Michigan Army National Guard
Michigan Army National Guard August
1991-present
Deployment Squadron Commander 126th Cavalry
Afghanistan Jan-Oct 2012

Chapter Seventeen

Always Ready Always There

ON THE SUNNY, CLEAR SKIES morning of September 11, 2001, everything changed. Islamic terrorist hijackers took control of four commercial passenger jets flying out of airports on the east coast of the United States. Two of the aircraft were deliberately flown into the twin towers of the World Trade Center in New York, with a third hitting the Pentagon in Virginia. The fourth plane never reached its intended target, crashing in Pennsylvania. Heroic passengers and crew overpowered the hijackers and took control of the plane.

September 11, 2001 brought new meaning to the concept of "always ready always there" for the National Guard. Following the attack on the World Trade Center, the New York Army and Air National Guard mobilized to secure the area, rush in supplies, and assist in the rescue and recovery. In September of 2001, President Bush authorized the use of the National Guard to increase security at airports, mobilized in either a federal or state status in order to secure airports and other vital facilities. Operation Noble Eagle commenced and it changed everything ... including the life of Colonel Mark Tellier. The US locked down borders, including Michigan, an important border and port state. Tellier was assigned responsibility to oversee a federal response to increase security at the airports in Lansing, Kalamazoo and Grand Rapids, Michigan and bridges, including the Bluewater bridge in Port Huron and the Sault Ste. Marie international bridge. The security mission would last until the formation and implementation of the Transportation Security Administration (TSA).

With the TSA in place, the airport security mission ended in June 2002. The Army National Guard returned to steady state, not knowing what the future would hold. "Steady state" is defined as preparing for two missions. The federal mission assigned to the National Guard is to provide properly trained and equipped units to fight in time of war, to protect the homeland, and build our global partnerships. That's a big job in and of itself. The National Guard also has a state mission. The state mission is to respond to the governor of the State of Michigan with individuals or units to provide trained and disciplined forces for domestic emergencies, natural disasters, or civil unrest.

In the years Tellier had served in the military, from the time he was commissioned at Federal Officer Candidate School in August of 1991 to the year of 2000 there was "little change." So much so that he considered by the late 1990s, and actively pursued, a civilian life outside of the military. His father, who had enjoyed a distinguished military career, tipped off his commanding officers of Mark's intentions. Mark's dad was an officer in Vietnam, earning a Silver Star for heroism on the battlefield. After the Vietnam War, Mark's dad served in the National Guard, including during the Detroit riots of 1967-1968, an example of civil unrest requiring involvement of the National Guard.

The National Guard needs people like Mark Tellier to be "always there and always ready." Adjustments were made to change Mark's mind, but none so big as the events of 9/11/2001. Since September 11, 2001, Mark tells me that four primary issues have materialized since that date. First, the military changed rapidly from 2001 to 2016. Second, much of that change was due to the military entering into a counter-insurgency war with Iraq and Afghanistan in 2001-2010. Third, by 2017 the military was changing again to a decisive action strategy to meet today's global threats on the "modern" battlefield. The military must learn to fight in all five domains: air, land, sea, space, and cyber. Finally, Colonel Tellier explains to me that today's threats are decisive action against "near-peer" competitors like China and Russia, and "asymmetrical warfare" against North Korea and Iran, as well as the ever-continuing counter insurgency against global terrorism.

Mark Tellier volunteered for military duty one year after high school. "I joined for the wrong reasons," Mark said, "It was a way to pay for tuition before I learned the meaning of service." Mark, in turn, was one of my veteran friends who taught me the meaning of selfless service this past year.

He went to Fort Benning for basic training. Mark calls it a place that is "hot with briar bushes and red clay." The opposite of what he had expected happened. He had seen the videos of calisthenics and chow lines. It turned out to be much tougher than that. He was a kid coming from Lansing Catholic Central in Lansing, Michigan to join the infantry at Fort Benning and "the environment was tough," he said. "I woke up in life. I never had, prior to that point, experienced five or six people yelling at me." He said, "They learned to march as one unit, 40 people doing the same thing at one time." It wasn't until close to graduation of Initial Entry Training, otherwise known as basic training, that Mark and his teammates got their first compliment. They finally understood.

"An ah-ha moment," says Mark. He added, "success is about the team being successful, not individual actions."

Following basic training, it was more of Fort Benning to do his advanced infantry training, which included 2 years of officer's training. He was motivated, but, as Mark says, he had a lot to learn. He recalls a dark, rainy night on a land nav course as part of his training. You had to find four or five points on the map in the dark, and, "young and dumb" and full of energy, he bolted out of the gate only to hit an intermittent stream bed falling around 8 feet to the creekside. There he was face-to-face with the outline of a snake. "Snakes at Fort Benning are not good snakes," Mark said, "and I wanted to be done. What am I doing here?" he asked himself. But the answer in his mind always was that someone before him had completed this, that he was not unique or special, and that he could now do the same.

Mark advanced to become the Platoon leader, Combat Support Company, 3rd Battalion, 126th Infantry of the National Guard in August of 1991 in Wyoming, Michigan and advanced his career from there. Leadership skills were learned as a Platoon leader, and Mark learned his leadership skills as a 2nd Lieutenant in the Army.

Colonel Mark Tellier (back row second from right)

The Army National Guard is the oldest component of the United States armed forces. Militia companies were formed with the first English settlement at Jamestown in 1607. The first militia regiments were organized by the General Court of the Massachusetts Bay Colony in 1636. From the Pequot War in 1637 until the present day, the Army National Guard has participated in every war or conflict this nation has fought. The militia stood their ground at Lexington Green in 1775 when the opening shots of our War of Independence were fired. They fought the British and their Indian allies from the Great Lakes to New Orleans during the War of 1812, and provided 70% of the troops that fought in the Mexican War.

The National Guard of the United States is a reserve military force. It is comprised of National Guard military members or units of each state and the territories of Guam, the Virgin Islands, Puerto Rico and the District of Columbia. National Guard units are under the dual control of the state and the federal government. The majority of National Guard soldiers and airmen hold a civilian job full-time while serving part-time in the National Guard Reserve.

Mark describes the National Guard as a military force of citizen soldiers here to support state and federal governments. In the United States the general threat is natural disasters like hurricanes or flooding. They provide relief efforts, domestic response operations and whatever the mission requires. On the federal side they are an available tool when the government needs a "blunt" object, and they are very visual when called out. The uniqueness of the National Guard is: one day soldiers could be passing out water in a state disaster relief, and that same week could be called to serve in another country.

That's exactly what happened to Mark Tellier in 2012. It was off to Afghanistan as the 126th squadron commander. The squadron was identified by the Department of the Army to provide support to Afghan police as part of their rotation. They were to conduct three missions: support of the Afghan National Police, support the Afghan National Army and support the US Special

Operations Command, known as USSOCOM. The cavalry squadron Tellier was responsible for consisted of 450 men and women in the National Guard. This was their call to active duty.

"Afghanistan was one of the most beautiful countries," Mark said. "From mountains and mud huts to variable climates and temperatures, I thought it was beautiful, except a war was going on which gave it an ugliness," he said. "Many Afghans I met were simply farmers, and all they want to do was farm and take care of their tribe, even though many granted were poppy farmers. It was all about some bad people mixed into a community of good people."

His unit arrived on Jan 4, 2012 and it was cold and snowing. "Only 3 months later, traveling south to Kandahar, it was over 110 degrees," says Mark.

"A country of extremes," I said.

He nods his head. "We could be in the red sand and extremely arid Rigestan desert with temperatures of 128 to 130 degrees and then fly over mountains to Mazar-i-Sharif moving from 130 degrees to less than 30 degrees. The Rigestan desert also known as Registan is an extremely arid plateau region and Mazar-i Sharif is very cold climate in the winter. As commander of our unit I got to move around the country," he said. Their base of operations was at Bagram with 12 out-stations spread across the entire country. Non-conventional forces were not pocketed into a region, and were staged where they could best respond to meet the needs of the combatant commander.

"You were never out of harm's way," said Mark. This was especially true with the ever-constant threat of IEDs as they moved about the country. He particularly recalls a couple of rocket attacks and one specific attack where two squadron soldiers were blown into a bunker.

"The environment will kill you if not prepared," he said.

When it was all said and done, they returned every one of the 450 soldiers alive back to the US. A total of 18 purple hearts for wounds during active duty were awarded in his squadron.

There were many close calls for loss of life in that environment. The date of May 20, 2012 stands out in his mind as two vehicles that day were hit by IEDs. Mark's thoughts turn to United States Army National Guard Sergeant Eric Lund who lost both arms above the elbow after an IED explosion hit his convoy in Afghanistan. He was flown to Germany, where his arms were amputated above the elbow. He spent the next two years in San Antonio, Texas, recovering, before returning home to Ludington, Michigan. After numerous surgeries, prosthetics and two Purple Hearts, Eric received a double-arm transplant at John Hopkins University in Baltimore in November of 2017. Eric Lund served his country, he was ready, he was there, he sacrificed.

Tellier's squadron also worked with Special Operations Command, known as USSOCOM; they learned to serve and understand that it's "one team one fight" from those men and women. They were taught to survive in their environment. Colonel Tellier speaks highly of the Special Operations people who accepted and taught his men and women of the National Guard how to survive in their area of operations as a team.

"Little Bird" helicopters, nicknamed the "Killer Egg," are light helicopters used for special operations in the United States Army. It's what special operations used to support ground-based operatives, so you had to train to be a gunner on the platform of an AH-6 tied in with a strap around your waist. With a top speed of 175 mph and a cruise speed of 150 mph and range of 267 miles, this agile, helicopter is outfitted with outboard "benches" designed to ferry commandos outside the cockpit on each side. It can conduct rapid insertions and extractions of special operations forces in and out of a challenging terrain such as what is found in Afghanistan. They became one team, one fight, learning to survive in a hostile war-torn region.

Mark explains to me that the majority of these men and women are volunteers called to service. The majority have a civilian job and are paid to wear the uniform and train two days a month. They must find ways to support themselves in their homeland environment and need civilian employers to also make sacrifices to make it work. He reminds me that families also sacrifice. A family sacrifices because Mom or Dad, a spouse or a brother or sister can't be there. Mark is not unique, but his family moments are. Over the 31 years of service, Mark's family has celebrated many birthdays, anniversaries, births of children, graduations and other special events without him.

Mark and Andrea Tellier

"It takes a supportive family and a supportive employer to make it work," says Tellier.

In today's world, it takes a partner with industry and other civilian agencies to maintain a technological edge. As CIO or Chief Information Officer, Colonel Tellier understood the need for the help of civilian businesses with the best technology. Network and cyber security, walking side by side with the IT industry, is a vital part of national security. The military must keep pace with a changing world, and partnering with industry leaders gives the United States the tactical edge. As the cost of technology has dropped off, adversaries capitalize on low-cost technologies, known as Anti Access/Area Denial (A2/AD). These are technology or weapons used to prevent foes from occupying or traversing an area of land, sea, air or cyber. Information and technology is readily available in today's world more than ever before. What once was exclusive intellect and competencies of the military, is now information spread rapidly through technology. Partnership with the best civilian businesses can begin to fill the information and technology gap between the military and IT industry.

It's an essential element of being always ready, always there. I see those same characteristics in Colonel Tellier as we chat over a cup of coffee. His "drive" is a sense of accomplishment; always obtaining new skills; the desire to contribute and achieve to the next level. Just like the older World War II veterans I spent time with, he seems to have that same characteristic, the same common thread" … continual goals." To see the end result of actions.

"When you receive a higher rank, you often don't see those fruits until later, maybe not until I'm gone," says Tellier. "But the drive is always to take that hill as part of a winning team."

OPERATION RUMINATION

WHEN BENJAMIN DISRAELI FIRST BECAME PRIME MINISTER of the United Kingdom in 1868, upon being congratulated, he said, "Yes," to a friend's congratulations, "I have climbed to the top of a greasy pole." It was also Benjamin Disraeli, twice the Prime Minister of the UK in the 1800s, who said these words that are completely relevant even today:

"Change is inevitable. Change is constant."

I thought of that quote while considering the service of Mark Tellier. Once frustrated by the lack of change in the Army, I'm sure he would admit that Disraeli's sentiments soon proved true to form in his life. Once in a position with processes that seemed rigid and immutable, he sought change. Sure, as the day follows night change happened. But the principles of service and sacrifice do not seem to change; they remain the same. Humility. Empathy for your fellow man. Making a difference.

I recalled a fellow worker who would always use the Boy Scout motto as his litmus test for associates being considered for advancement within the company ... Trustworthy. Loyal. Helpful. Friendly. Courteous. Kind. Obedient. Cheerful. Thrifty. Brave. Clean. Reverent.

I noted that Colonel Tellier is the recipient of a Bronze Star, a United States decoration awarded to members of the United States Armed Forces for either heroic achievement, heroic service, meritorious achievement, or meritorious service in a combat zone. True to form, as I have found with other veterans, Mark is quick to change the subject and not dwell on a personal medal of honor; rather he focuses on the sacrifices others have made and are making even today. Yet I thought of the meaning of "heroic service" and realized that he lives, every day, the National Guard motto, "Always ready, Always there."

With this in mind on one of my "basic training" runs, I spent the duration with the two phrases in juxtaposition in my mind. "Change is inevitable and constant" juxtaposed with "Always ready, Always there." It caused me to think about the irony when juxtapositions like success and failure, calm and chaos or weakness and strength can work *together* for the common good. There can be calm in the midst of chaos, and you can find success in a failure to move on and weakness can partner with strength when vulnerability benefits others. The men and women of the National Guard live among us with everyday occupations, families and activities. But they commit, train and stand ready to protect us and our nation living the motto "Always ready, Always there." That is a big commitment of service.

Now as an older man approaching my 60s, I chuckle to myself thinking, that in day-to-day life I can't be always ready and always there. My chuckle turns to outright laughter when I think truthfully; it's more like 'sometimes I don't want to.' But I can be *sometimes ready* and *sometimes there* to help another when in need, if I am willing to serve others. If we all do that, there is strength in numbers. When disillusioned by daily news events, I remember there are ***many,*** who, day after day, quietly and without fanfare serve others. ***Collectively,*** as a group, we too can use the example of the men and women of the National Guard and can be always ready, always there, in our own corner of the world.

She came from a small Michigan town
To serve, not seeking renown,
Her path she would envision
With skill and precision
As she flies keeping it greasy side down.

Kathryn Prater

US Army

UH-60M Black Hawk Helicopter Pilot

Commander, Company B,

1-147 Air Assault Battalion

Deployed to Camp Bondsteel Kosovo 2005

Deployed to Camp Taji Iraq 2010

Chapter Eighteen

Keep it Greasy Side Down

L**ULLABIES HAVE SHORT AND MEMO**rable musical intervals, a tempo and predictable structure or cadence when sung to a child snuggled in their bed. Parents and cultures across the world have used the lullaby, once books have been read and lights are switched off, to lull a child into peaceful sleep. Twinkle, twinkle little star, how I wonder where you are. In music theory, an interval is the difference in pitch between two sounds. It's the rhythm and cadence which makes that tune memorable, long after the child has outgrown their parents crooning. For Kathryn Prater, the lullaby her dad sang to her years ago is still memorable for a reason you might not expect.

Kathryn Prater comes from a military family with a big brother who went to West Point, and a dad who served in the Army 101st airborne as an engineer and paratrooper. She says God led her to Fort Knox for basic training, the same place her dad had done his basic years ago. It was there she learned the lullabies he sang to her as a child were not of the "Somewhere over the Rainbow" or "When you wish upon a Star" typical melodic lullaby genre. They, instead, were songs troops used for singing cadence to stay in step when marching, like the one below, first copyrighted by George A. Norton in 1917.

Around her hair she wore a yellow ribbon
She wore it in the springtime, in the merry
month of May
And if you asked her why the heck she wore it
She wore it for her soldier who was far, far
away.
Far away,
Far away.
She wore it for her soldier who was far, far
away.
Around the block she pushed a baby carriage,
She pushed it in the springtime, in the merry
month of May.
And if you asked her why the heck she pushed it,
She pushed it for her soldier who was far, far
away.
Far away,
Far away.
She pushed it for her soldier who was far, far
away.

Kathryn grew up on a Christmas tree farm, and graduated from high school with a senior class of only 42 graduates in the "booming metropolis" of Litchfield, Michigan. Litchfield is a city in Hillsdale County, known for its unique history and for being a productive farming area.

After high school, proficient in math skills and seemingly destined to become a high school math teacher, I asked Kathryn what would cause her to want to become a pilot?

"It was the *Top Gun* movie poster hanging in my bedroom," she says laughing. It is true that when the blockbuster movie came out in 1986, polls showed many Americans had doubts about the post-Vietnam military and about "saber rattling" from the Reagan White House. Then came *Top Gun*, the highest-dollar grossing film of 1986. Its impact went well beyond dollars and cents and the silver-screen. It had an enduring cultural legacy, even today in reruns.

Kathryn was accepted into the Air Force Academy, but did not feel it was the right place for her. She decided instead to enroll at Western Michigan University to study for a teaching degree. She was drawn to the ROTC program at WMU in 1999, and, recruited by the Michigan National Guard, utilizing their scholarship program. It was in the summer between her sophomore and junior years at Western that she went to basic training at Fort Knox, Kentucky, the same place her Dad had done his basic training years before.

Basic training with ROTC recruits is mostly comprised of college kids, everyone heading off for officer training.

"It was cull the herd to see if you're tough enough," said Kathryn. "Leadership courses, lots of running, getting yelled at, rappelling off structures, shooting, that kind of thing."

"Was it difficult?" I asked.

"It was more so that feeling you don't want to let people down," she said.

Early in our conversation, I realized she had that same recurring characteristic I had found with the other veterans I interviewed … continual goals.

She sprained her ankle 4 weeks through and was not about to quit. She was going to complete the 6 weeks and did.

"800 mg of Motrin is the Army's cure for everything," she says laughing.

In the fall it was back to college to study to be a teacher. Prior to nine-eleven, Kathryn felt she could "straddle the fence" by being both a teacher and serving in the National Guard.

"One year before nine-eleven, I could get some strange looks wearing the uniform," she said. That changed to vocal support and encouragement after September 11, 2001."

She completed her Junior year at Western Michigan University and that summer went to Fort Lewis, Washington, which is an Army training facility south of Tacoma, Washington. There in ROTC training she competed against other officers. "PT" or physical training, rope climbing and obstacle course, infantry tactics, squad-level tactics, all were used to evaluate your leadership ability. That is how you are selected into your branch. For Kathryn Prater, the young lady who had flying in her blood, and her dad a recreational pilot himself, it meant her orientation guided her towards aviation.

As a senior at Western Michigan University, she was on the four and a half year plan and a student teacher. Her goal was to teach advanced mathematics. Having been selected by the Army aviation unit she knew she wanted to be a pilot. She still figured she could do both, juggle two personal goals, to be a teacher *and* a pilot. After testing and medical screening, she was accepted and told "we are going to send you to flight school."

She was excited. Who wouldn't be? She headed to Fort Rucker, Alabama where rotary wing pilots are trained. Army pilots like Kathryn are trained at Rucker and go back there to continue their training. They affectionately call the place "Mother Rucker." There they train on the Bell TH-67, which is a military variant of the famous Bell 206-B civilian helicopter, and is used for flight training by the US Army. The helicopter is not hard to miss; it's painted orange.

"They do that so you don't hit each other," said Kathryn laughing.

"The first time your instructor hands you the controls and you try to hover you're all over the place," she said. "They take the controls from you and set it down with fingertip ease." Like anything else … practice makes perfect.

The key is practice with the cyclic, or, as some would call it, the "stick." This sensitive practice of changing the pitch angle of the rotor blades with the net effect to tilt the rotor disc. The disc then moves in the direction of tilt, and since the rotors are attached to the helicopter fuselage, the body of the helicopter then follows. Moving the cyclic forward causes the rotor disc, and the helicopter, to tilt forward. The helicopter pitches nose down, and speeds up. Moving the cyclic or stick aft has the opposite effect, and moving it sideways causes the aircraft to turn. As they say, practice makes perfect, so Kathryn spent hours with a handy makeshift "stick" at the library. It was simply a small wooden "shelf" with a marble supported by a stick or practice "cyclic" in the center. She spent hours developing her touch, keeping the marble centered with fine tuned corrections.

After initial flight training in the "orange" helicopter, it was on to the OH-58. The Bell OH-58 is a single-engine, single-rotor, military helicopter used for observation, utility, and direct fire support. After that it was on to the Black Hawk helicopter, an icon of modern aerial warfare and the stuff Hollywood movies are made of. The UH-60 is powered by twin General Electric engines, and is the Army's primary medium-lift utility transport. A Black Hawk is capable of carrying 11 combat-equipped troops. With armor-protected seats and armored fuselage, it has a host of advanced avionics able to fly in almost any weather conditions. This is what the young lady from Litchfield, Michigan was meant to fly.

Kathryn trained for a year at Fort Rucker. The training was hard. She never had been academically challenged by the Army before, so she went into it "maybe a little overconfident." She studied day and night. It was only a two-hour drive south to Panama City beach for a little R&R. She went only twice in that year.

"I would put tin foil on the windows so I could sleep," said Kathryn. "We did a lot of flight training at night with night vision goggles, so you had to get some sleep during the day."

When you graduate you're officially a pilot. She graduated with honors. Your family comes to Fort Rucker for the ceremony and the Army pins wings on you. Now a qualified aviator, she returned to her unit in Grand Ledge, Michigan to be trained in the Air Assault unit, and was simultaneously teaching math at Huron High School. Kathryn and I laugh as I try to juxtapose the image of a classroom teacher and one wearing an Army uniform, conducting mission tasks in a multi-million dollar helicopter in flight practice with "bambi buckets" to put out fires.

Kathryn had been teaching for a year, doing just fine grading papers and flying military helicopters. Just like nine-eleven changed everything, notification her unit was going to be deployed, changed everything for her. This was big. It was her Grand Ledge unit's first deployment since it was called to go to Haiti years before.

They were to go to Kosovo in June of 2005 for 18 months. Kosovo is a strategic and disputed territory located on the Balkan Peninsula, the subject of a territorial dispute between the Republic of Kosovo and the Republic of Serbia. Because of the conflict in Iraq and Afghanistan, many active duty Army were in the Middle East, so National Guard mobilizations were needed. She was single and would see the world, traveling to Kosovo, flying in a United Nations mission and working with Polish, Ukrainian and French forces.

They flew commercial airlines to Germany. From there they flew their Black Hawk helicopters through Austria, Croatia, Bosnia and into Kosovo on Christmas eve. "It gave me the travel bug," she said. "Croatia was beautiful to fly through, and I did it before it became the noted travel destination it is today," she said with a smile.

Her home was Camp Bondsteel, named after James Leroy Bondsteel, a US Army Staff Sergeant who served during the Vietnam War and received the Medal of Honor. Camp Bondsteel base served as the headquarters for Multinational Task Force East led by the US Army.

They were in Kosovo to help keep the peace. When not flying, 25-year-old Kathryn would also volunteer at an orphanage. Poverty is widespread and persistent in Kosovo. It is a "young" and poor society, with an estimated 27 percent of the population under the age of 14, and half under the age of 25. Poverty particularly affects children. When flying at night she could recall the rolling blackouts in the troubled area. Part of their responsibility was to also help monitor the issue of illegal logging, an issue with a long history and checkered past in the forests of Kosovo.

Approximately 42% of Kosovo is covered by forest. Some 32 % of this area is owned by small landowners; 68% is publicly owned. Illegal logging in Kosovo includes logging from public forests without permission, logging in protected areas and smuggling. It was the country's lack of capacity to fully protect forests in Kosovo, making forests vulnerable particularly at the border, and a prime target of wood thieves. The instability in Kosovo led to more opportunity for criminals to act with impunity.

A COMMANDER AND AN INSTRUCTOR

UPON HER RETURN FROM KOSOVO, KATHRYN HAD DECIsions to make. "I was going to be a teacher, but the National Guard offered me a full-time job in the Army National Guard. I was 26 years old, and, in reality, saw more deployments in the future based on world events. I didn't think I could be successfully good at being *both* a teacher and a soldier, a pilot, a leader."

My immediate impression in talking with Kathryn was that she has a sense of duty to do her best and excel in what she does. She has focus. If I were to apply one word to my personal impression of her, it would be proficiency.

> proficiency
> noun_- pro·fi·cien·cy | \prə- ˈfi-shən(t)-sē \
> 1: advancement in knowledge or skill :
> PROGRESS
> 2: the quality or state of being proficient

In other words, I thought to myself *I would be very comfortable and confident with Kathryn as a pilot, a leader, my commander if I was a soldier. Her proficiency instills confidence.*

Kathryn said, "The opportunity to be an active-duty soldier

focused my efforts."

She would be working for the Governor and the State of Michigan, as well as her country, instead of teaching advanced math. Her teaching days, however, were not over.

Kathryn was chosen to go to back to Rucker, this time to learn to be a Black Hawk instructor. After 5 years of college and teaching experience, the Army was going to teach her how people learn. "They had it figured out with an acronym-based system," she said with a laugh.

The Army was modernizing and engaged in a couple of wars long term. The new Black Hawk helicopter awaited her, the UH-60M; it was the "newest and best, everything digital, fancy computer-based helicopter," she said.

It was a big deal. Not only was she now trained to fly and be an instructor in the upgraded, digital, state-of-the-art, brand new, iconic Black Hawk helicopter, she would be a commander. Her teaching and leadership skills would come full circle. She was now a "15B" or Aviation Combined Arms Operations.

I read the job description and thought, *wow I'm quite sure none of my high school math teachers had these qualifications.*

"Commands or serves in leadership positions in aviation units. Plans, coordinates, and directs employment of aviation assets as an integral member of the combined arms team. Serves in staff positions, at various levels, which require knowledge of, and training in, the doctrinal and organizational facets of aviation and the other combat arms."

She was assigned to the Air Assault unit at Grand Ledge and retraining, when notified of her unit's Iraq deployment. The unit had 10 brand new aircraft, 43 flight crew members, chiefs and door gunners and one unit commander … Kathryn Prater. They left during June of 2010 to Fort Hood to continue training, then "folded em up" (the helicopters) to transport them to Kuwait on C5 military transport airplanes. There they would "unfold" the helicopters and give the pilots the "dust test," to make sure they could safely land in the brownout conditions which were common in Iraq. The endless dust conditions of the Middle East tested a pilot's proficiency to land in the wind and dust. Because of low humidity, extreme temperatures and little vegetation, dust and sand storms are persistent problems in Middle Eastern regions. The dust can pose health issues for soldiers and maintenance issues for helicopters.

From there it was off to Camp Taji Iraq. Al Taji was an airfield and supply depot for Saddam Hussein's army prior to the invasion of Iraq. It came under American control following the invasion in 2003. The camp, in addition to US military, houses soldiers of the new Iraqi Army and the Iraqi National Guard. One of the soldier's in her company under her command was born in Iraq. What a sight it was, flying over Baghdad during day. She had seen pictures from her brother's deployment, but there is nothing like seeing it in real life. It was a poignant realization for her that most communities were simply families just trying to make ends meet.

"There was no grass, little green and sad looking cows," said Kathryn, born and raised in the heart of Michigan's farming country. And the heat was oppressive. The *average* temperature in summer is 34.4 Celsius or 94 Fahrenheit at Taji. That's the *average,* with many days easily exceeding the century mark.

"It was middle of July oppressive take your breath away heat," said Kathryn, "and redheads don't like heat."

There was danger. They could see the tracer rounds while flying at night, visible with their night vision goggles. There were the sand storms and the oppressive heat to deal with, but due to the volume of missions they were to fly, her closest calls dealt with mechanical issues, due to the extreme environmental conditions of the Middle East. Kathryn told me a number of times how thankful she was for having the best mechanics who professionally and expertly cared for the helicopters. She has great respect for *their* proficiency.

She recalls flying over Fallujah with infantry men to secure and take them back to Taji. Suddenly, out in the middle of the desert, instrument panel warning lights came on, the type of warning lights where you've been trained to land the helicopter

… immediately. She wasn't going to put it down in the middle of desert, but, instead, flew to an unsecured medevac pad outside of Fallujah. She put it down fast and shut it down quickly. "Our company had the best mechanics and I had complete trust in them," she said. The check light was indication of metal in the tail rotor gearbox. A magnetic insert could be pulled by the mechanic to check for metal shavings. Grinding metal and bits on the magnetic detector means something is making metal in the tail rotor and indicative of a failure. The magnet has to be pulled by a mechanic and then a determination, a judgement if they could go on. As a helicopter pilot she wears a 9mm pistol under her arm with the goal, always try hard not to end up on the ground in "bad guy land" as she put it.

It caused me to think of the action/war drama *Black Hawk Down,* based on a best-selling book, detailing a mission in Somalia on October 3, 1993. US Army Rangers were dropped by helicopter deep into the capital city of Mogadishu to capture two top lieutenants of a Somali warlord. A firefight ensued, result-

Kathryn Prater in Iraq

ing in the destruction of two US Black Hawk helicopters. The movie focus is on the heroic efforts of the Rangers to get to the downed Black Hawk helicopters. Over the course of Operation Rumination, it has been my sentient realization that each military person I spent time with always has the backs of their fellow soldiers. I have become cognizant of their ingrained sense of duty, honor and selfless willingness to have each other's back … being invested in a common goal that is bigger than your own. Needless to say, I have often seen the opposite in the daily business world. Whether a veteran 100 years old, middle age or young, retired or active duty, when you take the time to talk to them you quickly pick up on this "have each other's back" characteristic.

In my conversation with Kathryn, I quickly recognized in her the same characteristic as the other veterans, including the 90 to 100-year-old veterans I became acquainted with. Quick to deflect praise, she was more interested in talking about "her guys," or talking about "the expert mechanics," and those with whom she served. I thought … it is true. It is a band of brothers and sisters.

"I'm 30 years old, and the punched-in-the-stomach anxiety you feel are the decisions you make for others," she said. " I am making judgements and calculations on how much of a maintenance risk this problem is out here in the middle of nowhere and whether we keep going."

Then she added, "Our mantra as helicopter pilots is keep it greasy side down, right side up."

As commander of her unit flying 15-million-dollar helicopters "you watch your guys fly off 6 to 8 flight hours every day and you worry about them." They flew so much in Iraq the ear plugs everyone wore eventually gave them cuts in their ears. From Balad to Baghdad and all the way to the west coast of Iraq, from Ramadi to Al Asad and Sadr city the troops have to go places and they were going to get them there and back.

They worked in coordination with the Iraqi army, and Kathryn said that gives you hope. It generally worked well, except for one mission she recalls in particular. They were conducting planning to insert a group of Iraqi Army soldiers into Western Iraq. Kathryn was one of the Black Hawk pilots and the Air Mission Commander. The Iraqi general they were working with did not like it. "Why is she here?" she hears via the interpreter in her headset. The General was unhappy and not familiar working with a female pilot or commander for that matter. Kathryn pushed back.

"This is what you get sir. Take it or leave it. I'm not going to put my men in danger because you want to change a deliberate mission plan." She told the interpreter, "I can leave ... but the helicopters go with me."

A MOTHERLY INSTINCT

THE UNITED STATES NAVY SEALS SPECIAL FORCES IN Operation Neptune Spear killed Al-Qaeda leader Osama Bin Laden in Abbottabad, Pakistan on May 2, 2011. Al-Qaeda confirmed the death on May 6, with posts made on militant websites, vowing to avenge the killing. This created a big uprising of terrorist cells and coordinated attacks. Early in the morning at Taji, they felt the avenge attacks with lots of mortar rounds and rockets fired into the base.

"I'll never forget being inside my room, trying to muster the courage to open the door and look outside to make sure my guys were OK." The shelling lasted for 3 minutes. Kathryn was laying on the floor by a T wall and grabbed her body armor with a pillow over her head. She laid there and counted the shells. No time to run for the bunker.

"My motherly instinct was with my crew, and, when I went outside, I told the first sergeant I wanted to lay eyes on all my people. My first sergeant and I worked well together, and our unit identified problems and solved them; it was a very professional group." They were the 1-147 Aviation Air Assault Battalion. They were the Bravo company Silverbacks, 43 men and women from Michigan serving their country. Everyone in her unit was

OK, even the missing EMT who had grabbed his bag and gone out looking for casualties.

She took the safety of all her unit very seriously. "We were flying so much while stationed there. I have a degree in math, so I know with the volume of flying time we were doing statistically something was bound to go wrong."

Over the 10-month deployment, each pilot put in an amazing number of hours in flying time. Taking troops to conduct ground operations, in transport as many as 600 to 700 hours of flying time each. Flying in an unforgiving environment, as their commander, Kathryn took their safety seriously to heart.

"It was the hand of God," she said. "OK, Jesus, let's talk. While deployed I had lots of conversations with Him. It made my faith stronger. It's like having a toddler and having to let them go; it's hard when you do that, but you're never going to get those days back. These are guys in the civilian sector, some having a tough time paying the mortgage. They have families at home."

Back home the Family Readiness Group Secretary was Kathryn's mom. Her mom wrote the newsletter, with input from Kathryn, to keep families posted. Her mom stayed after her so the info kept coming. The group arranged to have a Christmas tree mailed to Iraq, to be enjoyed by the National Guard unit of 43. I'm sure, being from Michigan, a fresh evergreen tree felt a little like home out in the dusty desert.

"Did you name the helicopters or have a special name for them?" I asked.

"We would name them by their triple digit number stenciled below the tail rotor," she said. "I remember helicopter 111 was called triple sticks."

"So back to that *Top Gun* movie poster, just out of curiosity," I said. "Do you feel the need for speed?"

"Not really," said Kathryn. "We would generally fly at about 120 knots, and, remember, 20 to 30 knot head winds were not unusual along with copious amounts of dust. The commander sets the standard for everyone else, so I would always be conservative and err on side of caution. Being a commander can be lonely, you have to allow your guys some space for camaraderie and an opportunity to complain about you," she said with a smile. "I wanted to be fair, firm, consistent."

The other great thing about National Guard people is they have many varied skillsets they bring from the civilian sector. She said in her unit the electricians, builders and other trades got together to build a deck out of packing materials. "They would hang out and drink fake beers and smoke cigars on the deck they'd built, giving them a little taste of home while in Iraq," Kathryn said.

I asked Kathryn if she was glad she served, and, without hesitation, she said yes. "It was always the plan and God kept bringing me back. And I've seen the world. My favorite part is working with other soldiers. They have your back and all you have to do is ask. They exemplify selfless service. And I've wondered, does the service attract that type of person or does it make them? In the civilian sector people can't always say that about their co-workers."

Kathryn met her husband in the Army. He also was a UH-60 pilot. Together they have a daughter, now 4 years old. With two Army Black Hawk helicopter pilots as parents, she laughs when she tells me, her daughter's favorite color is pink. Her daughter tells her, "Your camouflage is not beautiful Mommy," says Kathryn laughing.

I laugh and I sit there thinking that Kathryn, with a Bronze Star for heroic and meritorious service in a combat zone, as well as other Meritorious awards, will have a daughter that someday understands why she wears that camouflage to work. In the interim, for now, at night she can sing lullabies to her daughter dressed in pink … and, during the day, work in her camouflage to keep it all greasy side down.

OPERATION RUMINATION

I WAS OUT RUNNING TO RUMINATE ON MY CONVERSATION with Kathryn Prater. Serving as a Black Hawk helicopter instructor she feels as she says "not being a natural" makes her now a better instructor. She teaches others, starting at the very beginning as a pilot just as she did She knows what the training pilots are going through. She can relate, it's the old been-there-done-that scenario. Kathryn is a teacher and knows how to teach. But it's the real-life experience, the walk a mile in another person's shoes that makes her a special teacher. The combination of her piloting skills and her teaching skills are *enhanced by her experience.* Having the discipline to use that experience to help others is a highly valuable component of selfless service. We are all better for it, and her high standard for service became evident to me early on in our conversation.

> *I understand I too have the opportunity to use my experiences and roads traveled to help others along the way.*

The road we run can be bumpy with twists and turns. Kathryn tells me active duty personnel have to take the PT test every 6 months … the test that I'll be taking soon . Always the teacher, she coaches me on the proper order of push-ups first, then sit-ups and finally the run when testing. She made a New Year's resolution this year to run a half marathon, and she just accomplished it in the Capital City Marathon. She learned, just like I did, that when life comes at you, exercise can provide some valuable solitude and stress relief. Both she and her husband live their lives on the go. Her husband flies a corporate jet, and Kathryn in her full-time service to the National Guard, both maintain an active schedule. I learned personally that at some point your health, mentally and physically as well as getting a good night's sleep cause you to take notice. Kathryn had the same experience, and it was a friend at her daughter's day care that gave her good advice. Her friend is an avid runner and suggested, before you seek the help of a doctor … give distance running a chance. It has benefited her, and I share that same experience with Kathryn. It reminded me that, just like Kathryn Prater, I can be a teacher too, **and have the opportunity to use my experiences and roads traveled to help others along the way.**

Even as a high school teen
His drive was far from routine
You hear it in the way he talks
You see it in the way he walks
Destined to be a Marine.

Matthew "McDizzle" McDaid

Sergeant US Marine Corps

US Marines Infantry First tour Ramadi, Iraq
2004-2005

MEU Marine Expeditionary Unit Okinawa Japan
Sniper School 2005-2006

March 2007-October 2007 Sniper section leader
Ramadi and Karma Iraq

Chapter Nineteen

A Hammer or a Toolbox

H E KNEW HIS WHOLE LIFE FROM A young age he wanted to serve in the military. He remembers watching Operation Desert Storm at the age of 5 years and looking up to the US military. Even his high school yearbook noted his future plans were to be a sniper. His baseball coach at Paw Paw High School, while having teammates out running, gave him a pellet gun to crawl around on the field "low crawl" shooting gophers. Paw Paw was named by the indigenous population from the paw paw fruit that grew thickly along the river's banks. The watershed includes Great Lakes marshes, swamps and floodplain forests, which serve as habitats for migratory birds, butterflies, the massasauga rattlesnake, whitetail deer, spotted turtle and other wildlife. Paw Paw is wine country with acres of water and woods. Young Matthew grew up on a dead-end of a dirt road with hundreds of acres of swamps and wooded area to explore.

The Almena swamp or the "big swamp," for initial settlers of the area in the 1830s, was a challenging place. Nearly every pioneer of Almena was lost in its mazes at one time or another, until they learned that following the streams up would be sure to lead to an opening. Almena township is in Van Buren County Michigan, and at least one-third of the township is covered by a great swamp. Good water-power, which attracted the attention of the first white settler, is found on a fork of the Paw Paw river flowing through the town towards the west. Matthew McDaid planted the seeds of his early development, observational skills and adventurous characteristics in that historic swamp.

"I loved to go into the swamps and woods to disappear, to observe, to become part of the environment," Matthew said.

After high school it was off to Camp Pendleton, California for basic training. It was hard but it was no surprise. "My parents had trained me to be comfortable with being uncomfortable," Matthew said with a grin. Sixty young men in his group "shuffling" to learn where they were going to be and where they fit in. He soon was put in a leadership position, one of four in his platoon.

At boot camp they break you down. He remembers on one occasion all the recruits were to take off their underwear or "whitey tighties" as Matthew called them, and throw them in the center of the room. No room for modesty or selfish preservation, their instructors mixed and tossed the underwear in front of them. They were given 10 seconds to retrieve their underwear. It gave you just enough time just to grab a pair. "I wore a medium," said Matthew, "but I think I got a 2 XL."

He recalls marching up front to a rifle range. His drill instructor didn't want to carry his pack, so he made Matthew carry his for him along with his own. With his pack on his back, he strapped his instructors pack on the front, and they marched. A strange smell emanated from the instructors pack. Matthew could swear it smelled like McDonalds chicken McNuggets. He found an occasion to unzip the bag and sure enough there they were, chicken McNuggets. Matthew doesn't know but surmises he did it intentionally. Matthew took one and ate it, quickly zipping the bag. I asked him if his drill instructor knew.

"He would have been kicking my ass for months if he saw it. He would have kicked me to the IT deck for push-ups, squats, jumping jacks and more until I was in a pool of my own sweat," Matthew said. Incentive training (IT) is one of the tools drill instructors use to instill discipline and motivation. The IT deck, or quarter deck, is roughly 10' X 10' and used by drill instructors to instill discipline and motivation, and correct minor disciplinary infractions. It instills self-discipline and motivates you to check yourself and make sure that everything around you is right, so you don't spend time on the quarterdeck.

Boot camp was about discipline and physical fitness, especially upper body strength. "When I got home from boot camp everyone thought I was taller," said Matthew. He had perfect posture drilled into him … no more slouching, and it was noticeable to those who had known him before his boot camp experience.

After graduating from boot camp, he went back home for a month, and then on to California for SOI or School of Infantry for 4 to 5 weeks of tactics training and more discipline. This would prepare him for what was to come in Iraq. At the end of this training and evaluation, the 100 Marines were lined up for a roster rundown, names called off on where you would go next. Matthew anxiously waited for his name to be called. "Call my name" he was thinking quietly, and was thrilled when he found his next assignment was the "Two-Five." Founded just over a hundred years ago, the 2nd Battalion, 5th Marines had earned and maintained a tremendous reputation for its professionalism and performance. One of the most decorated in history, the 2nd battalion, 5th Marines had found itself wherever the Marine Corps was making history.

The battalion motto - "Retreat hell we just got here" - comes from the 1918 battle of Belleau Wood. The Belleau Woods, near the Marne River in France, was the site of the fighting tenacity of the Marines in June 1918, pushing back the German spring offensive in World War I. As the Marines approached the site of what would be one the Marine Corps' most famous battles, retreating allied soldiers told the Marines they must retreat before the German onslaught. Captain Lloyd Williams, at the time a company commander in 2nd Battalion, 5th Marines, replied, "Retreat? Hell, we just got here!" The motto reflects the fighting spirit of the Marines who have served in 2/5 ever since, including Guadalcanal, Okinawa, Korea, the battle of Hue City, Iraq and Afghanistan. Joining the "Two-Five" meant Matthew would be trained to go to Iraq.

I asked him why he wanted his name to be called?

"Imagine being a painter and never being able to paint," said Matthew, "the Marines are the best fighters in the world."

The buses arrived and he was nervous to meet his new squad, leader wanting to make a good impression. "Now I'm in the real Marine Corps," he thought, "and you can count on me." It was a short trip to the "Two-Five" from Camp Pendleton. 2nd Battalion, 5th Marines is located in Camp San Mateo, California. The "Two-Five" had just returned from the Iraq invasion and was picking up new Marines. He felt the weight, it was a lot to live up to; the seven months of training was very hard. "You were always tired," said Matthew.

There he was, wearing sunglasses. You couldn't see his eyes. You were scared to look at him just out of respect. His name was J.R. Lott and he was Matthew's new squad leader. "Everyone was scared of him," Matthew said. Golf company 2nd platoon squad was broken into teams, and Matthew's squad leader for the next 7 months would be J.R. Lott. "He treated us like Navy Seals," says Matthew, "he hammered us." Running miles on the beaches, climbing mountains near the San Mateo base so steep you had to use ropes, swimming in their gear in the Pacific Ocean.

Today J.R. Lott is one of his best friends, traveling to Michigan for Matthew and Sarah's wedding. I ask him about the 7 months of training with him, and I can see the respect he has for his squad leader, preparing him for what lie ahead in Iraq.

"Some point to their stripes, or their rank, J.R. was never like that," says Matthew. "When we were out training, he was out front. He never asked us to do anything he didn't do better or first." I said that sounds like the definition of leadership. Matthew nods his head.

The training did, indeed, prepare him for what lie ahead. He was deployed to Ramadi, Iraq, known as the city of death. Since the fall of Fallujah, Ramadi had become the center of the insurgency in Iraq. Law and order there had broken down and street battles were a common occurrence. IEDs (Improvised Explosive Devices), small arms and RPGs (Rocket Propelled Grenades) were a part of everyday life in Ramadi.

"Ramadi was a good fight," Matthew said, "lots of enemy contact and IEDs small arms and RPGs." He said even today he missed the camaraderie of "after-mission sharing" with the others in his group. They shared a bond. They had just survived a 12-hour gunfight and were sitting around together sharing their stories.

Matthew's first tour of Iraq was from September 2004 to March of 2005 in Ramadi. Of the 700 in his "Two-Five" battalion 15 were killed in action and 300 wounded. A few months after his arrival he became one of those wounded in action.

On October 28, 2004 Matthew McDaid and his team were involved in a gunfight on the streets of Ramadi, Iraq. The insurgents were shooting at them with RPGs. Near the Humvee, he remembers clearly the feeling of the moment. An explosion; it felt like someone had just punched him in the face. Pulled around to the backside of the Humvee by Lieutenant Downs, he was bleeding heavily from his upper lip. They pulled the metal out of his upper lip and slowed the bleeding. Shrapnel was later removed from his leg.

Matthew received a Purple Heart for being wounded in action. The Purple Heart is awarded to members of the armed forces of the US who are wounded by an instrument of war in the hands of the enemy, and, posthumously, to the next of kin in the name of those who are killed in action or die of wounds received in action. It is a combat decoration. As we talk of the incident, he pushes his lunch aside and seems uninterested in the decoration or even talking about it.

"When your Humvee hits an IED it is an awakening ... people are trying to kill you."

"We had many close calls with roadside IEDs" he said, recalling specifically one time his whole squad was blown into the ditch by an explosion. A very close call. He was reminded by his dad later; it was the same day on the calendar that his Uncle John had died in Vietnam years earlier. He quickly detracts and downplays the importance of *his* Purple Heart with a somber sad look on his face and says, "Others like my Uncle John die or some lose a leg or an arm and they get a Purple Heart." He implies *they* are the true heroes and we change the subject continuing with our lunch.

His 7-month tour in Iraq was over. In March of 2005, Matthew returned home from Iraq with a month off. It was then off to sniper school at Camp Pendleton with, as he put it, "open tryouts." There were 50 guys, and everyone was "hard ass" as he put it. They push you in sniper school, lots of homework, study, memorization, physical activity and carrying the weight, reading notecards and memorizing morning noon and night, during any break that you have in your day.

"It was all about *Observe, Recall, Recite,*" says Matthew. He recites an acronym "KIMS" or keep in memory system.

Of the 50 original, only the top three advance to sniper school. They were dropping like flies. Down to 18...12...10. "I had to do it," he says, "I said in my high school yearbook I was going to do it!" We laugh together as I can see even now that drive in his eyes and his demeanor. Sure enough, Matthew and two of his "buddies" saw it all the way through.

Sniper school was all about learning what is "baseline" and then having the ability to pick out what's not normal. The power of observation ... a keen eye, a calm approach, an awareness of what's going on around you. It seemed natural to Matthew, as a young man he liked hiding in the swamp and woods "becoming a part of the environment."

"Snipers do much more than shoot," says Matthew. "They observe and report. They paint a picture of what is going on around them and then report those keen observations so others can plan."

> **"A sniper is trained to do so much more that shoot. Imagine if building a house and you're only given a hammer (gun) versus the whole toolbox. You can defend yourself and others with the toolbox. As a Marine sniper you are taught to use the whole toolbox."**

Marine Sniper Sergeant Matthew McDaid

He shares a couple stories to support the training and work of a sniper. He and the other sniper trainees were given 2 minutes to look at 10 random items dumped out of a box in the morning. They were given 2 minutes to look at and memorize the contents, 10 items in all. Their instructors try to distract them. They spend the day on the run … training and classes. Meanwhile he tried to build a story in his mind throughout the day of what he'd seen earlier. A "song" in his head he can recite throughout the day while occupied with other tasks. Late in the day they are given a minute to draw and write on a piece of paper the 10 objects that were dumped from the box hours before. Observe and report. Paint a picture. Observe, recall, recite. This practice, or mental exercise, pays off for a sniper down the road. He recalls from his position on a roof in Ramadi, observing a man in the marketplace, dragging his heels as he walks. He would repeatedly move across the road to shake hands with others or move about the marketplace, all the while dragging a heel. The training kicks in. Know what is baseline, or normal, and pick out what is not normal. He calls it in requesting permission to engage. A team is sent out to the location under his watchful eye pinpointing the area. A trip wire is lifted from the road. The dragging heel insurgent was burying wire for explosives in the marketplace and Matthew's powers of observation noted it.

Urban sniper school was next, and, upon graduation in September of 2005, he was off to Okinawa, Japan as a sniper school graduate for further training. He was part of a MEU pronounced "Mew" or Marine Expeditionary Unit, the 31st MEU to Japan, Korea, Philippines and Guam. He was there not for combat, but, rather, training as a Corporal and sniper section leader. A MEU, however, is always ready for quick deployment and immediate response to any crisis. Upon completion of a deployment, the Marine expeditionary unit remains "special operations capable," prepared to respond to events around the world. In the case of Matthew, after his assigned MEU, his time was up. He had served his time and it was back to the States. Restless, when asked if interested in extending his service, he volunteered. There was unfinished business and "bad blood" in Iraq. It was late 2006, and he decided to re-up his commitment as a Marine and a trained sniper. "Most parents aren't thrilled when you do something like that," Matthew says with a grin.

It was back to Camp Pendleton to train as a leader. Promoted to sergeant rank in the "H&S" company...or Headquarters and Services Company, he would lead and prepare a sniper team of six for service in Iraq. He had 7 months to pick and train a team that was technically sound with skilled minds. "What makes a sniper is the small details," says Matthew.

Before his final deployment to Iraq the "Two-Five" snipers were issued new rifles. They would be the first to use these smaller rifles called the XM3. It was a big deal. The brand new rifle came out of the box and had to be custom painted. Matthew named his rifle "Chelsea," after a young lady he was dating at the time. Years later he got a phone call from someone in Idaho. When the military is done with rifles they can be decommissioned and sold. The CMP or Civilian Marksmanship Program sells the rifles with a certificate and this person had bought "Chelsea" paint job and all for $16,000. The caller said he looked through the data book, and was informing him he had his sniper rifle. He wanted to tell him if he ever wanted it back, he would sell it, but only to him. We laugh … yes … $16,000 dollars. "I didn't have that kind of money laying around," said Matthew.

In March of 2007 it was back to Ramadi, Iraq for his last deployment. Recalling what he had experienced in his first tour, he had trained his team for a firefight. Things had changed significantly by 2007. Serious gains had been made with some rebuilding and some pride, far different from his first go around. He spent 3 months with his team on sniper missions seeking out insurgents, the mujahideen or "Mooosh as we called them" said Matthew.

Three months into the tour his team was needed elsewhere. A sniper team was needed in the city of Karma outside of Fallujah. The patrols with his sniper team were "textbook," Matthew said. "It was hunting, house to house learning, a cat and mouse game, by then the dumb ones were dead."

And then it was over. Time to go home. October of 2007 it was "thank you for your service" and a flight back home. He started college at Western Michigan University for sports medicine while working at Bronson Hospital. He got a call from a friend asking him if he missed what they did as Marine snipers. There was an opportunity as US embassies needed snipers to protect the Embassy. He was flown to Washington DC to interview and got the job. Working on finishing his Bachelor of Science degree while attending a sniper school in Arkansas, he was nicknamed "Old School" by the others, achieving top shot and honor grad status in 2012. Paid as a private security civilian, he found himself on top of the US Embassy in Kabul, Afghanistan from January to August 2013 as a hired sniper protecting the embassy.

Today Matthew McDaid runs a company he founded called Section 1776. Matthew put an idea he had for a long time into action. He built a business that reflects his nature, patriotic, active, and adventurous. With no background in marketing, business, clothing or making a brand, his personal characteristics were perfect for the entrepreneurial risk involved in starting a business. It also reflected his lifelong discipline of service and giving back. Section 1776 events are organized and called "Section Collections" that help veterans with food, clothes and household items.

Matthew's thriving business, Section 1776, sells only apparel made in the US with each sale donating a portion to Team Rubicon. Team Rubicon unites the skills and experiences of military veterans with first responders to rapidly deploy emergency response teams. Team Rubicon's primary mission is providing disaster relief to those affected by natural disasters such as hurricanes or floods, domestic or international. Matthew, as founder of Section 1776, has deployed on two separate "Operations" since he joined their volunteer ranks.

Our lunch is over, and Matthew is off on his next adventure. The brisket tacos were delicious. When we were shown our table on the patio at the start of lunch, I chose the chair facing the door, the exit, so Matthew had his back to the door. I suddenly realized that wasn't the right move when having lunch with a highly trained, keenly observant Marine sniper. We laugh in the recognition of my faux pas and Matthew acknowledges he conceded "that is how it's going to have to be." I'll do better on my next lunch mission with McDaid. For now, he is off on his next mission: to manage the business and then marry his fiancé, Sarah, that weekend, opening a new chapter in his life. We stand and shake hands, "Welcome to Section 1776," he says.

OPERATION RUMINATION

As I ruminate on my time with Matthew McDaid I reflect on risk … my ability to stomach and engage in risk at this point in my life. Calculated risk. Smart risk as someone willing to lead to benefit others. My ability to "observe, recall, recite" and to help others in simple ways. Am I engaged in life as a man and making a difference? Am I observant of what is going on around me and the needs of others? Am I using a hammer someone else gave me, or, am I tapping into my full toolbox? Not only for my personal benefit, but for the benefit of others that cross my path on a daily basis. Imagine if building a house, you're only given a hammer versus the *whole* toolbox? Thanks to Marine Sergeant Matthew McDaid, I resolve to help others with *my* whole toolbox.

Semper Paratus

Always prepared to say yes
With aid to those in distress
By water by air
They serve everywhere
And rush to the call SOS.

Roland Ashby
US Coast Guard
Chief Warrant Officer 4
RAID team Middle East
Search and Rescue Coxswain

Chapter Twenty

Say Yes ... You Never Know

What Will Happen

T IS APRIL ON LAKE MICHIGAN AND spring is in the air. Winter-weary residents with cabin fever appreciate the daytime temperatures, finally approaching 50 to 60 degrees. On some random days a bonus of 70-degree temperatures might occur. In Muskegon, Michigan the April average is around 56 degrees. The earth slowly comes to life, but the lake called "Michigami" by the native Americans of the Ojibwe and Potawatomi tribes, meaning "big lake," is slow to wake from its winter slumber. The variance, between warming spring air temperatures and almost freezing Lake Michigan water temperatures, can cause difficult navigation conditions for those who venture out on the "big lake."

April 16, 2000 had conditions perfect for advection fog to form near Muskegon, Michigan. Water temperatures were in the frigid 30s, while air temperatures were warming up and contained more moisture. The east side of Lake Michigan is primed for advection fog due to horizontal westerly and southerly winds blowing across the water. The fog is called advection fog, because warmer, more moist air advects, or blows, over the cold water of Lake Michigan. As the warm, moist air moves over the cold water, the air cools down rapidly. The cooler air can't hold the moisture it could at the former warm temperature, so condensation forms. The invisible water vapor condenses the dew point, which rises and forms fog.

On April 16, 2000 a single-engine plane lifted off from Muskegon airport en route to Illinois. It didn't get far. The Cessna 172 single engine plane, carrying a father and son, crashed into Lake Michigan about 5 miles south of Muskegon. A 49-year-old Illinois man and his 12-year-old son were in the nearly freezing waters, shrouded in fog and clinging to life.

Petty Officer Roland Ashby, a Coast Guard reservist, responded to the call for help. Hampered by dense fog, Ashby and crew, when they got close, found the pair by turning off their boat engines and listening for their calls for help. There they were, the father and son, clinging to one of the plane's wheels, floating in the frigid Lake Michigan waters. In the water for over 20 minutes the two were rescued by the Coast Guard and treated at the hospital for hypothermia. An example of Semper Paratus, always prepared, what a United States Coast Guard member will say is his motto and is the reason he or she is ready for any emergency, including fog. "We couldn't see anything," Ashby said. "We heard screaming. Mostly from the boy." The father told rescuers that he lost the horizon before the plane crashed.

Years later, I sit in an airport hanger with US Coast Guard Chief Warrant Officer Roland Ashby, chatting about the work of the Coast Guard. I live near a Coast Guard station on Lake Michigan, and I mentioned to Roland that, as I stand knee deep in the water on the shoreline near my home in mid-summer, I watch the bright orange Coast Guard helicopter roar by at a low altitude. I tell him that I would love to go for a ride.

"We're all jealous of the helicopter pilots," says Roland

laughing.

Roland spent time stationed in Grand Haven, Michigan and Muskegon, Michigan as a "Search and Rescue Coxswain," the boat captain in charge of the crew. We laugh hard as he says, "A requirement is to be 6-foot-tall so you can walk back to shore." Well I'm never going to meet that requirement and training for it would be a stretch. I also gathered my odds of a ride in the rescue helicopter, short of my personal rescue, was remote at best. Roland notes he deals with his jealousy by reminding himself there are more helicopters in the bottom of the ocean than there are boats in the air.

On a 352-acre peninsula along Cape May Harbor, Coast Guard Training Center Cape May, New Jersey has trained many Coast Guard recruits through the years. Basic training for Roland Ashby was at Cape May; he the grandson of a Coast Guard veteran who retired from the ferry-boat system in Clinton, Washington.

Roland Ashby

"When in basic training you're held to a different standard; you stay very active," said Roland.

Even today Roland hasn't stopped running yet. He has done four Ironman triathlons, and, at the time we met, he had just signed up for one the following year. We talked about running and why he is driven to do things like train for a triathlon.

"When you get a desk job it sneaks up on you, you have to stay active," Roland said.

"Why so driven?" I ask.

"I've been that way since I was a kid. I would be devious if bored," said Roland with a self-deprecating laugh and twinkle in his eye. "People need to have a goal and purpose, something that is bigger than themselves," he said.

I smile and think to myself, *there it is again*. That reoccurring thread I have found with the veterans I hang around … continual goals.

Roland did meet a personal goal by becoming a pilot. While deployed in Virginia for 4 ½ four and a half years, while he was in and out of the Middle East on the Coast Guard RAID team, he trained as a pilot, taking flight training at Langley Air base. He earned his pilot certifications through the US Air Force Flight Training Center at Langley Air Force Base, and now shares his passion for aviation as an aircraft broker and a volunteer mission pilot with the Civil Air Patrol. We stand chatting in an airport hanger with tools, metal and plans spread out on benches. He is in the process of building his own airplane.

I live on the shores of Lake Michigan and near a busy channel and port on the lake. I have seen the role of the Coast Guard in action, but, of course, it's just a glimpse of the purpose of the men and women of the US Coast Guard. The Coast Guard is a unique branch of the military, responsible for an array of maritime duties, from ensuring safe and lawful commerce to performing rescue missions in severe conditions. Nearly 42,000 men and women are actively serving in the Coast Guard to defend America's borders and protect the maritime environment.

Roland Ashby is a Chief Warrant Officer and a veteran of

the US Coast Guard Reserve. He served on active duty for four years in support of Operation Iraqi Freedom and Operation Enduring Freedom, managing the Coast Guard's RAID Team (Redeployment Assistance and Inspection Detachment) in Iraq, Afghanistan and Kuwait. Roland has also served as a Search and Rescue boat coxswain on the Great Lakes and Puerto Rico.

Most people do not realize the Coast Guard was involved in the military effort in Iraq and Afghanistan. The Coast Guard Redeployment Assistance and Inspection Detachment Team (RAID) is distinct and the most forward-deployed task force of the Coast Guard. The job was created in 2003 by the Department of Defense to ensure hazardous materials are properly prepared

Roland Ashby as part of Coast Guard RAID team

for shipment and re-entry into US ports as part of the military redeployment process.

Since 2003 hundreds of Coast Guard personnel have been deployed to the Middle East as members of RAID Teams, where they inspected cargo shipping containers to make sure the containers are serviceable and seaworthy, and to ensure that all requirements and regulations are followed. These inspections helped to eliminate delays in shipping of material and equipment back to the states. Forces in the Middle East use standard containers to move equipment and supplies. Freight containers hold several kinds of products, from food to ammunition, and the Army efficiently supplies its forces by using such containerized cargo. The Coast Guard has long specialized in effective container inspections, which is the reason the Coast Guard received this mission.

On March 1, 2003 the Coast Guard became part of the newly created Department of Homeland Security. For Roland Ashby, this included his work on Lake Michigan, managing the traffic of intoxicated boat operators. They watched for "erratic boating," including boats operating in the evening without their lights on. He recalls following a large Sea Ray boat into the weeds after a fireworks show without its lights on. When they caught up to it, they saw the 8-year-old daughter at the wheel. Roland told the man "we'll follow her from here and watch her dock." They decided instead to anchor there for the night. No one was arrested.

His work in the Coast Guard dealt with the civilian population outside of his work with the RAID operation in the Middle East.

"Military people can be rude to each other but it's different. There is a saying that often a military person can be rude or direct to your face and *have your back*. A civilian can be nice to your face and stab you in the back," says Roland.

In military training, including the Coast Guard, you are trained to have each other's back. When stationed in Muskegon, Roland recalls a new, young 19-year-old arrival fresh from boot camp and basic training. Roland and the others stationed there, decided they were going to initiate the young man and have a laugh or two in the process. They sent him out on the pier at the Muskegon channel with ping pong paddles and had him hold them with heavy welding gloves. They told him they were going to "re-tune the radar" and wanted him to hold up and move the paddles based on their direction.

Waving the paddles at sunset, I can only imagine the entertainment this provided the beach-goers awaiting one of the classic and anticipated sunsets I have enjoyed on the pier in West Michigan. Adding insult to injury, they had cracked open the contents of chemlights and dumped it into the fingers of the gloves. This caused his fingers to glow in fluorescent green when he took off the gloves. They told him they hoped he wasn't planning to have kids someday as his hands glowed in radioactive green.

We laugh together at his memory. But I also reflect on that same pier in Muskegon, Michigan that I have loved for its amazing sunsets. Warm summer evenings, stormy fall fronts, ice-covered brilliance and the promise of spring. I've watched the Coast Guard as they exit the channel in their boats or roar overhead along the coastline in a helicopter. I'm glad they are "always prepared" for an emergency and have our back.

> *From Aztec Shore to Arctic Zone*
> *To Europe and Far East,*
> *The flag is carried by our ships,*
> *In times of war and peace;*
> *And never have we struck it yet*
> *In spite of foeman's might.*
> *Who cheered our crews and cheered again*
> *For showing how to fight.*

> **Chorus**
> *So here's the Coast Guard marching song,*
> *We sing on land and sea.*
> *Through surf and storm and howling gale,*
> *High shall our purpose be.*
> *"Semper Paratus" is our guide,*
> *Our fame and glory too.*
> *To fight to save or fight and die,*
> *Aye! Coast Guard we are for you*

OPERATION RUMINATION

I THANKED ROLAND ASHBY FOR HIS SERVICE WITH A handshake. "I feel guilty when thanked," says Roland. "The military has done more for me than I've done for it."

Again, the characteristic of selfless service as I have found in other veterans. He also shares with me his philosophy and attitude in life is this, "Say yes, you never know what will happen."

I ruminate on his philosophy and think *I've learned to take that approach at this point in my life too.* Functioning based on fear or worry, something I've done from time to time, is no way to operate or make a difference. I thought, *bring on that new challenge, that new adventure.* I thought *Semper Paratus..... always prepared.... for something new.*

Roland Ashby as co-host of Frontlines of Freedom
Radio, the largest military veteran talk show in America

No venue needed to formalize
Impromptu he could organize
With the word scholastical
He would be ecclesiastical
In the field he could sermonize.

Chaplain Major Larry L. "Chappy" Vollink
Army Chaplain 1980-2000
American Legion State Chaplain 1991-2008
National Chaplain 2008-2009
Michigan Wing Chaplain Civil Air Patrol 2012-
2018

Chapter Twenty-one

The Lord Answered His Prayer

T WAS A HUMID, BALMY SEPTEMBER evening. I arrived at the YMCA and dragged both myself and my gym bag into the locker room after a long day at work. Hungry and tired, I had to talk myself out of skipping my "basic training" workout that night in lieu of a hot meal. I plunked down on the locker-room bench and began pulling my running gear out of the bag: shoes, socks, shorts and an Army PFU that didn't smell very good. "Lord what am I doing this for?" I asked myself. With visions of a chicken sandwich and cold drink dancing in my head, I willed myself out of my work clothes and into my workout attire. Running shoes, black shorts and the grey cotton shirt with the word ARMY emblazoned across the front that I had worn all year in my journey. I decided to get the 6-mile run outside done first, so I could finish my workout of weights, push-ups and sit-ups indoors in the cooler environment of the YMCA.

I head outside, set my watch and begin running west into the hot, setting sun. My dog tag and cross necklace jangle as they bounce in rhythm on my chest to the beat of my feet pounding the pavement. On an upward climb up a busy street, ironically named "Health Way," I pace myself, lost in my thoughts.

I see a car to my left, stopped in the middle of the road and with the door open, the driver is outside the car waving and calling to me. Thinking he needs help or a push I stop to talk to the man. It is Chaplain Larry Vollink, known to some as "Chap" or "Chappy" or "Hey Padre." I realize he, like others over the course of this summer, took notice of the grey shirt with large, black ARMY letters across the front.

"Are you an Army veteran?" asks Larry.

"It's a long story," I said. "Do you have a business card?"

As traffic tries to get by, I become traffic cop while Larry digs for a business card out of his car. I take the card and zip it into a zippered pouch in the back of my running shorts and continue off into the sunset. Larry pulls up alongside me and rolls down his window as I run. We agree to meet for coffee sometime down the road. We both have stories to share. I thought to myself you never know who might just cross your path on any given day.

The next day I dig the now-sweaty and soggy business card out of my shorts, and I email and call Larry. I'm thinking *Lord I was faithful in putting in the miles last night even though I didn't want to, so maybe it's a sign you put someone in my path to learn a lesson*. It's been like that all year since Operation Rumination commenced. I guess you could say I followed His leading.

Larry Vollink was 33 years old when he experienced Army basic training in 1980. It was Chaplain's basic training in Fort Monmouth, New Jersey. The US Army Chaplain school was first created out of need to adequately train chaplains for the large fighting force that the United States was creating in 1917 for service in World War I. Since then, many chaplains have experienced basic training, and gone on to be there for men and women in conflicts ever since. For Larry it was 6 weeks of basic training. He did all the physical training, and it helped to be with other chaplains that had experience. They helped train to be an officer, wear the uniform and get you in physical, mental and spiritual shape. For Larry, a 1965 graduate from South high school, he initially was encouraged by his family to enter the ministry. He didn't want to enter the ministry, but he didn't want to go to the Vietnam War either. A conundrum.

Prior to basic training Larry had been grounded by "failure" in his words, something we all have to experience, it seems, to find our way. After high school he acquired a "4D status" because he opted for Bible college in Lansing at Great Lakes Christian college. Upon completion he was ordained in Grand Rapids, Michigan on May 3, 1970 as a pastor. Larry's wife at the time was an Air Force "brat." And. as his fiancé. Sharon now explains to me they have "itchy feet to move." As a military brat, Sharon understands itchy feet and the lifestyle of living on the move. After three churches and "unsuccessful" years in the pastorate, it was time to make a change. He needed his masters, so he went to Grand Rapids Baptist seminary. After 10 years of ministry, now at the age of 33, he found his "calling" and he volunteered to be an Army chaplain.

Larry tells me he said a prayer at that time. "Why is it Lord you can't keep me in a long ministry? I'm a failure. Lord is there any way you can help me be successful? I would like to be in a long ministry." God answered his prayer.

The requirements are high to be an Army chaplain. You need to have three things: a masters, an ecclesiastical endorsement and pastoral experience. In addition, you have to be willing to rappel out of helicopters. Really. When at Fort Campbell, they had to experience and train, just like the fighters who were going to Operation Desert Storm. That included rappelling out of helicopters.

Larry, at the age of 33, was finally ready to meet his calling. Army ministry has been his true calling. "If you ever have an issue go to a military chaplain," says Larry.

Fort Campbell in Kentucky was Larry's first assignment as a chaplain beginning his military career in October of 1980. On a typical Sunday, he would be at the Stockade at 7AM to counsel, then teach Sunday school at a high school, give a sermon at the chapel, and, in the afternoon, meet a battalion out in the field for a small impromptu service. Taking the jeep and a chaplain assistant, they would give a 10-minute sermon, serve communion and sing a song or two.

The Army has chaplains of all denominations, but, as a chaplain in the military, you learn to work with pastors of other faiths. Theology is not the issue. Meeting the needs of the soldier and families is the priority. Over the years Larry has learned the same applies in a VA hospital setting.

After Ft Campbell it was off to Germany as a chaplain, visiting with troops across the country for 3 years. He motored around Germany in a van ministering to the troops. That all changed one day when his commanding officer, Colonel Sterling, asked to see him for a private session. The colonel asked him to close and lock the door so they could talk. It seems the colonel was stressed out and nervous when flying. He had a small plane to get around Germany, but came clean that flying was not his thing. It caused him anxiety, now magnified by the tragic event of the DC-8 crash at Gander International Airport in Gander, Newfoundland on December 12, 1985. On that day, tragically, a military chartered Arrow Air DC-8 crashed into the cold, damp landscape at the end of runway 22 at Gander International Airport in Gander, Newfoundland. All Two-hundred and forty-eight military personnel and eight crew members perished in the accident. The flight was made up of three legs, with refueling stops in Cologne and Gander, then on to Fort Campbell. As members of the 101st Airborne division, stationed in Fort Campbell, Kentucky, the servicemen were assigned to rotation as a peacekeeping force in Egypt's Sinai Peninsula, in the multinational force and observers peacekeeping mission, enforcing the Camp David Accords of 1978.

Today at the Fort Campbell memorial are the names of the 248 "Screaming Eagles" who were killed in the crash; and the Bible passage from Isaiah 10:30-31, which reads:

"They that wait upon the Lord shall renew their strength:

they shall mount up with wings as eagles."

Colonel Sterling told Chaplain Larry to get rid of the van. From now on he would be flying with the commander as they made their rounds throughout Germany.

After his stint in Germany, Larry was the chaplain at Fort Carson, which is located just south of Colorado Springs Colorado. "Camp Carson" was established in 1942, following Japan's attack on Pearl Harbor. The city of Colorado Springs, Colorado purchased land south of the city and donated it to the War Department. Construction began immediately, and the first building, the camp headquarters, was completed January 31, 1942. Camp Carson was named in honor of the legendary Army scout, General Kit Carson, who explored much of the West in the 1800s.

Chaplains in the Army are rotated every three years, so just as the Army was gearing up for Operation Desert Storm, Larry was transferred to Selfridge air base near Mount Clemens, Michigan. His old unit at Fort Carson called him to ask if he could come back to help prepare for the battle ahead. Larry was preparing, in his mind, if he would be called on to go to the Middle East. At the time, no one in the midst of sabre rattling and threats from Saddam Hussein, knew how long the conflict would last.

In the last months of 1990, the United States participated in the defense of Saudi Arabia in a deployment known as Operation Desert Shield. Over 500,000 American troops were placed in Saudi Arabia in case of an Iraqi attack on the Saudis. The US further sought multilateral support in the United Nations Security Council. President Bush, remembering the lessons of Vietnam, sought public support as well. When all the forces were in place, a line was drawn in the sand for Saddam Hussein. Leave Kuwait by January 15,1991 or face a full-on attack. When Hussien balked at leaving, Operation Desert Storm commenced with bombing sorties and a world-wide audience. The Persian Gulf War was a television event. CNN broadcasted round-the-clock coverage of unfolding events. Americans saw footage from cameras placed on smart bombs as they struck Iraqi targets. The stealth fighter, designed to avoid radar detection ,was put into use for the first time. General Norman Schwarzkopf and General Colin Powell became household names as citizens watched their direction of the conflict.

It was all over very quickly, so quickly that the work of chaplains was needed to work with civilian communities in transitioning the soldier when they came back to their families and hometowns. Again, painful lessons learned from the Vietnam War ... we didn't ever want a reception experienced like those who fought in Vietnam to happen again. Military families have difficulty adjusting and need help from chaplains, civilians as well as businesses.

As Grand Marshall of the Eastpointe parade in eastern Michigan, Larry made a speech at a cemetery on Memorial Day which resulted in him being called on to be a chaplain for the American Legion in 1991. He became State chaplain of the Michigan American Legion for 15 years. The American Legion was chartered by Congress in 1919 as a patriotic veteran's orga-

Chaplain Larry Vollink

nization. Focusing on service to veterans, service members and communities, the Legion evolved from a group of war-weary veterans of World War I into one of the most influential non-profit groups in the United States. Membership swiftly grew to over 1 million, and local posts sprang up across the country. Today, membership stands at over 2 million in more than 13,000 posts worldwide. The posts are organized into 55 departments: one each for the 50 states, along with the District of Columbia, Puerto Rico, France, Mexico and the Philippines.

The highlight for Larry was as National Chaplain in 2008 and 2009. His service included prayers for national meetings and an opportunity to pray before the US House and Senate. When Mike Rogers introduced him before Congress, he said Larry was a graduate of South High, where former President Gerald Ford attended.

The process of praying before Congress is interesting, as the prayer is written months in advance, and committees review the contents. The chaplain is to follow the script. I chuckle, thinking *there is no room for improvisation or divine momentary inspiration.* I didn't ask Larry if they passed the collection plate. Larry had the opportunity once for both the House of Representatives and once for the Senate. The prayers are documented in the national archives. His prayer before the Senate was during Boys Nation on July 13, 2009. The first Boys Nation – then called Boys Forum of National Government – convened at American University in Washington in August 1946. The 1946 American Legion National Convention adopted the event as an official youth activity. Three years later, it became American Legion Boys Nation. Boys Nation is an annual forum concerning civic training, government, leadership, and Americanism, that is run by the American Legion. Ninety-eight boys, "Nation Senators" are chosen from a pool of over 20,000 Boys State participants, making it one of the most selective educational programs in the United States

At the event, each delegate acts as a senator from his "Boys State." The young lawmakers caucus at the beginning of the session, then organize into committees and conduct hearings on bills submitted by program delegates. In addition, they participate in a memorial service at Arlington National Cemetery. Along with the national commander, as they did with Larry on July 23, 2009, there is the laying of the wreath at the tomb of the unknown soldier.

The week of government training also includes lectures, forums and visits to federal agencies, national shrines, institutions, memorials and historical sites. On Capitol Hill, Boys Nation senators meet with elected officials from their home states.

Every state has juniors from high school, narrowed down to two individuals from Boys State American Legion, to go to Boys Nation the end of July. I looked through the notable alumni list of names and found the likes of Tom Brokaw, Bill Clinton, NBA star Michael Jordan and others.

"You got the chance to rub shoulders with some pretty influential people, didn't you?" I asked Larry.

Larry smiles and recalls for me an American Legion National Convention in Washington. The speaker was retired Army General David Petraeus.

"I'm going backstage to shake his hand after the dinner, because I have some questions for him," said Larry.

"The proverbial I'm going in," I said. Larry laughs. He did just that and challenged the general in the process.

"I've got a question general, veterans are upset because our new President doesn't wear the American flag on his suit lapel? And while I'm at it can you get him to improve the salute to the Marines as he steps off the Marine One helicopter?"

Petraeus acknowledged him and said "Chaplain I hear your concerns," and walked on with his entourage. Larry has no idea if he followed up on his request, but likes to think he helped make a difference because things improved shortly after that encounter.

He also remembers praying over the noted author, personality and economist Ben Stein, putting his hand on his shoulder in an impromptu prayer at a national breakfast event. Mr. Stein sought him out afterward to tell him he appreciated the divine intervention.

After active duty he became a veteran's chaplain and looked for ways to serve his calling as a hospital chaplain.

"Veterans want to be welcomed and respected. They need community and employer support that a job will be there. The community needs to be patriotic and be behind military families," he said.

"Many Veterans struggle with loneliness and depression that can lead to homelessness. Veterans help other veterans," said Larry. "They learn the importance of helping other fellow comrades to thrive and survive."

"So, you, like anyone else, have had low points in your life too," I said to Larry.

"I remember praying *Lord is there any way you can help me be successful*? At a low point in your life it's your special friends that get you through it. Your comrades," said Larry.

For "Chappy" Larry Vollink, the Lord answered his prayer.

OPERATION RUMINATION

I BELIEVE WE ALL HAVE A CALLING IN LIFE. HOW DO WE identify that calling? Even an ordained minister doesn't have a direct line or guiding light that appears from heaven and makes it clear. You find your way through all of it, the old trial and error thing during the journey. I've had people ask me how I found my calling. I think it's more like *stops along the journey* than one clear-cut calling. At each stop you try to make a difference and improve yourself along the way. You don't *prove* yourself, but, rather, *improve* yourself. If you do, you'll help others along the way. I hope and think I've made a difference so far ... more miles to go. Remember ... it's about continual goals? Just like Larry, we all have to believe God has answered our prayer in one way or the other. We just have to be willing to put ourselves in that position.

To their letters I replied
And with them worked alongside
I enjoyed each letter
They made me better
In them I have great pride.

Private Joshua Korhorn
US Army 3rd PLT Bravo Company 2-13th INF REGT
193rd BDE
Fort Jackson, South Carolina

Sr Francisco Gabriel
Ship 14 Div 343
Recruit Training Command
Naval Training Center Great Lakes, Illinois

Chapter Twenty-two

My PT Friends

WHILE I TRAINED TO MEET THE physical requirements of my APFT score (Army Physical Fitness Test) I corresponded with my "PT friends" Joshua Korhorn and Gabriel Francisco, who gave me a sense of what basic training was like for them. Full disclosure … I'm their proud uncle … both of them. I thought about them as I ran the miles and did the push-ups and sit-ups at the end of the pier on Pere Marquette Beach. I knew with the heat we were experiencing in Michigan that summer, it had to be that much hotter and humid in South Carolina for Joshua and Illinois for Gabe. I would train for my test knowing I had it a lot easier than them. At my age I made sure I got more sleep than they did. Also, there was no one yelling at me. I took long, hot showers, as long as I wanted. Based on our correspondence, I quickly understood they got the tougher end of the deal this summer.

Joshua Korhorn took the time to correspond with me, and is an excellent letter writer. His Mom had forewarned me he would be a good and detailed letter writer. I looked forward to my mail call because of Joshua. My mail call was much different than his mail call. My postal carrier would walk to my mailbox, and I could leisurely retrieve my mail in my bathrobe and slippers. He would get mail at 9 o'clock at night after a long day, then "toe the line" because his day wasn't done yet. Along with cleaning and hygiene, he still had lonely fire guard duty. Myself, I would try to stay awake to watch the 10PM news, with mixed results. In Joshua I made a friend and I learned something. He did something I never did; he completed Army basic training. I am proud of my PT friend, Joshua. He helped me get through my personal basic training while he serves his country. He inspired me to keep running the beach, to keep hitting the push-ups and keep doing those difficult sit-ups. He truly was an inspiration in the process. If he was going to do it, I wasn't going to let him down. I would keep going. No ice cream sundae for me tonight.

Joshua Korhorn

Gabriel's correspondence was colorful and fun to read. Based on my correspondence with Gabriel, he became an expert at the 60- to 90-second shower. He gave me a real sense of what boot camp was like. When I would run Operation Rumination beach and stop at the end of the pier, I would think about him while looking across the water of Lake Michigan in the direction of the Great Lakes Naval Training Center.

I knew Gabe before he left for basic training. A fine young man, caring and quick with a smile. I enjoyed my conversations with him. I could tell as the summer wore on, that basic training took what was already a fine young man, and further ingrained the characteristic of selfless service, or, as he called it, "servitude" caring for others.

We got through the summer together. I made a friend and I learned something. He did something I never did … completed boot camp. I am proud of my PT friend, Gabriel. He helped me get through my personal basic training while he serves his country.

In an age of digital correspondence, you quickly forget how much fun it is to get a handwritten letter. I learned that young recruits enjoy mail call when at basic training or boot camp. I enjoyed it too, finding mail in the mailbox. Half the fun is trying to figure out some of the words due to penmanship, or following the line of thought as you move from page to page. You can picture the individual sitting at a table writing the letter. The fact they invested that time is encouraging alone. And words are powerful for painting a picture. Theatre of the mind. As the French would say La stylo plume est plus forte que l'epee … the pen is mightier than the sword. Interestingly, the phrase is credited not to real-life conflict resolution, but, rather, was first written by novelist and playwright Edward Bulwer-Lytton in 1839 as part of a play. It obviously resonated with us all and has been passed on through the ages. What follows is a sampling of the letters and correspondence that Joshua and Gabriel penned me during our summer and fall of PT and basic training.

Gabriel Francisco

LETTER FROM GABE 23 JULY, 2018

23 July 2018

Dear Uncle Rick,

If war movies were anything like how basic actually is no one would watch them because basic reaches the extremes of activity. One minute we have Petty Officers screaming at us to go from PTU (physical training uniform) to a NWU (Navy working uniform) within 30 seconds flat. I've never sweat putting on clothes before now. We shower so fast you sweat while showering. On the other hand we will also spend hours standing at attention or sitting at a desk staring at the chain of command memorizing every sleeve rank or insignia while fighting the losing battle between studying for our test and sleep deprivation. There are good things however, I am more organized than I've ever been as everything has its exact place. Also in the two weeks I've been here I've lost 6lbs. We eat pretty healthy here and exercise vigorously. That's all for now, please write any specific questions you have.

SR Francisco G.C.

LETTER FROM JOSH 10 AUGUST, 2018

10 August 2018

Dear Uncle Rick,

I received your letter about an hour ago and now we have about 20 minutes of personal time so I'm starting my response. I have fire guard duty tonight for an hour and a half so that should be enough time to finish responding.

> *Authors note: Every night, at least two recruits from the platoon must be awake at any given time, patrolling their barracks area, watching for fires, cleaning the barracks and watching for recruits attempting to leave the barracks area. They wake the next pair of recruits at the end of their shift. This duty is called fire guard. Fire guard stems back to the days of wooden barracks and wood-burning stoves. The fire guard would watch the stoves to make sure that the barracks would not catch fire. Since open flames are not generally used to heat sleeping areas any longer, present-day fire guard during Basic Training is more an exercise in discipline than a practical necessity. Fireguard duty is not fun. When all you want to do at basic training is sleep, you have to wake up in the middle of the night and stand in an empty hall.*

Basic has been the hardest 10 weeks of my life. The first week of basic is called reception and the first 24 hours of reception were the worst 24 hours of my life. I questioned a lot of things in life, especially why I joined and left an amazing life at home. It's not gotten a lot better from there, but it has improved. I think the thing about basic that is so frustrating is that even the easy things are hard. Lack of food and sleep can make anything a challenge.

> *Authors note: While physical training this summer I picked days of fasting to feel hunger like recruits told me they experienced. The big difference was mine was self-induced and I could eat anytime I wanted whatever I wanted at the pace I desired when I was ready to not be hungry anymore.*

Basic is broken down into three phases that are each three weeks long. Red phase is the first and hardest phase. Drill sergeants are constantly smoking everyone for small things that one person does wrong. They treat us really poorly and food and sleep are minimal. 5-6 hours of sleep a night but often less with three small meals a day and about 5-6 minutes to eat, with drill sergeants constantly screaming at people. Shower drills are a red phase thing as well, where you have a minute to strip and shower and be out and drying off.

> *Authors note: I tried the strip, shower and drying off in one minute thing to mimic what they were experiencing. My conclusion was you have to be something between an Olympic track athlete and Harry Houdini to pull that off.*

After red phase is white phase. Almost everyday is spent at ranges trying to qualify. MREs (meals ready to eat) are a good portion of our diets because we're not back for the DFAC.

> *Authors note: Army uses DFAC as their term for dining facility or more specifically Dining*

*Facility Administration Center although many
soldiers will use the terminology "chow hall."*

Qualifying for me on the rifle range was a challenge at first. The challenge was learning to breathe and squeeze the trigger in rhythm. After I figured out how to shoot, I had to deal with faulty targets and bad ranges. On the official qualification day people on lanes 2, 4, 7 and 9 qualified every time with a score over 30 because the targets went down on their own. Every single person who shot on lane 12, the lane I was assigned, got a 10 because most of the targets wouldn't go down. In the end I qualified with a 31 out of 40 on a good rifle range. They gave an extra day for qualifications on a new range that was 100% functional because over half the company didn't qualify, mostly because of range issues. Not being qualified was stressful and frustrating but it worked out in the end.

Blue phase is an EOC (End of course) PT (physical training) test and a 50+ mile road march with all sorts of events that are designed to test us on what we've learned during basic. The march is called "The Forge." It lasts four days and four nights. We got an hour to two hours of sleep every night and spent a lot of time marching and doing crazy stuff for the rest of the night. We would work until 3AM then pull security for an hour and sleep an hour until wake up at 5AM. On the "Forge" we did things like a night infiltration course where they shot live rounds out of machine guns while we crawled towards the gunfire and mass cavalry where they threw smoke and gas bombs and told people they were injured or dead and made us carry the wounded for miles to a medivac site, just to name two of the 17 events. The sleep and nutrition deprivation was the hardest part of the "Forge." On the last night and day we were up for over 30 hours straight and marched 15 miles at the end which was by far the hardest part of basic. At that point I had crazy chafing and was almost falling asleep while marching. Over 100 people in our battalion passed out during the "Forge" from the heat. It was over 100 degrees every day. Now that it's over it feels like a big accomplishment.

Graduation is less than two weeks away. Family day is the day before graduation. I've never looked forward to anything more. Seeing my family after these two and a half months will be surreal and unforgettable. Physical training tests are now pretty straightforward and easy. I'm at the point where I'm maxing push-ups and the run, but I still need to work on sit-ups. My goal is to max the PT test with 300 when I get to AIT so that I can have special privileges when I actually get to my unit.

Days here start at 0430 hours with first formation at 0530 hours. We clean the bays and shave. If the bays (the place all males in our platoon sleep) aren't clean we get smoked and they throw beds and linens all over. Any unlocked lockers get emptied and their contents are spread throughout the bays. We do PT until 0700 hours then go to chow. Hundreds of soldiers are fed in 35 to 40 minutes everyday. We shower and change into OCPs (Operational Camouflage Pattern) and then go about our day. No day is the same. We're always back for DFAC or hot A's by 18:00 or so.

Authors note: In my research and experience this past year I have learned that military jargon is full of acronyms. Wait ... they're wearing OCPs to the DFAC for Hot A's by 6 o'clock? I had to look up the "Hot A's" out of curiosity. Hot-A's are hot chow. Hot food served to Soldiers while in the field. The 'A' comes from the meal's designation in the Army Field Food Service AR30-22 Chapter 4 paragraph 2. Roger, roger that. There seems to be an acronym for everything and I even find myself using them now. I'm wearing my PFU (physical fitness uniform) to the gym today for my PT (physical training). My COA (course of action) is IAW (in accordance with) my chosen OO (order of operations) to become an SME (subject matter expert) and I WILCO (will comply) to the physical requirements laid out in the APFT (Army Physical Fitness Test) and submit a verified SITREP (Situational Report). I even saw there was an acronym for what I have been trying to do all summer: CAPE meaning Corrective Action through Physical Exercise. Where's the DFAC now I'm hungry.

Add in with the acronyms all the slang like Charlie Mike: Continue mission, keep doing what you were doing. Or Lima Charlie: Loud and Clear.

After all that, I chuckled in my rumination that I'm sure the military doesn't use any more acronyms than the average 16-year-old does in a week's worth of text messaging. I guess if we're all talking the same lingo and it abbreviates communication then I'm A-OK with that.

After DFAC or Hot A's we clean weapons and usually take a class to learn for the next day's activities. Then we get mail and go upstairs around 21:00 for "toe to line" which is our version of a night formation. After that we shower and do personal hygiene. Then we often have fire guard for an hour and a half at night. (The food here tastes better than I thought it would but we get less than I thought we would.)

During my time here I have found a new level of personal relationship with God. Right when I wake up and before I go to bed, I read my Bible and do devotions. In the challenge that basic has been, God has been pushing me to rely on him and trust him. He's shown his grace and goodness through his word and provision. That is something I'm going to aim to continue to grow, even as I leave basic.

I have also learned to appreciate things, because things can always get worse. I realized I didn't appreciate all I had at home like I should have. I was tired of some of the aspects of home when I left, but now I would kill to be home. Perspective is a crazy thing.

I stay at Fort Jackson for AIT (Advanced Infantry Training) which is another 9 weeks. I'm excited for AIT, I'll have weekends off and my phone at night. I plan to read books, watch college football and go to the gym lots. I'm not a reader, at least not much, but I plan to work to grow in that. I lifted lots at home so I'm excited to get back into that. I also plan to make up for lots of lost sleep.

Thanks for your letter. I look forward to reading your book. I love US history so it will for sure be right up my alley.

Joshua

P.S. I passed my last PT test with a 271. Still need to work on sit-ups. I should max out at 300 during AIT. I'm doing sit-ups every night because AIT is only 2 weeks away and the PT test is in the first week of AIT. I'm in the 60s (sit-ups) but still have a lot of work to go.

LETTER FROM GABE 30 JULY, 2018

30 July 2018

Dear Uncle Rick,

I received your letter today during mail call which happens to be the best part of the day. I'm glad you found humor in some of the extremes of necessary measures to make us civilians into sailors. To answer your question, Taps (when one "goes to sleep") is from around 21:30 to 22:00 hours depending on the evening's activities.

Reveille is at 05:00-06:00 but we have to be up one hour before reveille to shave, make our racks, wrap up our homework and start cleaning the compartment. We stay up anywhere from 30 minutes to 2 hours past taps ironing, folding laundry, doing homework and writing letters like this one so in reality it is more like taps 23:30 hours and reveille at 03:30 hours. As for running we run about 4 times a week doing shuttle runs, dead sprints, and 30-minute sustained runs.

The food varies wildly with some stuff extremely good and other food downright inedible. The galley has a program called "Go for Green" which makes it very easy for recruits to eat healthy. All entree options are posted on an electronic board with basic nutritional facts for content (protein and carbs). They are assigned a color green, yellow or red for how healthy they are. I love the cranberry chicken chef salad and hate the bean burgers. I miss Grandma Francisco's roasts. About the showers I am actually the head PO which means I'm in charge of the head (bathroom) and I give everyone 30 seconds from when they hit the water.

> *Authors note: In my basic training practice this past year I tried the in and out in 1-minute shower to mimic what my boot camp friends were experiencing. It didn't go real well. It took me all of a minute just to get the water temperature right. Even if I ignored the water temperature, I still had soap in my hair and a film on my skin when I jumped out as the timer was going off. The real boot camp recruits shower in a tiled room with shower heads so I practiced at the YMCA for the communal group shower 1-minute drill. That didn't go well either. It made me glad I was being scored on push-ups, sit-ups and running, because if I would have been scored on the shower I would have failed. I found it precarious to quickly exit on a slippery*

> *floor with soap in my eyes. The drill sergeant*
> *would have had a field day with me.*

This has been a faith journey for me. I am closer in my faith than I have ever been despite not making it to chapel due to my job as head PO. I pray much more than before, not only much more but quality if you know what I mean. Also a lot of basic is sacrificing for the division chief, it's always ship, shipmate then self last in that order. You help your rackmate with his sheets on the bed before doing your own. When you go to the scuttlebutt to refill your hydrate tool you take six more for your ship-mates. Servitude and comradery has brought me to the best position I've had in my personal faith.

I'm sorry for my long letter, just thought you would want to hear about that. Feel free to write me with more ques-tions.

SR Francisco G.C.

EMAIL FROM GABE

Email September 6, 2018

I passed my PFT (physical fitness test) with 72 push-ups, 66 sit-ups and 10:42 in the 1.5-Mile run. That qualifies me as "good-low fit" Ha ha. I leave for Charleston, South Carolina after graduation.

SR Francisco G.C.

LETTER FROM JOSH 23 SEPTEMBER, 2018

23 September 2018

Dear Uncle Rick,

AIT (Advanced Individual Training) is much better than basic. Much more freedom. Having my phone is a huge difference and having weekends off is also really nice. Food and the time we are given to eat it is significantly better here. On the weekends from 11-8 we're free to go just about anywhere on post right now, and starting next weekend when we go to gold phase we'll be able to go off post during that time if we want. I have a PT (physical training) test this Tuesday that will be my record one, assuming I pass it which I should. I've been working on strengthening my core so I'm hoping for at least 80% on sit-ups which I think is very manageable considering the work I've been putting in. I should be able to max push-ups and the run. We'll see. After that I plan to start using the gym we can go to after classes are over everyday in addition to PT. That's something I am very much looking forward to.

Authors note: The Army reported this year that they would phase out the current physical test that Joshua and I took this year by 2020. One of the aspects of the new test is it drops the sit-up requirements. Full sit-ups with heels on the floor and hands intertwined behind the head have been a staple of the PT test, but have been suspect to strain and injury. I'm with Joshua, the sit-up standards are tough and, daily over the course of this year, not something I personally looked forward to. I did receive good coaching from my active duty servicemen and women; they coached me to do my sit-ups before my run, because that is how you are tested. Push-ups first, then sit-ups then run. The advice was good as 60-some full sit-ups cause your legs to burn before the two-mile run. By the time I got to my PT test, it was no surprise to me that, after aggressive sit-up,s you will feel the burn in your

quads. The next day I did sit-ups in bed, hitting
the snooze button.

I am going to be deployed to Korea for a year once AIT is over. That wasn't necessarily where I wanted to go, but I've heard good things about it so I am optimistic. It's far from home, and I still miss home, but it's the sacrifice many have made before me and many after me will make in the future. I miss home less than in basic because I'm able to text, call and Facetime my family and friends at home, but in a way that makes me miss it more because I see what's there. Overall though I am doing great.

Joshua

LETTER FROM JOSH 6 OCTOBER, 2018

6 October 2018

Dear Uncle Rick,

I still haven't been told my official PT score, all I know is I passed. Roughly around a 250 or 260. Definitely lower than I was hoping. I got better at sit-ups which was good. Push-ups I actually improved as well, but I got a grader who didn't like the way I did them so I only got 62 counted. She didn't count 22 of them. There are always 18 graders for the PT tests here and usually 2 or 3 of them try and be really strict about push-ups form. I'd never had one, just heard about them. Lucky I wasn't in a position where I needed every last one to pass. Run went down. Not sure why. Not a huge fan of the course. It goes uphill some which isn't helpful at all, but still not a good reason not to max especially since I was running mid 12's in basic. I ran in the mid 13's this time. Around a 90+ percentage. Not awful but not what I'm capable of.

Authors note: "Mid 12s in basic is hauling the
mail or in this case the "male." 13 minutes would

*get you a perfect 100% score and mid 12s on the
two-mile run is 6 minute 15 second miles which is
a very admirable pace.*

Now I'm just getting ready for the first PT test in Korea. Putting serious effort into being ready to max that. Giving it my all every morning at PT. School here is going really well. Got perfect on the last test. I'm in the running for an honor grad spot with three tests to go. I'm .07 percent off from being there. Three more tests to up my GPA just a bit more. Definitely doable. How is your PT coming along?

Joshua

EMAIL FROM JOSH 7 OCTOBER, 2018

7 October 2018

Dear Uncle Rick,

Good to hear you are still working on physical training. It's definitely not the most fun thing in the world but it's quite rewarding. I go to Korea for a year around the end of November. I graduate on November 2nd and then have 14 days of hometown recruiting and then will take an additional 10 days of leave home. After that I will be flying to Korea. I'll be there for a year. I should be back for Christmas next year. That's my hope.

Joshua

A WEDDING RECEPTION

December 26, 2018

Gabriel has a few days home for the Christmas holiday. By the end of the month he will report back for duty to the Navy in South Carolina. I attend a reception for Gabriel and Jade, newlyweds starting a life together. It has been a big year for Gabe. I approach him at the reception, shaking his hand and grabbing his shoulder with my other hand. He has the same stature people tend to comment about after basic training. Seems taller. His posture is straight … lean and strong, not the same person I visited with in the early summer at a graduation pool party. I walk away smiling, thinking we both did some growing up this year. I'm older and wiser and Gabriel is young, strong and wiser on the heels of his boot camp experience, ready to "sail" into a lifetime of potential.

OPERATION RUMINATION

I did some honest personal rumination thinking about Joshua after one of my summer workouts. I'm proud of him and what he accomplished this past summer. I can also say I'm not sure I could have done what he did when I was 18. In forthright mental gymnastics after one of my workouts, I thought back to my disposition and resolve at that age. Could I have been whipped into shape by a drill sergeant "smoking" me at boot camp? I'll never know. I do think I would have failed miserably with the 1-minute shower. I appreciated Joshua's honest, descriptive correspondence. He gave me insight into the discipline needed to make the grade. Joshua, at a young age, chose service to his country and the Army … and he saw it through. Thank you, my friend. Thank you for sharing your journey with me and serving your country.

Oh, to be young again. A fresh start, a clean slate. When you interact with young men like Gabriel you catch a glimpse of what you were, who you used to be, but, more importantly, who you wanted to be. What did you do with your opportunity? Now seasoned with experience and dusty from the long road, I can admire those beginning their journey. Gabe shared his lessons of discipline and growth with me, giving me a glimpse of the process. Gabriel, at a young age, chose service to his country and the Navy … and he saw it through. Thank you, my friend. Thank you for sharing your journey with me and serving your country.

"Understanding is a two-way street."

-Eleanor Roosevelt

Chapter Twenty-three

Denouement

De·noue·ment noun
dānoo̅ˈ mäN
The final part of a narrative in which the strands
of the plot are drawn together, and matters are
explained.

The epilogue, the climax of a chain of events,
usually when something is made clear.

DENOUEMENT COMES FROM THE
French for "untying" or "unknotting", as in untying a knot. A metaphor for a climax, where the
plot is unraveled. After my year of relationships, rumination
and physical training, I sat back and thought about what I had
learned. I already had a good handle on the emotion I was feeling. Humbled.

ru·mi·na·tion
/ ˌroo̅məˈ nāSH(ə)n/
noun - A deep or considered thought about
something.

I had made up my mind that over the course of the year my
mental and physical focus would be salubrious. A year of *healthy*
rumination. Relationships. Conversations. Friendships. Physical
exercise. Diet. Reflection. There were times over the course of

the year I wanted to be done. I was tired or wanted to do something else or take a night off from exercise. I told myself *run the mile you're in*. Even though I felt I was done, I was only 40% done. At least that's what a Navy Seal had told me. He told me "when your mind is telling you you're done, you're really only 40 percent done." There were days my legs felt like concrete and I didn't want to do any more push-ups. But I knew if I didn't follow through, later that evening I would feel like a failure.

There were days I stumbled through my basic training and reminded myself that Winston Churchill once remarked that "Success is stumbling from failure to failure without loss of enthusiasm." I would remain enthusiastic even on days I stumbled.

In the end it wasn't so much accomplishing a goal, there will be others (continual goals), in so much as it was the experience. The journey. Personal growth and stories to share for the benefit of myself and others. Rumination, in my experience, resulted in a positive experience of being humbled, of better understanding the meaning of selfless service.

humble
huhm-buhl

Not proud or arrogant; modest: to be humble although successful.
courteously respectful

Common Threads

There were similar threads with the veterans I spent time with this year ... the "thread" or the "denouement" was founded on a recurring theme, characteristics that emerged time and again. The key characteristics of the veterans I spent time with were this:

- Humility
- Honor. Strong faith. (a purpose greater than themselves)
- A sense of humor
- Selfless service (it is taught, a learned behavior and not innate, a discipline)

- Courage is not the absence of fear, it's doing what you have to do despite the presence of fear.

(there is that phrase again … "I did what I had to do.")

- Physical activity
- Continual goals
- Strong work ethic
- Camaraderie

You could say they fit the description of the adjective: Operose (Op-er-owss) which almost sounds like a military operation. The definition is: Industrious; diligent. It inspired me as a man to serve others, to love my brother and my sister who cross my path in my daily walk in life. In simple daily ways to serve. All the veterans young and old inspired me.

A characteristic that linked them in a thread was **continual goals**. I find myself humming to the tune of *Mary Jane's Last Dance*, "You never slow down you never grow old."

In Operation Rumination I learned from veterans, a driving force. One factor stood out: continual goals. I believe that if you **_don't_** set goals as targets, you're at least assured of hitting your "target" every time because there is nothing to miss. But that's not a very ambitious or admirable incentive. There is a discipline to setting goals and working towards them. There is a discipline to brushing off disappointments which are inevitable and moving forward. The fun is in the trying to get there. My conversations with three veterans, two a couple months shy of 100 years old and one at the age of 100 years and 7 months, is that throughout their life and *even now* at 100 plus, they have continual goals. One a dancer and an inventor, one a traveler, travelogue producer and painter, one a gardener and composter. It went well beyond just having something to look forward to; it was part of their makeup, habitual, second nature. These men and women are amazingly fit at the age of 100 both physically and mentally. All the more reason for staying fit … without it you don't have the energy and focus to chase your continual goals.

Some influences in my life had focused on the 5% of issues that were a problem instead of the 95% that are positive. Negative motivation can drag you down. Goals are your flotation device to keep you from going under. Not dreams, but goals. Creative, inventive, tangible goals. Goals that become reality. Or goals that "fail" but are used as springboard for new goals. Continual goals.

I sensed with the older World War II veterans they had the same "CAVU" spirit made famous by Navy pilot and 41st President of the United States George H.W. Bush. World War II pilots did not have the navigational instrumentation we have at our disposal today, so they thrived in a spirit of "CAVU" or "Ceiling and Visibility Unlimited."

I read with interest interviews with centenarians. One such lady, over the age of 100, said the key was refusing to run away from your problems, and maintaining physical activity, an active physical and social life. But my attention focused when she added that a specific food could be partly responsible for her longevity.

"I like my porridge. I have all my life."

Now that got my attention. I like "porridge" more specifically cooked oat bran with blueberries for breakfast. I'm told a good bowl of cooked oat bran lowers LDL or "bad" cholesterol. Soluble fiber in oat bran works to reduce cholesterol in a number of ways. When soluble fiber is consumed, it has the ability to bind with cholesterol and excrete it from the body. I know this from trying to clean the pan off the stove. Additionally, it may limit the cholesterol from foods within the diet. Healthy cholesterol levels, reduce the risk of heart disease, including stroke and heart attack. Now add to that my Army regime of push-ups, sit-ups and running as a lifestyle habit, and I'll hope I've found my fountain of youth.

It's not Ponce de Leon's fountain of youth, but I'll concur that the bubbling, cooking oat mass in a pan each morning and exercise at night make a difference for me.

MID 20TH CENTURY MEN AND WOMEN

MY DAD, WHO WAS ALMOST 11 YEARS OLD WHEN THE Germans rampaged through Europe along with countless other men, influenced me in my formative years. They fit a distinctive description. They were mid-20th century men

"who never complained and never explained."

"We just did what we had to do" was a refrain I heard often this year as explanation in their later years. They just did their jobs. Tested by extraordinary hardships like the Great Depression or a world at war, later in life they showed their softer side. A family of one of the World War II veterans explained it to me this way. "It was the example they set after the fighting was over, a strong work ethic and humble demeanor." I would hear from them when I would question them how they did what they did, "We just did what we had to do," with a shrug of their shoulders. They got through it. It caused me to think of the phrase penned by the poet Robert Frost.

"The best way out is always through."

- Robert Frost

That's the example that was exhibited to me as a young man. Work hard and don't complain. I run the beach to the lighthouse and think, "People are used for good when tested deeply."

Later in life I would realize the characteristics that I was taught by their example. I was a young man graduating from high school just after the Vietnam War. I realize now, looking back, there were a lot of things we were expected to do without questioning. Was this why I had the drive and work ethic I had? It's not genetic just like selfless service is not genetic. It is taught. Exhibited. Patterned. Ingrained. I have been told by others younger than me, that they don't want to be like me. An unquestioning work ethic. It took me to age 60 to deal with it. It was part of Operation Rumination. It hurt, but it was healthy. It was real.

PAYING ATTENTION

I LEARNED TO PAY BETTER ATTENTION TO THOSE AROUND me. Attention is not a critical act like judgment is. It is the opposite of distraction. It is an art and a discipline. You have to pay attention. Unless they are a celebrity, most people don't receive a lot of attention and some actually shun it, but all of us pay it. You choose how you're going to pay. You can receive it, pursue it, avoid it, but everyone pays. Attention is actually an act of loving kindness. Assiduity is another great synonym for attention.

As part of paying attention, I realized through my experience about the very real effects of PTSD with some veterans. Their feelings are generally kept "bottled up." It can cause worry, confusion, depression and anger, in some cases thoughts of suicide. A friend of one of these veterans told me it can cause her friend to "forget" or be disorganized which affects her work life. I found that the confusion disrupts the person's life, making it hard to continue daily activities or keep appointments. Our brains and our emotions are complicated and all wired differently. Only some will develop PTSD, and the reason for this is not clear. It made me thankful for the people I met whose life's work and passion is to help those with PTSD. And for me, to be aware, understanding, compassionate.

In 2016, the age and gender adjusted rates of suicide were 26.1 per 100,000 for veterans and 17.4 per 100,000 for civilians. In 2016, the suicide rate was 1.5 times greater for veterans than for civilians, after adjusting for age and gender.

I had some conversations with families who lost a loved one in the service. I particularly recall a conversation with a young man who had lost a brother serving his country in the Middle East. They deal with the reality and their sadness and grief. They deal with questions in their minds like "what if?" and "why?" In the process, I learned the most important things I can do for them.

> **Listen** *to their story.*
> **Honor** *their service.*
> **Respect** *your country and the flag.*

I could hear it in their voices. You see it in their eyes. As I run down Operation Rumination beach, I think about how disrespecting the flag or your country is like kicking sand in their faces at the beach. You honor their service when you respect your country and the flag. You honor their service when you listen to the story, because there are lessons to be learned.

I sat at a lonely chilly January bar in Fort Lauderdale Florida with a young man in his 20s who had served in Afghanistan. The sun had set and it was chilly and dark by south Florida standards. He told me his story of how his wife left him while he was overseas. You could hear the pain in his voice and see it in his eyes. He just needed someone to listen to his story. And respect him for his service.

Some were not willing to talk. They did not want to revisit or share their experience. I can respect that. It did not upset me at all. You also have to be ready to talk. It was roughly right down the middle. 50% said yes and 50% said no. I applied this wonderful quote from Henry Wadsworth Longfellow to my experience:

> *"Every man has his secret sorrows which the*
> *world knows not; and oftentimes we call a man*
> *cold when he is only sad."*
>
> **-Henry Wadsworth Longfellow**

I respect their service, and I certainly respect what these men and women are carrying with them. For those who did share we developed an understanding. As Eleanor Roosevelt was quoted as saying, "Understanding is a two-way street." A camaraderie so to speak of respect, me for their service and story, and they for my attempt to serve in some way at this point in my life. When they understood my intentions, I could tell they had my back. It was a good feeling.

I learned by talking to servicemen and women how important

family is. Many active-duty servicemen and servicewomen are married and many with children. I met the spouses and family members and learned of the sacrifice they make and have made. Issues like affordable family housing, child care and education, counseling, financial guidance, relocation help, health care and day-to-day needs are worries and practical concerns when a spouse is away, whether at a base, here at home or halfway around the world serving their country.

SELFLESS SERVICE

I had spent the summer reflecting on one of the most extolled virtues of all time: selfless service to others. I remembered my days in Bible school. In the book of Acts Paul quotes Jesus,

"It is more blessed to give than to receive."

You hear that phrase often, especially in November and December each year. Marketers surmise going in that, to a large extent people are egoists. Various studies, however, have suggested that no matter your lot in life, those who spend money on others experience a higher level of happiness. But it's easy to slip someone a five or buy them lunch. As important and necessary as altruistic tendencies are, giving of one's self is an ultimate act of selfless service. This "selfless service" is noted in the Army's core values. Not everyone can give a large sum of money to a cause, but anyone can give of themselves. Or can we? Are we wired as such?

It's about a soldier who stands with their comrades as the diametrically opposite example of a solipsist. They demonstrated to me it was others first, me last. How many times did I hear over the course of the year how the veteran "missed the camaraderie with those he or she served with?" They had their backs. I watched 100-year-old Sid Lenger reunite with David "Goldie" Goldsboro years after World War II. The bond they shared was immediately palpable, evident, tangible.

In selfless service you give to others without expecting anything in return. No reward, no recognition. Does it require a saint? No. We all have the capacity for selfless service. I would like to think everyone has a natural impulse to help a fellow human being in need.

> **The best basic training exercise is to lift someone up. It is good for both your heart and your mind.**

There will always be those who bask in the schadenfreude of another's misfortune. And, it's one thing to hand a buck to someone holding a sign at the street corner; it's another thing to volunteer a significant amount of time or risk your life for others. Maybe expecting to feel good or avoid feeling bad is the anticipated reward that motivates some charitable acts?

So, what you get back is feeling you are making a difference. It's not hopeless. To receive gratitude from those they serve and admiration from society at large. That was the painful reminder of the Vietnam conflict. The veterans I spoke with did not receive the gratitude of society at large. In fact, for many it was just the opposite. They were advised not to wear their uniform in airports or on their way back home.

World War II, in my mind, was the furthest thing from an amorphous conflict. I didn't experience it, but history demonstrates the enemy was clearly defined and recognizable. The battle lines were clearly recognizable in that war with the German Hitler Nazi atrocities and the Japanese gauntlet of the Pearl Harbor bombing. Because of this, public sentiment to defeat them was consentient once committed. From the bombing of Pearl Harbor to the end. When East met West on the River Elbe on April 25, 1945, and Soviet and American troops meet at Torgau, Germany. It was the end of the Thousand-Year Reich after 12 destructive years, as Germany surrendered unconditionally on all fronts in May of 1945. Then came the surrender of Imperial Japan announced on August 15 and formally signed on September 2, 1945, bringing the hostilities of World War II to a close.

For those, however, battling ambiguous enemies of the jungles or the terrorists lurking in the shadows, our gratitude for their service is just as important regardless of political or public opinion. All valiant veterans of American wars deserve gratitude and recognition for their selfless service to our country.

So, both givers and receivers can benefit from selfless service. There are individual differences in the strength of the impulse and the likelihood of acting on it consistently. When selfless individuals associate with each other, they build on that environment. It's a camaraderie.

Then there is the subject of equity theory. Equity theory predicts that people feel exploited when they give more than they receive, and they feel uncomfortable when they receive more than they give. Research supports those predictions. Selfless service is an admirable virtue in a society that, in many ways, encourages equitable relationships. I learned selfless service has nothing to do with equity. Those who served did so with honor, duty, loyalty and did so selflessly, expecting nothing in return. I learned this past year that it is about applying dependable core values, values that are dependable to those who cross your path. A veteran's example in risking their lives and serving was not one of reciprocity but one of *true* selfless service.

US ARMY SEVEN CORE VALUES

- Loyalty
- Duty. Fulfill your obligations.
- Respect
- Selfless Service
- Honor
- Integrity
- Personal Courage

Selfless service is not necessarily in your genes or inherited … it evolves through teaching example and is passed on through the generations. That's why it is so important to demonstrate it. Teach it. That is why it is so important to capture stories. Study history. It is civilian basic training. There is a heavenly host out there serving quietly under the radar each day, serving others without fanfare, recognition or remuneration. They do it because that's just what you do.

APFT ARMY PHYSICAL FITNESS TEST RESULTS

THE DAY FINALLY ARRIVED. NOVEMBER 28, THE DAY AFter my 59th birthday. It was time to put up or shut up. The phrase comes from boxing fights in the 1800s when one fighter would challenge another and require him to put up a stake for a match, or stop his fighting words. In this case I had challenged myself and "put up" the training time, now it was time to shut up and see what I could do. Out of a maximum score of 300 (100% for each of three criteria) I would need at least a minimum of 180 or better to eke by and pass the requirements for a 17 to 21-year-old Army recruit at the age of 59. Cindy, an administrator at the YMCA, has us sign our waivers and wishes me luck. Cindy and the other Y staff have been there through this journey, watching me train through the spring, summer and fall. Marine Vet, Sergeant Skip Coryell is there to certify the numbers and the run time, per the criteria and standards provided by the Army DA form 705. A DA Form 705 is used by the Army as an Army Physical Fitness Test Scorecard. It is used to keep a record of a soldier's physical fitness test scores. These tests are conducted at various points throughout a soldier's career, from the start, in order to make sure they are physically able to perform their job. With clipboard and timer in hand, Sergeant Coryell runs me through the paces.

First the push-ups. A 100% score for a 17 to 21-year-old is 71 push-ups in two minutes. 90% is 64 push-ups. 80% is 57. 49 push-ups in two minutes is good for a 70% score. 42 in two minutes is 60% for the minimum passing grade. I feel somewhat confident about the push-ups. All year I had dropped down and done push-ups, sometimes in unusual places resulting in unusual looks from bystanders.

Second are the sit-ups. The standards for a 17 to 21-year-old are 78 sit-ups in two minutes for a 100% score. Are you kidding me? That's more than one full sit-up every two seconds. 72 gets you a 90%. 66 sit-ups will score you 80% and 59 a 70% score. 53 sit-ups in two minutes gets you a passing 60% grade for the minimum requirement.

The third leg of my PT testing is the run. A 2-mile sprint with grading for a 17 to 21-year-old old is as follows. 13 minutes (which is absolutely ridiculous) would score 100%. For a 90% score I would finish the run in 13:42. If I were to run it in 14:27 I would have an 80% score. 15:12 gets me in at 70% and 15:54 scores me at the 60% minimum requirement for a 17 to 21-year-old.

We start with the push-ups and I take a deep breath. The push-up, or the "press up" if you're from the UK, is one of the most common of calisthenics, I always thought it was used as a common form of punishment in the military. Drop down and give me 30. I had wondered why the military uses the push-up as their measure of upper body strength rather than the bench press. I figured, as I had learned, a push-up can be done anytime and anywhere and doesn't require expensive gym equipment. Over the course of the year I had done push-ups in parking lots, my office, airports, in the kitchen while food is preparing and in the living room during commercials. It is better to do push-ups than watch the microwave waiting for it to hit 0:00. I'm told it is because the push-up uses more muscles than upper-body exercises that require weights. It necessitates tapping into whole body strength head to toe, including core and balance to do a sequence of push-ups. While training I thought, *who is Jerick Revilla and why was he given credit for modernizing and "inventing" the push-up as a form of exercise in 1905?* I'm sure ancient warriors years ago did push-ups. Now I have two minutes to knock out as many as I can. The push-ups were the favorite part of my physical training, because it was easy to measure progress and measures whole body strength, so I had focused on them all summer. I get into position and the clock starts. At the end of two minutes I had completed 72 or a 100% score. Off to a good start, but waiting in the wings in just a few minutes ... the sit-ups.

With feet and heels firmly planted on the ground and laying on your back, you lock your hands behind your head and stare up to the ceiling. Full sit-ups aren't a lot of fun, so you don't see many people doing them. It's hard to look stylish. For the purpose of this operation I trained to pass, not hurt my back and not throw up. The alternative to sit-ups are "crunches" which sound just as safe to a 59-year-old body. I position on the floor and the clock starts. I was warned the full sit-ups burn out your legs for the run to follow. I just want to get through it after a summer of sit-ups. At the two-minute point I had completed 65 sit-ups, good for a 79% score. I'll take it. That's more than one full sit-up every 2 seconds and my back was still intact. After basic training I'm going back to crunches and the ab machine.

The running was my favorite part of the physical training as it relates to time to reflect and ruminate and to be alone with my thoughts. That's why I tend to run alone. I loved my runs on the beach and the breakwater leading to the lighthouse. On this day

Army Physical Fitness Test Scorecard
For use of this form, see FM 7-22; the proponent agency is TRADOC.

TEST ONE			TEST TWO		
DATE 11/28/18	GRADE	AGE 59	DATE	GRADE	AGE
HEIGHT (IN INCHES)	BODY COMPOSITION WEIGHT: lbs. GO / NO-GO	BODY FAT: % GO / NO-GO	HEIGHT (IN INCHES)	BODY COMPOSITION WEIGHT: lbs. GO / NO-GO	BODY COMPOSITI BOD GO / N
PU RAW SCORE 72	INITIALS SC	POINTS 100	PU RAW SCORE	INITIALS	POI
SU RAW SCORE 65	INITIALS SC	POINTS 79	SU RAW SCORE	INITIALS	POI
2MR RAW SCORE 14:09	INITIALS SC	POINTS 85	2MR RAW SCORE	INITIALS	POI
ALTERNATE AEROBIC EVENT EVENT TIME GO NO-GO		TOTAL POINTS 264	ALTERNATE AEROBIC EVENT EVENT TIME GO NO-GO		TOT POI
NCOIC/OIC SIGNATURE Sgt S Kipling			NCOIC/OIC SIGNATURE		
COMMENTS			COMMENTS		

SPECIAL INSTRUCTION: USE INK
LEGEND: PU - PUSH UPS   2MR - 2 MILE RUN

my mouth was dry. I take a sip of water then toe the line on the track to run my two miles. I'm thankful I'm wearing my running shoes. My Vietnam vet friends had threatened me I would have to run the course in combat boots. I had checked out this detail and found running shoes were acceptable. My commanding officer had cleared me on this detail much to my relief. The clock starts and I take off. On this track 8 laps are a mile and the two-mile requirement would cover 16 laps. Halfway through I feel my time is tracking and settle in for a second mile. Sergeant Coryell is yelling at me as I pass by telling me to step it up. 16 laps, 2 miles complete and I ran it in 14 minutes and 9 seconds. A little over 7 minutes a mile gets me an 85% score.

My Army Physical Fitness Test Scorecard is tallied, and I total a 264 out of 300, a passing grade for a 17 to 21-year-old. I feel good that some 40 years after the time I should have taken the test, I finally took it ... and passed. More importantly were the lessons I learned while training to meet the requirements. Least importantly I got in physical shape by training with my PT friends. It was a side benefit to the important mental rumination I was engaged in.

You never know how thick the fog is until it lifts. The fog may be so thick you can only see a few feet in front of you, but you'll get there if you keep going. The same applies with the mind. I did my best to hone my perspicacity. I learned or was reminded that there is an absolute direct connection between the gut and the mind and mental clarity, that the digestive system is the second brain. As it goes, so goes both your physical fitness and your mental clarity. You reap what you put into both your brain and your gut. Exercise and proper diet can't be a New Year's resolution. It has to be a habit, a lifestyle in order to work. When I started running years ago a curious thing happened: The more I ran, the more I exercised, the more my body craved it. And fog lifted. For me, exercise has become a bodily need. Just like Drill Sergeant Johnny at the Y. That's how he explained it. I just don't feel right without it. And while I used to think I didn't have time to work out, now I don't see how I could get through my busy days without the energy I get from exercise. I know it helps people generate energy. It's like compounding interest. I know from experience it improves mood, focus and creativity. This, in turn, makes me better able to serve others. The benefits are both tangible and intangible when you move. So, it's not how much time you have in your life, it's how much life you have in your time. And if you invest in earlier years in your health, the life in your time later will be better. It's never too late to start.

STOP LOOKING FOR A MAGIC BULLET.

TEDDY ROOSEVELT SAID IT BEST.

> *"If you could kick the person in the pants*
> *responsible for most of your trouble, you*
> *wouldn't sit for a month."*

Sugar is a problem for me. I like sugar. In order to get back to late teens and early 20's weight I would have to cut back on sugar. I love Pecan Pie. That delicious gelatinous textural nutty-sweet goodness with crust was a comfort food and the perfect way to end a day, a reward at the end of the day before bed. I looked at the per serving calories one night. 520 calories, 26g of fat and 6g of saturated fat. 60mg of Cholesterol, 230 mg of sodium and 30g of sugar. And that's before a dollop of whipped creme. I mitigated my guilt by telling myself I was getting 3g of protein and 2g of dietary fiber in every serving. I knew I had to make a change. I knew I couldn't eat this and then lay down at night. So, I started eating it for breakfast. Just joking.

I found that, for me, exercise is easier than diet. Both are equally important to your goal of health and longevity. Both are challenged by a time-pressed lifestyle. But with exercise you just have to determine you're going to do it, take something out of your current schedule, and then do it. With diet, however, we have to eat, and, options out of convenience, generally are not good options. Sugar is all around us. It is not lost on me that years ago you had to chase your food or be chased. Today, everywhere you go, there are a multitude of fast, convenient options.

FEED TO FUEL NOT TO FILL

So, I DECIDED I WOULD USE FOOD FOR FUEL, NOT FOR filling. Smaller portions when eating. And following Drill Sergeant Johnny's recommendation, giving the digestive system a chance to rest. He would say stop eating after 4PM. The motivation for eating better should be to feel good and healthy. Do it for you, not for others.

It is about values and discipline. It's about consistency. Something like 60% of gym members never actually visit the gym, and 80% fail a fitness New Year's resolution by February. I believe it. I see it. If hard work is replaced by fads, false promises and magic pills we are doomed. Here is what you need: patience, repetition, commitment and reinforcement. That's it. It is about process. And there is no better day to start than today. Whether you are 20, 30, 40, 50, or 60, if you decide to do it, there is no better day than today and the rest of your days. You also psychologically need to see results. Surround yourself with like-minded, positive people. The key to success, I learned, is not to commiserate with complainers or those who engage in excuses. That is what I liked about the veterans I hung around with this year. They were jump and figure out the landing on the way down kind of people. They don't ask "what happened to me?" They ask, what can I learn from this. Where do I go from here? Make sure your goals are attainable. It's not how much time you have in your life, it's how much life you have in your time … and quality of life in your later years.

There is no magic bullet. No magic pill. I am not a doctor. But I learned the key elements for me were repetition exercise, reducing inflammation in the body and focusing on oxidation. The best way to maintain a healthy nitric oxide level and keep blood vessels healthy was my diet and exercise which helps enhance nitric oxide generation.

Social initiatives recommend 150 minutes of moderate physical activity or 75 minutes of vigorous physical activity each week, as well as muscle-strengthening activities at least twice a week. I have read of initiatives that hope they can get

20% of adults meeting those guidelines. One in five hitting the target. I recommend "basic training" to make exercise a lifetime habit, just like my YMCA Drill Sergeant Johnny told me he made his exercise habit since his Army days. I'm sure your basic training will look different than mine. Just start now. No better day than today to get started.

CURTAIN CALL
A GRAND JOINT SERVICES BALL
AND A GREEN BERET

Green Beret Command Sergeant Major William Schrader
US Army July 1948-November 1976
Korean War and Vietnam War

My year of rumination drew to a close on February 9, 2019 when I was given the honor of emceeing a Joint Services Ball at the Amway Grand Plaza Hotel in Grand Rapids, Michigan. I understood the committee was taking a chance on me. I'm a civilian. They were not in the habit of a "civilian" emcee for their annual event. Former Navy Seal Branden Minuth would be the keynote speaker. Standing at the podium, blinded by the spotlights, it was comforting to know I had veteran friends in the audience. US Navy Captain (retired) Paul J Ryan was there and had coached, encouraged and endorsed my involvement. My friend US Army Lieutenant Colonel Denny Gillem (retired) was there too (book foreword). Chief of Staff Michigan Army National Guard Colonel Mark Tellier (chapter 17) and US Army World War II veteran Virgil Westdale (chapter 2) and his family were there. I would emcee the event as a representative of the 92.7 percent of the American population who never served.

I quickly learned I had more friends than I realized. I was made to feel welcome and encouraged. It was an honor and a privilege to share in their night. I made new friends and learned once again about the meaning of selfless service. I was moved and inspired by the experience.

During the dinner portion, after the program and before the keynote address, I walked to the back of the Ambassador Ballroom to find Major Bishop, the chairman of the ball committee, to ask him a point of order question. I was intercepted by a gentleman seated at a table in the back. He was uniformed and decorated with medals.

He was Command Sergeant Major William Schrader. A Green Beret. It put a cap on my year of rumination. He listens to my radio show every week. He is my neighbor in my community. Yet, without this encounter at the back of the ballroom I would not know his story. At the podium, when blinded by the spotlights, the audience is not clearly visible. When you get on the ground and make one-on-one connections the real benefit of interaction is derived. Again, it was the realization that each random passerby is living a life with stories, and, yes, in some cases, epic stories you wouldn't know unless you asked or were told.

Counterinsurgency had become a keyword during the Kennedy presidency in 1961. With that in mind and a need for special forces in a changing world, President John F. Kennedy went to Fort Bragg on October 12, 1961. The day is known as the moment when special forces was awarded the Green Beret. It is said that President Kennedy sent a thank you message to the commander of special forces saying, "I am sure that the Green Beret will be a mark of distinction in the trying times ahead." Since that time Army Special Forces have been known as the Green Berets. At Fort Bragg at the time, Bill Schrader was among the first in our nation to wear the Green Beret.

A popular song in the 1960s was *The Ballad of the Green Berets* recorded and sung by Barry Sadler. Sadler was a twenty-five-year-old, active-duty Green Beret medic in 1966. After performing the song on The Ed Sullivan Show, it was number 1 in the country for five weeks in 1966 and sold millions of singles and albums.

Command Master Sergeant Schrader received a Silver Star for gallantry in action on March 17, 1953. While in the vicinity of Um-Dong, North Korea he was involved in a counterattack on enemy forces, which had penetrated friendly positions. The enemy was strongly entrenched, and one machine gun in particular was hampering the movement of the friendly unit and inflicting heavy casualties. Although he was suffering from a leg wound, he rushed the emplacement. He was exposed to enemy fire sweeping the area. Schrader overtook the objective, taking it out with grenades. He then led a group in a sweeping assault on the remaining positions, causing numerous enemy casualties and forcing the others to flee.

Wounded twice during the Korean War, Schrader received two Purple Hearts. He was awarded the Air Medal and Bronze Star for his service in Vietnam and the Iranian Jumpmaster Wings for finishing 15 parachute jumps with the Iranian Special

Command Sergeant Major Schrader receives a Silver Star Korea 1953

Forces. Schrader has made over 100 parachute jumps in seven countries. He has been stationed in Germany, Korea, Panama, Iran, Lebanon, Laos, Vietnam, and various posts in the United States including Alaska.

Like the other veterans I had met, he stayed busy in retirement with continual creative goals to the greater good, including, interestingly enough, as the organizing force behind a

Old worn pocket photo Bill Schrader in Korea

community 'Christmas Lite Show' for 21 years. Almost 2 miles of lights are exhibited at a West Michigan Ballpark where the baseball team, the West Michigan Whitecaps, play in summer. In November and December, it is transformed into a magical display of memories.

My visit with Green Beret Command Sergeant Major William Schrader was the perfect cap to a year of rumination. His smile, his story, his service, was exactly why I set out to learn more about these American heroes living all around us in our daily lives. He perfectly fit the thread, the characteristics of the other veterans I'd spent time with over the course of the year. Honor. Selfless service. Courage. A sense of humor. Now, almost 90 years old, he is active, sharp and fit. I ask him about it. Just like the other older veterans he remained physically active. Up early and running at reveille in the morning was a habit he carried over into civilian life. And it shows. Bill is a "morning person" and he would get up and run to "get the juices flowing."

Schrader was the perfect new friend to make at the conclusion of Operation Rumination.

At the close of the Joint Services Military Ball, a shield medal is pressed into the palm of my hand by Colonel Howard as a token of thanks, followed by a handshake from Command Sergeant Major Taylor. Later, another medal is pressed into my hand by the handshake of Colonel Mark Tellier. In a quiet moment, I run my hand across the inscription. Loyalty, Duty, Respect, Selfless Service, Honor, Integrity, Courage. Never Surrender.

I decide to apply the lesson taught me by the veterans and "do what I have to do." Invest in others through selfless service, even if it's something as simple as listening or offering an encouraging word. Invest in my physical and mental health. Ignore complainers. Move on from setbacks because they are inevitable. Set continual goals. Treat others with respect.

I walk from the hotel to my car in the parking ramp of the hotel. It had all started with a painful criticism a year earlier that I did not understand or care for veteran issues. It started with a storm and ended with a celebration. I reach my car and unlock the doors. I pull off my bow tie and pitch it into the car. I then straighten myself outside the car, take a deep breath in the chilly February night air and smile. I unbutton the top button of my white dress shirt. The operation has been a success. Bravo Zulu. Lima Charlie. But the rumination … it never ends. Not as long as there are stories to hear and stories to tell. Hooah. I got it. I understand. I'm with you.

Rick Vuyst is a businessman, radio host, TV personality, photographer, author, speaker and fitness enthusiast. After spending a year writing his first book *I Just Wet My Plants* that celebrated his 25 years in talk radio, he spent a year on the *Operation Rumination* project and book.